PRAISE FOR FRED TAYLOR

"Truly a very beloved man who was about the integrity of the art form and who knew how to present the music. A longtimer in this game. Happy and honored to have known him and worked with him since 1976, when I first played at the Jazz Workshop." —**Monty Alexander**, CD, DLitt, pianist

"I think the first time I met Fred was when I played the Jazz Workshop just after I joined Gary Burton's band in either late '74 or early '75. And my first real band, which was a trio with Jaco Pastorius and Bob Moses, got a week at the Jazz Workshop in '76, which was a huge thing. Fred took a chance on me with that and continued to support my thing in every way over the next forty-plus years.

"There is no way to compare Fred to anyone—he was an absolute original, an icon, and one of the best people any of us have known over the years and could ever hope to know. What always stood out to me with Fred was his genuine interest in the music. Think of the amount of great stuff he has heard in his life. He was around a staggering amount of good notes. And as a musician, there is an unusual benefit to hearing excellent players night after night after night. He shared that experience from a different perspective and was one of those people who really 'knew.' There are not a lot of non-musicians I can say that about. We all loved Fred!" —**Pat Metheny**, composer and musician

"When I began my thirty-year career as a journalist covering arts and entertainment for CBS Boston, it became immediately clear that Fred Taylor was as indispensable to the jazz scene as the artists he represented. Not only did he bring a deep love and understanding of music, but also a long and illustrious history of relationships with the artists themselves—legendary and young up-and-comers—and they trusted him as much as I did. The consummate professional and a very easy man to work with, Freddie was a legacy unto himself." —**Joyce Kulhawik**, Emmy Award–winning A&E critic

WHAT, AND GIVE UP SHOWBIZ?

SIX DECADES IN THE MUSIC BUSINESS

Fred Taylor
with Richard Vacca

Backbeat
Books
Guilford, Connecticut

Published by Backbeat Books
An imprint of The Rowman & Littlefield Publishing Group, Inc.
4501 Forbes Blvd., Ste. 200
Lanham, MD 20706
www.rowman.com

Distributed by NATIONAL BOOK NETWORK

Library of Congress Cataloging-in-Publication Data available

ISBN 978-1-4930-5184-7 (hardcover)
ISBN 978-1-4930-5185-4 (e-book)

♾™ The paper used in this publication meets the minimum requirements of American National Standard for Information Sciences—Permanence of Paper for Printed Library Materials, ANSI/NISO Z39.48-1992

CONTENTS

FOREWORD

Fred Taylor is a legend in the Boston music community. Perhaps no one has done so much for so long and for so many musicians. While rooted in jazz, he has booked artists ranging from Miles Davis, Freddie Hubbard, and Dave Brubeck to the Rolling Stones and Earth, Wind & Fire. He is associated with some of the most famous clubs in the city's history: Paul's Mall, the Jazz Workshop, Scullers, and more. He deserves credit for helping launch and promote the careers of a number of young artists, many from Berklee, like Danilo Pérez, Diana Krall, and Grace Kelly.

In 2015, we presented him with the first-ever George Wein Impresario Award for his role as a music promoter, and George himself, one of Fred's mentors, was there to be part of the fun.

Fred deserves another award—as an honorary Berklee faculty member. Over the years, so many of our students have used his clubs as classrooms, hearing Dizzy Gillespie, Bill Evans, Count Basie, Duke Ellington, Art Blakey, Weather Report, Pat Metheny, or Charles Mingus in a small venue where the music could be experienced in an intimate and immediate way. I can't tell you the number of stories I've heard from alumni whose minds were blown by seeing their idols at Fred's shows. Many of them have followed in those footsteps to musical prominence themselves.

This book is colorful, honest, instructional, and ultimately inspiring. Fred Taylor spent his life doing what he loves, through good times and bad, and having just recently celebrated the "20th anniversary of his 70th birthday" as he calls it, has some tales to tell. Not only do you learn about the joys and pitfalls of the crazy music industry; you see a man willing to go out to find a breast pump for a nursing mother so that the show could go on!

Fred is a treasure. Not only because of all that he's done, but because of who he is. He is a compassionate, caring man who loves not only the music but also the musicians who make it. I urge you to read and enjoy this book.

And do so with your favorite source of music ready, so that you can create a soundtrack for the story of the last several decades of music history. Fred will take you there!

Roger Brown
President, Berklee College of Music
August 2019

PREFACE

Fred Taylor never tired of telling stories. Whether his audience was one person or a hundred, Fred delighted in telling tales about the musicians, comedians, and other characters who peopled his showbiz universe.

And Fred loved to see happy faces. It deeply pleased him when his shows were a hit, and the crowd would be on its feet and clapping for more. He'd beam when a concertgoer would seek him out and say, "thank you, great show, keep the music coming." These thanks energized Fred, and kept him going, booking shows into his 89th year!

Thus this book. Fred saw it as a way to keep telling his stories and engaging with his audience even after he was gone. He very much wanted to see the book completed. He envisioned himself signing copies and handing them to his friends: "Here's my story. I think you'll enjoy it."

It was not to be. Fred Taylor lost his battle with cancer on October 26, 2019, not long after his 90th birthday.

Fred chose not to include the usual dedication you often see near the front of a book. However, I've chosen to upstage him with a dedication of my own, in his honor: to Fred Taylor, man of a thousand stories, friend to many, and a guy who never, ever gave up on showbiz.

Richard Vacca
February 2020

ACKNOWLEDGMENTS

A story like this doesn't happen overnight. I didn't think that it would take so long to write a book, but working with Richard Vacca, a wonderful writer and relentless researcher, we accomplished it. He's the guy who made this project go.

Bob Kelly, Irene Chang, and Grace Kelly formed the core of an incredible support network. They worked on the things that mean a lot to me, like the Fred Taylor Scholarship Fund benefit concerts—and they throw a pretty good birthday party too.

Laura Fillmore at Open Book Systems, my literary agent, made the match with the Globe Pequot Press. She believed in this showbiz saga, and worked tirelessly to improve and promote it.

Roger Brown, president of the Berklee College of Music, did more than just write a few words at the beginning of the book. He believed in this story too, and he honored it, and me, by creating the Fred Taylor Scholarship at that prestigious institution. Talk about a legacy to be proud of!

Hege Leyasmeyer has been my office manager and keeper of the calendar through 23 years and 5 office moves, and I simply could not have managed the whole shebang without her invaluable assistance. She has become my go-to and be-all person.

Finally, I would like to thank my parents, who always supported me through all my endeavors.

I've had a long life and long career. Countless people have inspired, helped, and counseled me, and I can't possibly name them all. But I thank every one of you, from the bottom of my heart. It's been a great ride. Thanks for sharing it.

WHAT,
AND
GIVE
UP
SHOWBIZ?

1

THIS COULD BE
THE START OF SOMETHING

On March 11, 2015, Roger Brown, president of the Berklee College of Music, presented me with their first George Wein Impresario Award. Berklee created the award to "recognize individuals who bring music to life through their dedication to discovering, mentoring, presenting, and promoting creative musicians and their music." That is exactly what I had been doing for 55 years. Wein, the founder of the Newport Jazz and Folk Festivals, made the presentation himself at Scullers Jazz Club in Boston, where I'd been the entertainment director for 25 years.

My name is Fred Taylor. Usually you'd see me backstage, but on this night I could sit in the front row and take it all in. And I let my mind wander a bit. Fifty-five years . . . countless names and faces and sounds. Dave Brubeck playing "Over the Rainbow" at Storyville. The Count Basie Orchestra, my favorite big band, wailing on Basie's 57th birthday. Bob Dylan striding onstage at Symphony Hall. Billy Joel's concert by flashlight at Paul's Mall. The Miles Davis comeback concerts at Kix. Cannonball and Mingus and Ahmad Jamal at the Jazz Workshop. Diana Ross conquering Boston from the stage of the Music Hall. Lily Tomlin's very special matinee for kids at Paul's Mall. George Shearing melting hearts with "You Must Believe in Spring" at Scullers. Sonny Rollins playing "In a Sentimental Mood" as an encore at Tanglewood. And there were more, many more: Duke Ellington. The Pointer Sisters. Bob Marley. Professor Irwin Corey. Flip Wilson. Nancy Wilson. Bruce Springsteen. Bobby Short. Diana Krall. Chris Botti. Marian McPartland. Aerosmith. George Benson. Esperanza Spalding. It's a list of musicians and singers and comedians that goes on and on, and I can tell you how I brought every one to Boston. It's what I do. And on this night, Berklee called it an award-winning performance.

I'm proud of this impresario award. It's both recognition for a job done long and well, and the entrepreneur's equivalent of a Purple Heart for the battering I've taken along the way. It's true that I've met great people, presented many musical giants, and accomplished some wonderful things. But I've also been threatened, tear-gassed at one of my own events, fired as artistic director of my own festival, and ruined financially more than once. I've battled union officials, shady promoters, and the tax man. I've had my share of nerve-wracking days. And nights.

Well, you might ask, if the going has been so rough, why not find something else to do? "What?" I'll answer, "and give up showbiz?" And that brings me to the story behind the title of this book.

There's an old industry joke that goes like this. A man works at the circus cleaning up after the elephants. All he does, week after week, year after year, is clean up elephant dung. He complains about his lot bitterly. He hates the job! One of his coworkers asks, "If you don't like it, why don't you just quit?" And our circus man, incredulous, replies: "What, and give up showbiz?"

Just like that circus man, showbiz has me in a headlock. I could never give it up, no matter how bad it gets. It's not that I haven't considered it. Shows fall apart, money runs out, the headliner is a no-show. Every day something happens that has me saying, "Okay, that's it, I'm going to look for a real job." But somehow I've always kept going. It's the magic of showbiz!

The music business turned out to be my dream job, but I didn't know it until I started to live it. It's not like I'm the star, because my world is behind the scenes. That's not where the glamour is, and as far as I know, there's never been a curtain call for the guy who booked the band. It can be frustrating, unpredictable, and financially precarious. But all that's forgotten at showtime. I couldn't possibly give this up.

That night at Scullers, George talked about impresarios and what it means to be one, and if anybody knows, it's George Wein. The original impresarios were Italians producing operas, and to this day, to be an impresario is to make a living in the music business. An impresario is part entrepreneur, part producer, part quartermaster, part talent scout, and part banker. I've worn all those hats. As George said, an impresario lays his own money on the line. You take a risk in the hope of turning a profit. Sometimes you succeed. Sometimes you don't. And that's another thing that George and I have in common: we've had times when we didn't succeed. Sometimes, to be an impresario is to fall on your face. There's nothing to do then except get back up and start working on the next show. It'll be a winner for sure!

But I wasn't thinking about failure in March 2015, when it was my night, in my club, surrounded by people I'd known for years. And from that vantage point, let's start our look back.

THE TAYLORS OF NEWTON

I was born in Boston on June 8, 1929, the only child of Frank and Ann Taylor. I can't say for sure if my music and humor genes came from my mom or my dad.

My father's father, Meyer, came from Russia, and the name Taylor is something of a family mystery. Meyer wasn't Taylor when he arrived on Ellis Island, but he was when he left it. Nobody alive today knows the story. He was a Jew, and perhaps he knew that antisemitism was strong in those days and wanted a name that would help him blend in. He wouldn't have been the first to do so.

He worked hard. He started a produce business, with a stall at Boston's Faneuil Hall market, and my dad worked with him, up at four in the morning and at the market before dawn. My dad came from that background of hard physical work, and he wanted something better for me, something that would keep me from a life of backbreaking manual labor. Sending me to college was very important to him.

My dad was a quiet man, while my mother, Ann Feinstone, was more outgoing. She attended the Girls' Latin School (it's called the Boston Latin Academy today), which was a college preparatory school, and she was the reader in the family. She was "the force" in the marriage, and she always struck me as a very practical person, what we used to call a homemaker. She was very supportive and didn't push. There were none of the "when are you gonna get married" kinds of questions, for which I was grateful.

Unfortunately, I seem to have acquired my pack-rat tendencies from mom. She saved *everything*. And I probably still have most of it!

My mom's father—my grandfather, Alexander Feinstone—started the family business, in partnership with a fellow named Moakler. They manufactured bedding and upholstered furniture. My grandfather married my grandmother Gertrude, and they had five daughters. Although I was young when he died, I have some vivid memories of him. He had been in an accident and lost a leg. He had a prosthetic limb but he didn't like it, and he usually walked with crutches or a cane. Sometimes he'd do things that would have gotten him in real trouble today, like give a woman a little poke in the rear with that cane.

Alex gave me my first job when I was a little boy. On Saturdays, Gayton, his driver, would pick me up and we would go to the Metropolitan Theatre downtown. Grandpa had decided, after some amount of research, that the Metropolitan was the most satisfactory place to take a nap, and my job was to wake him up when the show was over. Then somehow Gayton would find us, and we'd go home. After my grandfather died, Gertrude lived with my Aunt Laura. She was a hearty soul: she'd go out walking two or three miles every morning, whatever the weather. And she was an incurable romantic, in her 80s and swooning over the debonair leading men of Hollywood. "Oh," she'd gush, "*Charles Boyer!*"

I was four years old when we moved from Roxbury to an apartment on Eastbourne Road in suburban Newton. Then after a few years of renting, my father bought a house at 113 Brackett Road, and that for me was home. The house sat on a quarter acre of land, with a stand-alone two-car garage. My dad loved that yard. He dug up a lot of it and planted a big vegetable garden, and he'd be out tending it all summer long. I think it relaxed him.

MADAME CHALOFF AND OTHER MUSICAL PURSUITS

When I was eleven, I started piano lessons with Margaret Chaloff, and I don't recall people calling her "Madame Chaloff" at that time. She was a bit of a mystic and used to read my palm. I spent two years with her, learning the classics, at her home in Newton. I can't forget how I'd be laboring over the keyboard while she was off in some other room in the house. I'd play something, and then—"No, no. E-flat! E-flat!" She was a brilliant teacher, and two generations of jazz pianists flocked to her studio. Her touch technique was what was so special, and what so many pianists went to learn.

I was not learning trivial pieces—they were pieces like Edward MacDowell's *From a Wandering Iceberg*. After my first year I played Beethoven's *Moonlight Sonata* in recital. The jazz pianist Steve Kuhn was also a student then, and I played my recital at Steve's home in Newton.

I met the whole family. Margaret's husband, Julius, was also an accomplished musician who owned a music school. He seemed a bit pompous. And I met their two sons: Richard, who was studying engineering, and Serge, a saxophone prodigy who was about to go on the road with the Tommy Reynolds band. He was about 17 then. We'll return to Serge presently.

A few years later I studied piano again, this time with Sid Reinherz. He was not exactly a jazz player, more of a stride player with a little bit of popular jazz, and he had a show, *The 920 Club*, on WORL-AM, one of my favorite stations. On his program, Sid would play different pianos at the Stark piano warehouse, a little promotion for the piano companies as well as for Stark. I'd go to my lesson, and Sid would write out arrangements for me, complete charts, right and left hands, and that's what I'd practice. I've still got his arrangement of "Exactly Like You." I didn't stay long, and I didn't pursue the piano any further because I was too impatient—I wanted to be Oscar Peterson after one lesson.

Next I acquired a Vega jazz trumpet from a fellow in the Pierian Sodality Orchestra at Harvard (now the Harvard-Radcliffe Orchestra) and started taking lessons on that. I studied with Harry Kemler of the Boston Symphony, but it didn't last too long. To keep your lip up you've got to be dedicated, play every day, and as with the piano, I was too impatient and didn't stay with it.

Despite my lack of patience, these exposures taught me something about the instruments and the people who play them. That helped me build relationships with artists, made it easier to talk with them, because I knew how hard they had to work, and I respected them for it. I didn't become a professional, but I had some insight into professionals.

HANDS ON

I've always liked working with my hands, working with tools. I still do. That started in junior high school, when I took a woodworking class and learned how to use the lathe, band saw, and other tools. I made a cutting board in shop and I still cut bread on it. I had a little workshop of my own in the basement of the house in Newton, and I was always fixing or building something. I was so excited when I brought home a band saw from Sears, Roebuck. And I had a little bike repair business when I was about 14 years old. That interest didn't stop when I hit adulthood, either. I worked in a mattress factory and built storage racks, and the displays for the company's trade show booths. I became an expert at fixing toilets, which is a useful skill to have if you own a couple of nightclubs.

Doing things like that is very satisfying, especially on days when you spend all day talking on the phone and have nothing to show for it. I still get more satisfaction from repairing a broken hinge than I do from going out for a fancy dinner. One thing I haven't done that I've always wanted to do is create a fine piece of furniture from scratch, like a bureau or a chest of drawers.

In high school, I used to get my hands dirty working on cars. My mother inherited a 1936 V-8 Ford, but she didn't like to drive, and it ended up being my first car. It was a two-door coupe, with a V-shaped vertical grill and bullet headlamps. No rumble seat though. I loved it. It was gray, but I painted it red, and it became known throughout Newton as the Red Bomber.

I did all my own work on the Red Bomber, and this led to a very revealing conversation with my father. I was replacing the shock absorbers, which meant crawling under the car and covering myself with grease and dirt. My father happened by, and he asked, "Why are you doing that? Why not take it to a garage?" I explained that I liked working on the car and wanted to do it myself. He didn't approve. He saw it as unnecessary—if you didn't have to do this kind of work, you shouldn't do it. My dad never quite understood the difference between wanting to do something and having to do it. I'm sure he saw no difference between what I was doing under the car and what he was doing at the same age—hauling crates of vegetables at his father's market.

BIG BAND SATURDAYS

My Saturday ritual when I was in high school was to spend the day downtown at the RKO-Boston Theater, in what we call Downtown Crossing today. My mother would make me a sandwich, and I'd make the long trip on the trolley from Newton to Washington Street and the RKO, the home of the big bands. Twenty years later, that part of town came to be called the Combat Zone, but there was nothing X-rated about it back then. I wouldn't have noticed anything off-color anyway. I was just there to hear the bands.

I'd get to the theater for the early show—it started at 11:30 a.m. on Saturday—and settle in for the afternoon. The big bands might have been the top bananas at the RKO, but there were always opening acts. There might be acrobats or tap dancers or yodelers, and there was always a comedian. Finally the curtain would rise, and there was the band in their sharp uniforms, with all the glittering brass. I remember digging Jimmy Dorsey, Lionel Hampton, Woody Herman, and Louis Jordan and His Tympany Five. I saw the Andrews Sisters, who were big stars then, and they always had a swing band to supply the music.

After the stage show came the movie, with a newsreel first. These were mostly B-movies, most long-since forgotten. Then I'd watch the stage show again—even as a kid I loved the experience of seeing a live show. Afterwards I'd go to the Krey's record shop across the street to browse the latest 78s. It was a full day! Oh, I loved Saturdays. It would be suppertime before I'd finally get home.

BOSTON UNIVERSITY

Maybe it was my love of gadgetry and learning how things worked, but after I graduated from high school in 1947, I wanted to go to engineering school, and I applied to MIT. I was accepted, too, but there was a foul-up with the paperwork and I had second thoughts. I applied to Boston University and was accepted.

My major was economics, in the liberal arts school. I picked economics because it required the fewest number of credits to graduate of any major in the school. I didn't get much out of it. My clearest memory is of a professor named Hughes, who demonstrated the inverse relationship between bond prices and interest rates. "When interest rates are high" (he'd have his hands high over his head) "bond prices are low" (hands down to his knees). "And when interest rates are low" (hands still near his knees) "bond prices are high" (with the hands back up over his head). He looked like a toaster. But truth be told, I didn't have the chops to become an economist.

The Korean War started during my junior year, and I went for my physical, but I was classified as 4-F, not qualified to serve. I had flat feet, and that kept me out of the service. I did join the Civil Air Patrol, though, which was the civilian auxiliary unit of the United States Air Force. I ran for class vice president in 1950 too. I walked around campus passing out little cardboard triangles that said, "Let's pyramid to new heights with Fred Taylor as vice president." It might have been corny, but I won.

I might not have been a scholar, but I certainly enjoyed campus life. I joined a fraternity, Tau Epsilon Phi. I didn't join because I had a lofty opinion of the frat. I joined because one of the members, Al Sostik, talked me into it. Al was a great piano player and I loved listening to him. He was a good guy too, and he got me to sign up. As would happen so often in my life, I was following the music. I wasn't a rah-rah fraternity guy, but because of the people I met, it turned out to be an enjoyable experience.

Danny Kossow was a frat brother, and he was very enthusiastic about cabaret and musicals. Our frat house was at 488 Beacon Street, near Mass. Ave, and close to the old Hotel Fensgate, which had a fine little club called the Satire Room. Danny would go there to listen to the Jones Brothers. They were among the most popular entertainers in Boston in the pre–rock 'n' roll years, and sometimes Danny brought them back to the house after their shows. I got to know the Jones Brothers at that time. Clyde, Max, and Herb Jones really were brothers, and they all played an instrument, and they all sang. They took their inspiration from the great harmonizers, like the Ink Spots and the Mills Brothers. They could sing any kind of music, but they did best with jazz, and they were crowd-pleasers, very polished, real professionals. They had that magical ability to make it seem like they were performing just for you. Ten years later, when I started as a booking agent, the Jones Brothers were one of my first bookings. Clyde and I actually became good friends.

I graduated with a bachelor of arts degree in economics in 1951, and I didn't know what I wanted to do, so my mother suggested I go to work in the family business, which I did. I still had my nights free to roam the jazz clubs.

MY LIFE AS A SAILOR

When I was in college, I fell in love with sailing, and after I graduated, I bought my first boat. The seller was Birdie Tebbetts, the Boston Red Sox catcher. The Sox had sold his contract to Cleveland, and Birdie wasn't taking the boat with him, and I got a good deal on it. I thought it was ready to sail, so I hauled it down to South Boston, near the yacht club, and lowered it into the water. It promptly sank. Eventually, I got it out to my folks' back yard in Newton, and I worked on that boat all summer. I finally relaunched it the next year. I named it Old Smuggler, because that was the scotch we were drinking in those days. I had a sign company paint the Old Smuggler label on the transom—the transom was yellow and they painted Old Smuggler in black, just the way it looked on the bottle.

I liked to think it was an ocean-going vessel. We'd sail from Boston up the coast to Rockport and stay overnight. We'd knock on a door and ask, "Do you have any rooms, we just sailed in." "Oh, you sailed in!" That was the magic word, and you were welcomed. There was just something about coming from the sea. Sometimes we'd meet lobstermen coming into port, and we'd make a deal, and they'd throw over a couple lobsters, and we'd wrap up a couple bucks and toss that over to them. I had an alcohol stove, and we'd boil up the lobsters, and eat them with melted butter, and throw the shells over the side. Those were good times.

Eventually I sold Old Smuggler and bought a beautiful boat called Stardust, a 28-foot cabin sloop. That became my real pride and joy. We had many excursions, sailing north to Maine and south to Connecticut. When I became involved with the clubs in 1965, though, I suddenly was busy seven days a week, 18 hours a day, and the boat stayed in dry dock for the year. But that was wrong, so the next year I sold it, and that ended that. I gave up sailing for the business. And you know, that's not all I gave up. I think that's one of the reasons I never got married—I was married to the business. I was just consumed, working day and night. I'd meet somebody, and I'd think, "she's really nice, I've got to call her." Then I'd get busy, and three weeks later I'd come to, and tell myself, "I should have called." I never committed. I was never around long enough to commit. The clubs, the work, the concerts—it was seven days a week, every week. But it came at a cost. Anyway, I'm getting ahead of myself, so let's get back to that first job after college.

THE PLAYGROUND OF AMERICA

Grandfather Alex ran the family business, a bedding manufacturer named Enterprise-Moakler. They bought a franchise from Serta to manufacture their mattresses under the product name Serta-White Cross. They also built upholstered furniture and made Kapok life jackets during the war. I was there all through the '50s. My father was working there, too. He was the treasurer.

Right away I got my hands dirty. I'd walk around the plant, and if I saw something that I could improve, I did it. I became the plant's Mr. Fixit. For instance, we had big racks for storing bolts of cloth, 10 feet high, one divider in the middle. There would be four bolts piled on top of each other, and if you wanted the one on the bottom, you had to move a lot of cloth to get at it. One day I rebuilt the whole thing. I pulled everything out, and rebuilt the racks with two more dividers to make it easier to move bolts of cloth in and out. I would just see things like that and think, I ought to do something about that.

It wasn't a happy family situation after Alex died and my cousin Bill Ginsberg became president. There was a lot of turmoil. Bill was a Harvard man, and I thought he was rather full of himself. I don't think Bill wanted me there. He saw me as some kind of threat, and we had a contentious relationship from the beginning. There was nothing between us out in the open, but it was there, a continual aggravation. Sam Blake was the plant manager; he was a fine man, and we got along great. He was the buffer between Bill and me.

I learned the business. I did every job. When the cutter got sick, I learned how to cut mattress panels. I drove a delivery truck, hauling mattresses into the R. H. White department store. I got involved in advertising and promotions. Some time later in the decade, I came up with a new ad slogan: "Serta: Playground of America." The family wasn't amused.

My starting salary was $30 a week, and at the time the norm was more like $50 or $60 a week. But I was family, so Bill started me at $30. After a year I was all the way up to $35.

After a year, though, something else happened in my life, and it turned out to be more important to me than mattresses ever were. I met Dave Brubeck. So I'll get back to the Serta story a little bit later.

2

OVER THE RAINBOW WITH BRUBECK

I was a year out of college when I had an encounter that changed the course of my life. In 1952, I got to know Dave Brubeck, an up-and-coming piano player who became one of *the* legendary figures in American music. At the time, I was delighted to be involved with Dave and his group, but as the years went on, I realized what a milestone it was in my life. It led to things that I could never have anticipated. I'm not being dramatic when I say the meeting was momentous. And it was set in motion by an unlikely chain of events that began in June 1949.

HEARD THE ONE ABOUT THE BUSBOY WHO DID STANDUP?

That summer, after my sophomore year at BU, I was hired as a busboy at the Strawberry Hill Hotel in Bethlehem, New Hampshire. It was a small hotel, maybe 90 rooms, and it was one of those places where the hotel staff doubled as weekend entertainers. Ted, another busboy, played pretty good piano. There were two bellhops, Eddie and Herbie, and Eddie played clarinet and Herbie played trumpet. Eddie also played a stand-alone drum, what they called a cocktail drum, during Ted's or Herbie's solos. I was the emcee, telling jokes I wrote myself and introducing the tunes. On Wednesdays, Fridays, and Saturdays, we provided the hotel's entertainment.

Another hotel, called the Park View, was next door. Some of their entertainers, like the comedian Henny Youngman, were well known. I'd go over and listen to Youngman, and then, when I did my show, I'd have some new material. I told Youngman I stole his jokes when I hired him 16 years later at Paul's Mall. He didn't seem to mind.

Murray was the boss at the Strawberry Hill, and as I remember it, to walk with Murray was to walk under a rain cloud. No glass was ever half full for

Murray. On a Saturday night we'd have a packed house, but Murray would still be glum. "Murray," I'd say, "what are you worrying about? We're full."

"Yeah," he'd say, "but what about next week?"

And he kept a close watch on the expenses. I'd mention his tightfisted ways in my routine: "Ladies and gentlemen, I just wanted to let you know, we had a little accident, our manager Murray fell off his wallet, but he'll be alright."

I had eyes for Eddie's cocktail drum. It was pearl white, standing on three legs, about 3 feet tall. You played it while standing. It was tuned like a snare drum and played with sticks or brushes. I liked it. After a couple of weeks I asked Eddie if I could play the drum while he played clarinet, and he said sure. I started with the brushes and it just clicked, it felt natural, I could keep a nice rhythm. The guys liked it, and I became the drummer. At the end of the season, Eddie said he didn't want to take the drum back home, so I offered to buy it. I think I paid about 40 bucks for that cocktail drum. I still have it.

THE DON CREIGHTON ORCHESTRA

Come September, my first summer in show business was over, and I was back at Boston University for my junior year. And Herbie—Herbie Vaas, one of my fellow Strawberry Hill minstrels—also lived in Boston, and he led a band called the Don Creighton Orchestra. Herbie was leaving town, though, moving to Syracuse, but before he left, he asked me if I wanted to work with the band. Of course I said yes. It was a Strawberry Hill reprise, but without Murray. I'd introduce the tunes and play the drum. I became the Don Creighton Orchestra's front man. Most of our jobs had some connection to the university—campus events, frat house parties, a few engagement parties.

Now, there was nobody named Don Creighton in the band, but we did have Creighton Hoyt, a pianist going to school at BU on the GI Bill. Ed Udell was on bass, and Andy Greco on guitar. Mostly it was the four of us, but sometimes we'd add Chuck Wells, who doubled on vibes and trumpet. Chuck was a good trumpet player; he played around Boston for years, but I loved it when Chuck played the vibes. We were all crazy about George Shearing, the blind British pianist who was one of the most popular names in jazz in the early 1950s, and when we'd add the vibes to our band, we'd go after what everybody called "that Shearing sound." Shearing didn't use horns in his quintet—his front line was piano, vibes, and guitar. And they played together in a very tight harmony. The sound was instantly recognizable, and no one else had it. The Don Creighton Orchestra sure didn't have it, but we had a lot of fun giving it a try.

I sat out on the Don Creighton Orchestra's finest gig. In 1950, we played at the Tufts Winter Carnival as the Woody Herman All Stars, and although that was a bit of an exaggeration, we did have two guys who played in Woody's band: Serge and Joe MacDonald, the drummer. I gladly stepped aside for Joe. And we added a tenor saxophonist named Bill Wellington, an unbelievable player, who added a lot of bop licks. He was eventually brought down by a drug habit.

Even though I wouldn't be onstage that night, I still had an important role to play—I got Serge's horn out of hock. When we picked Serge up on the way to the show, he didn't have his horn. He said he had spilled some ice cream on the pads. I asked him where it was, and eventually he told me, and thank God we found the pawn ticket. We raced down to the shop, and luckily it was still open, and I got the horn back. Why had Serge pawned his horn? I won't mince words. Serge was a drug addict, and the money went up his arm. But he played very well that night. And I'll never forget, Serge was dating a woman named Linda then, and she had a younger sister, and they fixed me up with her, and the four of us went out to Boots Mussulli's club in Milford to hear the bop group of saxophonist Charlie Ventura. That was something special. On the way home, my date wanted to know if I would give her an engagement ring. That caught me by surprise. "Uh, didn't we just meet tonight?" She moved fast, that one.

Meanwhile, I found another diversion to keep me from my schoolwork: the tape recorder. In about 1950, the Revere Camera Company began making tape recorders for the consumer market. I was already a gadget guy, and I bought one. It came in its own carrying case, so it was portable, but it wasn't what you'd call lightweight. It was self-contained—it had a microphone and speaker built in, so you could both record and play back with it. It had 5-inch reels, and recorded 3-3/4 inches of tape per second, which was okay for a hobbyist but not nearly good enough for a pro. I thought it was the greatest. I started taking it with me to the clubs.

I made one memorable recording on a Sunday afternoon in late 1950, of my friend Serge Chaloff at the Hi-Hat club's weekly jam session. There I was, a college senior barely of legal drinking age, in a bar with a tape recorder, taping my piano teacher's son—who happened to be one of the finest baritone saxophone players in jazz.

Thirty years later, Bob Sunenblick of Uptown Records got wind of this tape and contacted me. He was assembling a collection of Serge Chaloff recordings from that period, and he wanted to know if my tape was available. I hadn't heard it in years, hadn't even thought of it, but I dug it out of the back of the closet and sent it to him. It gave his engineer some trouble—the reel had warped over the years in storage, and that led to an uneven playback—but they solved the problem and were able to use the music. I agreed to sell Bob the rights to it. Four of my tracks appeared on an Uptown compact disc in 1994, *Serge Chaloff: Boston 1950*. It was a fine CD and Bob credited me for my contribution in the liner notes. He even said I did pretty good for an amateur with a tape recorder.

Twenty-five years later, though, I'm still waiting to get paid.

THE STORYVILLE TAPES

But back to the Brubeck story. In 1952, I upgraded my operation. I bought a new TapeMaster recorder, with 7-inch reels, and it recorded 7-1/2 inches of tape per second, which was getting closer to a professional standard. The TapeMaster did not have a built-in microphone, so I bought an Electro-Voice 630, which was a real good one. It didn't have a built-in speaker either, so to hear what I recorded, I had to plug the machine into some kind of system with an amplifier and speakers. With the TapeMaster, I was recording in the clubs even more. I was having a ball with it.

Creighton Hoyt was always talking about a guy he knew when he was in the service, a jazz pianist who was already well known on the West Coast.

Creighton said if he ever came east, I should be sure to catch him because he was really, really great. He was talking about Dave Brubeck.

In October 1952, I read in the newspaper that Dave Brubeck's group was in town, at Storyville. This was Creighton's guy! I immediately made plans to catch Brubeck and his quartet. I went to Storyville on Sunday afternoon for the matinee with my TapeMaster in tow, and asked George Wein, who owned the club, if I could do some recording. He said it was okay with him, but I had to ask Brubeck.

I introduced myself to Dave and asked him if I could record some of his set. Then I mentioned my band and Creighton Hoyt—and as soon as I mentioned Creighton, Brubeck perked right up. He said, "Oh man, Creighton, how is he, he saved my life in the army, is he here?" I had to tell him that Creighton couldn't make it that day, but he wanted me to say hello. That was good enough for Brubeck. A friend of Creighton's was a friend of his. He told me to go ahead and do anything I wanted to do.

The group started playing and I moved around the bandstand, looking for the sweet spot for the microphone. All I had to guide me were my ears. I finally located what I thought was a good spot, and I switched on the machine and let the tape roll. I recorded a set of standards, which included "Take the 'A' Train," "Over the Rainbow," "You Go to My Head" and "Oh, Lady Be Good."

I knew nothing about this group when I walked into Storyville that day. I had never heard them and was only there on Creighton's recommendation. But my enthusiasm for Brubeck's music was immediate. There wasn't anybody else playing like Dave, and right away I liked how that set him apart. And Paul Desmond, the alto saxophonist, was another one going his own way. A lot of alto players were trying to sound like Charlie Parker. Not Desmond. He had a sound, a tone, all his own. I became an instant fan.

A funny thing about that session—we didn't hear the whole group. The club had booked Dave's quartet, but that afternoon it was just a trio with Dave, Paul, and Lloyd Davis, the drummer. The bass player, Wyatt Ruther, nicknamed "Bull," was absent. Lloyd didn't seem to miss him, though. He was a rock-steady timekeeper, but he only stayed with the quartet for about a year. He made his mark in the music world as a percussionist with the San Francisco Symphony.

When the session was over, Dave said he'd like to hear what I'd got. I explained that it was only a tape deck, and we needed something to amplify it, and that was back at my home in Newton. So Paul and Dave and I jumped into my car and we drove to Newton, and I plugged the tape into my hi-fi system. Dave loved it. He said he'd never been caught playing quite that way—because there was no bass player, he was doing things a little differently.

We couldn't talk long because I had to get them back to Storyville for the evening sets, but on the way Dave asked if I could make him a copy of the tape. I told him that I could do it the next day. He couldn't wait though, because the band was heading to New York for an engagement at Birdland. On Monday I went to Trans Radio Productions for the copy, and I sent it off to Dave.

The Brubeck Quartet moved on to Philadelphia, and Dave sent me a letter from there. They were recording for Fantasy Records then, and Max and Sol Weiss, who owned the company, had listened to the tape. Dave wrote: "We all are very pleased with the sound of the recordings and are very anxious to see them come out as an LP as soon as possible." And he wrote, "As for the Jazz at Storyville album, I think it is a wonderful idea."

Dave was all for doing the album, but there was some red tape to work through with Fantasy, and Max Weiss wanted Nat Hentoff, the Boston correspondent for *Down Beat* magazine and host of the live broadcasts from the club for WMEX radio, to write the liner notes.

Fantasy made the album, and two of our tunes, "Over the Rainbow" and "You Go to My Head, " comprised one side of *Jazz at Storyville*. The second side included our "Give a Little Whistle" and "Oh, Lady Be Good," which were actually played that day as a medley. It also included an additional track played by the full quartet (a swinging version of "Tea for Two"). Dave was reluctant to include music that wasn't played by the trio at Storyville, but nothing else on our tape met his high standards.

I sold Fantasy the rights to the tape for $70. That would be about $650 in 2018. For this, I was listed as the engineer in the liner notes.

Right on the front of the album it says, "George Wein presents Jazz at Storyville," and this marked the beginning of George's long relationship with Brubeck. Wein was not paid for the use of his club or his name; his interest was strictly in the publicity. Nat Hentoff did indeed write the liner notes, but he got the date of the session wrong, and it's been plaguing discographers ever since (it was October 12, not his date of October 2).

Fantasy released the album in spring 1953. That November, in a *New York Times* article, John Hammond complained about the sound on jazz LPs in general, but he did identify one bright spot: "The most intriguing disk is one by Dave Brubeck's trio and quartet, taped on amateur equipment (one mike) from an actual performance at Boston's Storyville Cafe. Some flutter is evident in the tape mechanism, but the balance is natural and the playing inspired." And in March 1954, John S. Wilson, also writing in the *New York Times*, praised the album for embracing the "new technology" of the long-playing record: "Although the LP format has been out for a while, artists are still tending to do three-minute cuts, except for a live recording done at Storyville with Dave Brubeck and Paul Desmond, where there is a seven-minute cut of 'Over the Rainbow,' one of the first to take advantage of the expanded LP format."

The Brubeck Quartet and that album were creating plenty of buzz, and I can tell you, it made for some smiling faces down at Storyville!

Dave was unhappy with Fantasy Records, and partly on the basis of the success of *Jazz at Storyville,* he was able to sign with Columbia Records in 1953. Our improvised recording session at the club really paid dividends for Dave. There were changes for Storyville that year, too—in September Wein moved from Kenmore Square to the Copley Square Hotel on Huntington Avenue. Dave's group came back to play for a week in the new Storyville in January 1954, and he called and asked if I could do some more taping. I was happy to, and I recorded on several different nights that week. Later, Dave said, "Let me have the tapes, because the Columbia engineers will just throw them away if they learn they were made on an amateur's machine. Instead, I'll just say they're mine, and they should check them out." That's what we did.

I sold the tapes to Dave himself. I asked if I could get $150 for them, and Dave said yes. Unbelievable! I made back all the money I spent on the tape recorder and microphone!

Dave's second album for Columbia was *Dave Brubeck at Storyville: 1954.* Two of the cuts, "On the Alamo" and "Don't Worry 'Bout Me," were from my tapes. The remaining tracks were taken from a radio broadcast done from the club that same week. Brubeck mentions in the liner notes that he thought "On the Alamo" was the best thing he'd done on record to that point.

Dave was on the cover of *Time* magazine shortly after that. He wasn't a legend yet, but he was very, very popular, especially on the college campuses. What was puzzling in those years was how the jazz purists never quite accepted him. They said he didn't swing, that he was too heavy-handed. That and the fact that the jazz purists don't like it when an artist becomes too commercially successful. They claimed he "sold out." It was only years later that the purists acknowledged how special Brubeck was.

WITH BRUBECK THROUGH THE DECADES

I never recorded Dave again, but we remained friends. When I started producing shows, I presented Dave many times in concerts and at festivals. In July 1998, he even played a long weekend for me at Scullers. That was a treat, because he rarely played nightclubs—he stopped initially because he couldn't stand the smoke. And of course he was doing very well on the concert stage, so he could be very selective when it came to club dates.

One festival appearance sticks in my mind because of something Dave told me. In 1978, I got involved with the Green Mountain Music Festival at Sugarbush, in Vermont. It was a series of summer concerts, all different types of music, and one weekend we had Maynard Ferguson's big band on a program with Dave Brubeck's current quartet, featuring Jerry Bergonzi in the saxophone chair. Paul Desmond had died about a year before, and when I saw Dave backstage, he said, "Fred, there's something I think you should know. I was with Paul in his final hours and he was still very lucid. And he said his favorite recording of his own playing with the Quartet, of all time, was on that Storyville album that you recorded." It was the ballad "You Go to My Head."

I was speechless. That was a very emotional moment.

Dave wrote some great music, and not just the things that became standards, like "In Your Own Sweet Way." He also wrote beautiful classical music, which was more popular in Europe than in the States. I had Dave at the Tanglewood Jazz Festival three times, in 2002, 2004, and 2006. He closed the festival in 2004, first playing a set with the quartet, and then performing some of his classical pieces. For this performance he assembled his "Symphonette," a 23-piece string ensemble recruited from the ranks of the Boston Symphony Orchestra and under the direction of his longtime associate, Russell Gloyd. He finished with the quartet joining the strings onstage for "Take Five," and I guarantee no one in the crowd ever heard Dave's standard closing tune played quite like that.

Brubeck didn't play at the Newport Jazz Festival every year, but he played it more often than anybody else, and I heard him there many times. I'd always make a point of catching up with him to say hello. In 2009, he had a small surprise for me. He said he'd been somewhere in Maryland to play a concert earlier that year, and he struck up a conversation with the piano tuner. This turned out to be the son of his old army buddy, Creighton Hoyt, my pianist in the Don Creighton Orchestra, and the man responsible for Dave and me first meeting way back in 1952. Maybe it is a small world at that.

My last date with Dave was in November 2010. It was a benefit concert at the Shalin Liu Performance Center in Rockport, Massachusetts. Offstage at the Shalin Liu there's a little room with a few benches, and we were sitting there just prior to going on, and I asked, "Hey Dave, do you ever play 'Over the Rainbow' anymore?"

"Oh, once in a while," he replied, and he didn't say anything else.

Showtime. Dave goes out onstage and I take my seat in the audience. And after he greets the audience and thanks the concert sponsors, he says, "There's someone here tonight I've known for many years," and he relates the whole story about me coming to Storyville and making the tape and how important that was and what it meant to him. Then he and his saxophonist Bobby Militello played "Over the Rainbow." It brought me to tears.

I know of no other artist in the world of jazz who had Dave's charisma and strong convictions. And to me, he was much more than a jazz legend— he was my good friend for almost sixty years.

3

WILD ABOUT BASIE!

In the mid-1950s, after my Storyville recordings with Brubeck, I was still working in the family business, and liking it less and less. Then our salesman who worked the accounts up north left the company. His territory was New Hampshire, Vermont, and western Massachusetts. I talked my way into becoming a salesman. I went on the road. I got along with the buyers and started to bring in some business. I had three or four accounts in Worcester, opened it up, I really did well in Worcester. I was still on salary, making $80 a week. If I had been working on commission, as most salesmen do, I'd have been making $300 a week.

When our senior salesman retired, I took over his accounts. I sold more mattresses. I was bringing in 40 percent of the company's business, but I was still only making $80 a week. I was pretty unhappy about it, and there was a lot of tension. That friction, from about 1956 on, got to be too much. It disrupted the family. As 1959 came to an end, I made the decision I'd been thinking about for a long time: I quit my job. The situation had deteriorated to the point of where it was time for me to do something else. I gave my notice and hopped on a plane to Florida. I needed a little time to relax and clear my head, and the Blue Bay Motel on Miami Beach sounded like the right place for it.

Miami was the perfect getaway after I left Serta. It's always a pleasure to escape New England's winter for a few weeks, and I spent my days swimming and relaxing in the sun. I also found a lively nightlife scene—Miami was jumping in the late '50s. Those were the glory days along Miami Beach, with shows in the big hotels like the Fontainebleau and the Montmartre, but that wasn't really my style. I found a couple of jazz clubs along the 79th Street Causeway that were more to my liking. Buddy Greco had his trio at one of them, and I hung out there every night until two in the morning. Then I found another club where Lenny Bruce was playing, and that's the only time I heard him live. He was incredible. I later hired many comedians at Paul's Mall who were deeply influenced by Lenny Bruce.

I couldn't stay in Miami forever, tempting as it seemed, and I came back to Boston in January 1960, tan and rested. There was one small problem: I didn't know what I was going to do. I didn't have a job, and in fact I hadn't even figured out what kind of job I wanted. I did know I wanted something with variety, where I wouldn't be doing the same thing day after day. I liked the idea of going to work and not knowing exactly what I'd be doing that day, where a phone call might completely change whatever was planned. I just didn't know where to look for such a thing.

TAYLOR MEETS BUCCI

While I was thinking about all this, I got a call from a friend of mine named John Sdoucos in March. I'd met John a few years before at Storyville; he was another Boston University alumnus and diehard jazz fan. John went to work for George Wein as a publicist and later as an advance man for his festivals. John knew I'd done quite a bit of recording, and he needed someone who could do some taping in a nightclub. He was excited: "I found this great jazz organist named Joe Bucci at Jackie's Game Bar in Lynn. He plays a Hammond B-3, and he works with just a drummer, and the two of them sound like the whole Basie band. You've gotta come out and record them." I've always liked big bands, and I liked Count Basie's best of all, so I was intrigued and said I'd do it.

Jackie's Game Bar was on Spring Street in downtown Lynn, a Boston suburb on the North Shore. I went out there and recorded Joe Bucci with his drummer, Joe Riddick, for four nights. And my friend John wasn't kidding, this duo could *play*. With the tapes in hand, I went to John to settle up. Turned out that John was broke at the time, but I had another idea. I shared his enthusiasm for Bucci. Joe's choice of material was perfect for his swinging style, and as a performer I thought he was really exciting. So I proposed to John that we become partners in managing and promoting him. We took the idea to Joe, and he was enthusiastic about it. So John and I became partners, and Joe was our first client.

That agreement marked my official entry into the music business, when I changed from being an amateur with a tape recorder to an artist's manager working for commissions. In 1959, I had been selling mattresses. Now I was going to be selling entertainment.

I liked working with Joe. He was an upbeat, friendly guy from Malden, a working-class suburb north of Boston. Joe came from a big family; there must have been ten kids. He was 33 or 34 when I first heard him at Jackie's Game Bar, and he'd been a professional musician for more than 10 years by then. He'd started out on the accordion, and I think that influenced his approach to the organ.

The Hammond B-3 was very popular in jazz in the early '60s, with guys like Jack McDuff and Jimmy Smith the best known of a sizable group of organists. In Boston, there were clubs like Wally's, Connolly's, and the Big M presenting a steady diet of organ trios. But even in that crowd, Joe's playing stood out.

One thing that made Joe's sound so distinctive was the bass. He played bass with his left foot, and the pedals on the organ were attached to a Krueger bass unit, which gave the bass pedals the sound of a string bass. It mimicked the way the bass sound decays, the "dummmmm." It gave his bass a different sound, and when we started promoting Joe, we called it the Joe Bucci Duo with the third man who wasn't there—that being his left foot. That foot was the bass player, and his hands were free to play the manuals—the keyboards.

But Joe needed more than a bass attachment to sound like 15 musicians, so he had a lever on the lower keyboard that engaged another attachment, a Maas-Rowe Vibrachord. This was a big box that contained a set of solenoid-operated vibes. Joe would throw the lever and launch into a vibes solo.

In about 1960, the Hammond company came up with a small organ called the Extravoice, which incorporated even more instrument sounds and features. Joe and Bruce Williams, an engineer with Hammond, married an Extravoice to the B-3 as a third manual. Now he was really cookin'! Joe called his customized Hammond "the Monster."

Joe considered himself a big band organist, and that's what made his sound distinctive. He didn't want the sound of an organ trio. He wanted to be the Count Basie band, the whole thing, and with all the sounds he conjured from his B-3, he just about did it. Joe Riddick's drums, providing fills and adding color, were the perfect complement to the organ. They were on to something that set them apart.

When Joe would do the Basie band, he could come in with the sax section on one hand and the trumpet section on the other hand, then change up the stops and come in with a trumpet solo, then change up and come in as a guitar, and those changes were always quick—he looked like he was playing handball on the keyboards, the way he would change up stops. To this day I don't know of any organ player who could exploit all the capabilities of the Hammond as well as Joe, with its stops and sounds and changes. He was a master. And he could *swing.*

BUCCI MEETS BASIE

Through his Storyville connections, John Sdoucos learned that the Basie band was coming through the area during the summer of 1961. I had never been involved in booking anything as big as the Basie band, but John and I decided to go for it. We found an open date on the band's calendar and booked the Count Basie Orchestra into the Starlight Ballroom on Route 128 in Lynnfield. In fact, it wasn't just any day, it was August 21, the Count's 57th birthday. And we booked Joe Bucci as the opening act. It was a great way to promote Joe and his music.

The summer of 1961 was dry. It seemed like there had been no rain for about three months. Come the day of the show, though, it started to rain. And rain. This was a problem for us, because the Starlight Ballroom wasn't really a "ballroom" at all—it was a big, open-air dance pavilion, a throwback to the heyday of the big bands. The band would stay dry under a canopy, but everybody else would be drenched. Here I was, staging my first big-time production, and I started to panic. Should we cancel the show? And the rain just kept coming down.

What, and give up show business?

Meanwhile, John was working the phone. He knew somebody at the Agganis Auditorium in Lynn, who told him the date was open. That was lucky for us, and John made a deal to move the show indoors at the Agganis. We scrambled to get the news out that afternoon, calling all the radio stations and asking them to announce that the concert had moved to the Auditorium. Somehow we managed to save the show.

Joe opened, the local boy made good, and played the biggest gig of his career. He pulled out all the stops—no pun intended—and hit the audience with the best of his Basie material. They loved it. So did Basie himself, and he loved Joe, too. Basie had a club in New York City at that time, up in Harlem, called Basie's Place, and he invited Joe to play a week there. John and I went down with Joe and Joe, Bucci and Riddick, for a truly memorable week of music.

I can add one culinary note to Joe's week at Basie's. The cook was serving platters of buttered roast beef with all the fixins'. And it was delicious! Of course if I even think about a dinner like that today, my arteries start to clog, but who was thinking about diet and cholesterol in those days?

RECORD DATE AT CAPITOL

About this time I met Al Coury, who was the Capitol Records promotion man in Boston. I played some of our Game Bar tapes for him: "We've got this Bucci-plays-Basie thing going, Al. What do you think?" He liked it, and he sent the tape to Capitol's A&R department in New York. They must have liked it too, because Al came back to me and proposed a deal. Al signed Joe to the contract that led to the *Wild About Basie!* album for Capitol.

It was the first of many encounters I'd have with Al Coury, who became a good friend and ended up as a major figure in the recording industry on the West Coast.

Joe was excited. He had a recording contract with Capitol Records! John and I were excited, too. Knowing that the duo would need to be sharp for the recording session, we started hunting for a place to rehearse where we wouldn't be moving the equipment all the time. John had a friend named Joe Baptiste up on the North Shore, and Joe loved jazz and knew every place in town where you could hear it. He knew about a joint on Route 1 in West Peabody with a good jukebox and a small stage, where the owner was a good guy and might be open to doing something with us. So we went to meet him. His name was Lennie Sogoloff, and his place was the Turnpike Club, a roadhouse out on the highway. I said to Lennie, "Look, we've got Joe Bucci and Joe Riddick, and they've just been signed to Capitol Records, and they need to rehearse." Then I sweetened the pot: "And if we can rehearse here during the day, we'll play for you at night." Well, Lennie went for that.

The place was jammed every night—Joe had a strong local following, and we got on the radio to promote him. Norm Nathan had the overnight show on WHDH, a program for jazz night owls called *Sounds in the Night.* It was a great show with loyal listeners, and because it was the middle of the night, the advertising rates were dirt cheap. We advertised every night on Norm's show, building the audience for Joe Bucci at Lennie's club. And Joe packed the place.

Norm Nathan thought Joe was the greatest, and after the album was released, Norm gave it a lot of airplay. Of course, it didn't hurt that Norm's theme song on *Sounds in the Night* was Basie's "Midnite Blue," which was one of the tunes Joe recorded on *Wild About Basie!*

In June 1962, just a couple of days before we were off to New York to record, Al Coury called—the recording session was postponed for a week. That meant I had to get some work for Joe during the week we were hanging. I happened to be on Dartmouth Street in Boston, near the Back Bay train station, and I noticed a bar and restaurant called Lindy's. I poked my head into a long, narrow room with a stage way in the back. I thought the room might work for Joe.

I went in and met the boss, Harold Buchhalter, a well-known real estate developer and nightclub owner. I said, "Would you put some music in here for a week?" I went into my whole Joe Bucci story. He asked me what it would cost and how much I wanted. I told him $350. He didn't agree to that, but he offered to split the receipts—the first $100 was for the bartender, and after that we'd go 50/50 on the register. I thought that sounded pretty good, but I said, "You do a little bit of advertising. Can I use those same dollars but place them differently?" He agreed to that, and again we advertised on Norm Nathan's show, and again the turnout was good. At the end of the week, we pocketed $480, and Buchhalter was pleased. He made me promise to bring Joe back to Lindy's after the New York trip, which I did.

Lindy's was my first encounter with Harold, but by no means my last. In fact I owe a lot to him—it was Harold who got me started in the nightclub business at Paul's Mall, a story I'll tell in chapter 5.

We finally got down to New York and into the studio on June 19, and over the next three days recorded Joe's first album. Tom Morgan was the producer, and I remember telling him it was important that we get the bass right, to get a mike on those foot pedals to pick up that bass line. He made sure of it.

Joe was playing a lot of Basie in the clubs and it was very popular, so our concept for the recording was to do an all-Basie program. Connoisseurs of the Basie band recognize two great periods in the band's history. The earlier one, from the heyday of the big bands, is the "Old Testament" band. The 1950s band is the "New Testament" band. Joe loved 'em all, and he recorded a dozen numbers, half from the Old Testament years, like "Taps Miller" and "Topsy," and half from the New Testament years, like "Shiny Stockings" and "Splanky." When *Wild About Basie!* came out in early 1963, it earned a three-star review in *Down Beat*, and was also favorably reviewed in *Billboard*. Capitol Records, like most of the major labels at that time, operated a mail-order record club, and it gave the album a boost by making it the alternate selection of the month in May. *New York Times* critic John S. Wilson wrote that Joe had total command of his instrument. "He plays it for its mellow tone, its rich timbres. And he swings in an easy, effortless fashion strongly reminiscent of the man whose band is the source of all the tunes Bucci plays in this set: Count Basie."

ON STAGE AT NEWPORT

Two weeks after the recording date in New York, we hit another milestone. Joe performed at the 1962 Newport Jazz Festival, on Sunday afternoon, July 8. Because of the outdoor setting, the festival organizers wanted to create a bigger sound, and we expanded Joe's duo to a trio by adding tenor saxophonist Eddie Stack, who led his own band around the New Bedford and Providence areas. I once read that Stack was the only musician actually born in Newport, Rhode Island, to perform at the jazz festival. I wonder if that's still true.

After Newport, we took advantage of the publicity and booked Joe wherever we could. In that 1962–64 period, he was often at Lennie Sogoloff's club, which he treated as his home base.

Joe and I went to Los Angeles in September 1964, when Joe was under contract to Capitol, to plan a second LP. While we were there, he auditioned for the *Steve Allen Show*, but he didn't actually get a chance to play on the air. Nor did he ever do that second album for Capitol, but I recorded Joe again in 1965, on my own label, Intro Records. That was *Bucci Goes Two for the Show*, where we selected two tunes each from six different Broadway shows. We also released four of the tunes on an EP.

I thought Intro was a good name for a label. I created it first as a way to release Joe's second album, and then I planned to use it as a label for introducing new artists. I got involved with Paul's Mall and the Jazz Workshop though, and I never really got going with Intro.

I got Joe some dates with Lionel Hampton's orchestra, and there was talk of a tour with Hamp, but it didn't pan out. However, when we took over Paul's Mall in June 1965, Joe was our first act, and he did great business for us into 1967. He still had a strong local following. Joe Riddick was gone by then, and Joe's drummers while he was at Paul's Mall were Harvey Mason and Jeff Brillinger. They were both students at Berklee then, and they've both enjoyed long careers in music since.

Joe kept playing, but as a jazz artist, he reached his peak by 1964–65. He never broke into the big time, despite the push by Capitol Records. Perhaps he wasn't ambitious enough. He had a family by then, and I'm sure that played into it. In 1967 Joe, needing steady work, accepted a position with another organ company, and he began making appearances on their behalf and playing their organs in performance. He retired the Monster, and lost much of his Hammond-inspired following. After the mid-'60s, he took some criticism for using too many gimmicks and electronic effects, but he kept performing into the 1990s. Joe was 81 when he died in 2008.

I loved working with Joe. He was a wonderful guy, and I've never forgotten the debt of gratitude I owe him. Because of Joe, I became an artists' manager and began my career in the music business. I met Al Coury and Norm Nathan and Lennie Sogoloff, who were friends and colleagues for decades. And because of Joe, I produced my first name-band event, the Count Basie show that was almost rained out.

Joe Bucci had the greatest mastery of the Hammond organ of anybody I've ever known, and I still shake my head in wonder when I listen to *Wild About Basie!* today. I've heard many jazz organists since, but as far as I'm concerned, Joe still stands apart.

4

FINDING MY WAY

I won't deny that a bit of luck played a role in shaping my career, especially in the early years. I never looked in the want ads for a job. Opportunities seemed to find me. When people ask me how I got started in the music business, I tell them that I just fell into it, and that one thing led to another, and another, and another. I wasn't much for waiting for somebody to tell me what to do. When I saw something that needed to be done, I jumped in and did it. Every day was another lesson in my on-the-job training. I had to find my own way in this crazy business, and one thing was for sure: it wasn't like selling mattresses. If anything, it was more like being a drummer: you paid close attention to what was going on around you, and when the situation called for it, you improvised. It was an uncertain living, but I was out on my own, learning the ropes, and going where my intuition told me to go.

THE BIRTH OF HT PRODUCTIONS

In 1961, John Sdoucos and I started booking other artists besides Joe Bucci. In the language of the industry, we became an independent booking agency, presenting talent to the buyers in the clubs around town. Generally the club owners did their own buying, and I got to know many of them. That paid big dividends when I booked advertising for the *Boston Herald* for a time.

So how do you get started as a booker? You don't just send in a coupon and $4.95 and get a book on how to be a band booker in 10 easy lessons. The answer is, I don't really know. My hero, Mel Brooks, talked about the invention of psychiatry. "How did you become a psychiatrist?" asked his straight man, Carl Reiner. The 2,000 Year Old Man answered, "I put my hand on a rock and said, 'I am a psychiatrist!'" Well, I put my hand on Joe Bucci's shoulder and said, "I am a booking agent!" Next question, how did I find work for

Joe? I called people. I went to clubs and schmoozed with the owners, tried to get a booking. Making the rounds like this, I learned what was going on.

I started using HT Productions as my company name at about this time, but it already had a little mileage on it. Back in the mid-1950s, I thought I might find my way into the world of comedy as a writer. There were two of us with that idea, actually. The other was a college friend, Ed Halian, who was writing ad copy at Gillette. Ed and I shared an apartment on Beacon Street near Kenmore Square. We started HT Productions (for Halian-Taylor) to produce and sell our material, but nothing much came of it. We kept our day jobs. Then I started in the music business, and one day somebody asked for my card. I didn't have one, so I gave him an old HT Productions card instead. I still had no better name in mind, so when those were gone, I ordered another box of HT cards. It's been my company name ever since.

John and I started getting calls from artists who heard we were booking. I'd tell them, Okay, I'll see if I can find you something. One thing led to another. We got to know the big agencies, like Associated Booking Corporation and Shaw Artists, and started working with them. We'd take an artist from their roster whom we thought might do well, and try to sell him (there weren't too many women on their rosters yet). I remember booking saxophonist Zoot Sims in 1963, and flutist Herbie Mann, too. I booked a string of musicians at the Tic Toc, a joint on the corner of Tremont and Stuart in Boston. Alan Schwarz's place. There was a big oval bar in the middle of the room with a stage in the center of it. The musicians shared the stage with Schwarz's strippers. Maybe he thought if he added jazz, it'd make the place respectable. So I put jazz in there, good acts, like the great trombonists Al Grey and Vic Dickenson, who both had roots in the Basie band. So there were places like that. All part of learning my way around.

In the early '60s, I met the Boston singer Mae Arnette, who was equally at home singing jazz or R&B, and I became her agent. I found her nightclub work south of Boston and in Rhode Island. Then I got her into the Meadows, a big suburban supper club in Framingham that once was owned by Vaughn Monroe. I'd drive home late at night on Route 9, and I'd start nodding off at the wheel. If I started drifting out of my lane, Mae would wheel her car up right behind me and lay on the horn to wake me up. She kidded me about that for years.

I had Mae at Caribe Club in the Theater District, and they liked her and kept extending the engagement. Mae was a great ballad singer, and she'd sing "Danny Boy" and bring everybody to tears. There was a detective with the Boston PD who used to drop in at the Caribe. When Mae would see him coming, she'd call for "Danny Boy," and he'd always leave a big tip. Mae and I had some great times. By the 1970s, people were calling her "Boston's First Lady of Song."

We sometimes put Mae together with the pianist and composer Sir Charles Thompson, who was "knighted" by the saxophonist Lester Young, who decided Thompson needed a nickname. He settled on "Sir," and it stuck. Young was well known for coming up with memorable nicknames— he's the one who first called Billie Holiday "Lady Day." Anyway, Sir Charles and I became friends when I helped him straighten out a little problem with the musicians' union. In those days I had an upright piano in my apartment in Brookline, and he used to come by and play it.

One of the musicians we met through George Wein was trumpeter Howard McGhee, nicknamed "Maggie," who had been off the scene and was just getting back in action. He made a name for himself as a pioneering bebop trumpeter with blazing speed. We put him together with Phil Porter, a talented young organist from nearby Somerville. Like Joe Bucci, Phil played the Hammond B-3, but with a totally different conception. This was the early 1960s, when the clubs were booking organ trios as fast as we could find them.

Meanwhile, John Sdoucos was working for George as an advance man for his festivals. When George's company had a festival in Cincinnati, for example, John was out there working the press, contacting radio stations, and generally greasing the publicity wheels in southern Ohio. I was mainly a stay-at-home guy, but John liked the travel. George, though—I'd known George for years before he started the festivals.

George Wein and I both grew up in suburban Newton. My family lived on Brackett Road, and his was four or five blocks away on Ward Street. We've known each other for 65 years and been friends that long. George is four years older than me, so we didn't hang out together as schoolboys, but we both attended the John Ward Elementary School, Newton High School, and Boston University. We both studied piano with Margaret Chaloff. George opened Storyville in the Buckminster Hotel, a short distance from the BU campus, during my senior year in 1951. I met John Sdoucos at Storyville. And in 1962, when the powers that be in Newport invited George back to town to produce the Newport Jazz Festival (they tried another producer in 1961, without success), I put some seed money into the festival to see George on his way. He said thank you by putting Joe Bucci on that year's program—a prized place on the biggest stage in jazz. We've had a good working relationship through the years. And in 2015, he was at Scullers to personally present me with Berklee College's first George Wein Impresario Award.

THE WEST PEABODY CONNECTION

John and I had early success as booking agents in West Peabody, a North Shore suburb of Boston. Two clubs were across the Newbury Turnpike from each other: Wagon Wheels and Lennie's-on-the-Turnpike.

Jazz never had a better friend than Lennie Sogoloff, and he was my friend for 50 years too. We met Lennie back in chapter 3—Joe Bucci rehearsed in his club before his session with Capitol Records, played every night, and developed a strong following. Joe was a big success, so we followed with Mae Arnette, singing with Sir Charles Thompson's trio. Mae also became a fan favorite, and Lennie invited her back many times. I continued to work with Lennie on his club bookings over the holidays and into the new year—I'd tell Lennie about booking bands, and he'd tell me about making roast beef sandwiches. Lennie made the best roast beef sandwiches!

In February 1963, we brought in trumpeter Roy Eldridge as Lennie's first "name" jazz act. I told him, "Lennie, I think you got the message." He did, and Lennie's became one of the area's great clubs.

Even though he closed his club in 1972, Lennie never stopped loving the music. He *had* to hear it—it brought him joy. Twenty, thirty years later, when I was at Scullers, he'd come down from his North Shore home to hear his favorites. When he started having trouble getting around, I'd arrange for transportation. He came even when he was in a wheelchair, and he loved to banter with the musicians and tell war stories. Like I said, he was a true friend of jazz.

Meanwhile, across the highway, Steve Drougas ran the Wagon Wheels, a place that looked like a big red barn. It might have looked like a place for country and western music, but that's not the kind of entertainment John and I supplied. We had a great idea in 1963. We knew the Woody Herman band was headed up to New Hampshire for a weekend date. We thought they might take a Thursday night at the Wagon Wheels, which was right on their way up. They went for it, and we booked them for $900. Steve charged $5 at the door, and more than 300 people showed up. It was a big success, and Steve asked us if we could do this once a month. We could, and we proceeded to book Stan Kenton, Harry James, Maynard Ferguson, and the other road bands. They were all represented by the Willard Alexander Agency, the big band specialists back then. Putting big bands in a club midweek like that was a new idea, and it started a whole new booking concept.

INSIDE THE JINGLE MILL

In 1962, I started dabbling in the production end of the business, running a "jingle mill"—a recording studio that produced advertisements for the radio market. It was called the Raycraft Recording Studio. Before we get to Raycraft, though, we need to meet a few people at the Ace Recording Studio, Raycraft's owner and the best-known and busiest recording studio in Boston.

The Ace Studio was across the street from the Boston Common and down an alley. It was hidden away in an old office building, four flights up, and it usually looked like a tornado had just blown through. It was owned and operated by the Yakus brothers, Milt and Herb, known around town as "the Yaki." The engineer was a wizard named Bill Ferruzi. He was the engine that made Ace go.

I first walked in the door at Ace as a customer. John Sdoucos and I needed a professional demo for Joe Bucci to send to the record companies, and we worked with Bill to record a few of Joe's tunes. While we were there, I brought in Mae Arnette to record a few things with Joe. It didn't take me long to get the sound I wanted on tape. This yielded a gorgeous version of "I Should Care," and I still regret that I couldn't interest a record company in that song.

All this gave Herbie Yakus an idea. He told me, "We've got this jingle mill running. We have a salesman who sells commercials to radio stations around the country. The stations have sponsors, and our guy gets descriptions of the sponsors' products, and we make a demo for the station. If the station likes it, we produce a commercial, using a full band and four voices." I don't remember what a commercial cost, but it was cheap money at the time. And Herbie was doing all the work on that.

Herbie had a good operation. He knew what you needed for a jingle: voices to tell the story and a band to set the mood. He'd brought a big band into the studio to record backing music, and built up an inventory of more than 100 tracks. The sponsor would tell him what they wanted, and Herbie would pull one of those tracks off the shelf and put the vocal on top of it. Ace was selling a lot of commercials, and it was taking a lot of studio time. So Herbie said to me, "Listen, we just bought this recording studio in Cambridge, Raycraft Recording, and we'd like you to manage it. We want to produce a cheaper version of the jingles. You'll be the producer, and we'll give you the tracks." It was one of those things. I didn't look for this work, it found me. Never mind that I had no experience with jingles—I knew I could step right in because I knew how to get sound on tape and mix multiple tracks.

The "Ray" in Raycraft was Ray Fournier, who opened the studio in 1959. He started out recording country and western music and releasing the records on his own label. He was the studio engineer and a pretty good singer too. Fran Deveneau was the house pianist and also a singer, and both of these guys were blind! It didn't seem to slow them down, though. Gene Raschi, their promotions man, could sing too. I put them all to work on the jingles. And I brought in a fourth singer, Margot Shea, who played piano. Tony Texeira played bass and wrote most of the jingle lyrics. We'd bring in other musicians if we needed them, but this was our core group.

First we'd produce a demo track, with just a piano and one or two voices. We'd send that out, and if the sponsor gave the go-ahead, I'd bring in the other singers, put all four voices together, and pick a band track. And we'd do the full commercial. Actually, we'd do three commercials—the full 60-second version, then a 30-second version, and finally a 10-second spot.

Herbie Yakus hired me because the jingle mill was taking up too much of his time. The same thing started happening to me. Between the booking agency and artists' management, I had enough to do, and I decided to leave Raycraft. But it was a worthwhile experience—I sure learned how to write a commercial spot for radio airplay.

ONLY THE BEST PLACES

If the Number 3 Lounge were opening today, we'd call it "upscale." But we didn't use that word in 1963, so we just called this Park Square club "sophisticated." For a time in 1963 and 1964, they gave jazz singers a try, and I booked them—singers who would be at home in that kind of room.

Our first booking was a homecoming for Boston's own Teddi King, the globetrotting singer who straddled the line between jazz and pop. We backed her with an excellent trio of local jazzmen led by pianist Rollins Griffith. Talk about a performer who could get an audience eating out of her hand! She took a couple of days off in the middle of the engagement to fly to Los Angeles to tape an appearance on Steve Allen's TV show. Her fill-in was a New York singer making her first Boston appearance, Marge Dodson, who became an audience favorite, and a favorite of mine, a few years later at Paul's Mall. Teddi sang at Paul's Mall too.

Our biggest coup at the Number 3, though, was the husband-and-wife duo of Jackie Paris and Anne Marie Moss. Jackie had a big hit record with "Skylark," and I loved his version of that tune and jumped at the chance to bring him in. This was top-shelf entertainment, exactly what you'd want in a room that called itself sophisticated. Jackie was a great guitarist, Anne Marie was a wonderful ballad singer, their stage banter was witty, and they could *swing*. People took notice—even *Down Beat*, the national music magazine, sent a reviewer to cover their show.

IT'S SAND, MAN

Another place where I booked talent in the early '60s was Basin Street South, on Washington Street in the South End, in the shadow of the elevated tracks. Andy Martorano was the manager there. He was also a bookie on the side. One of his sons, John, became a notorious hitman for the gangster Whitey Bulger. That was bad business. But Andy was a good guy, I got along with him, and I booked some major singers at his club. Nancy Wilson was one, and Joe Williams, and Lambert, Hendricks & Bavan. Yolande Bavan had recently replaced Annie Ross in that trio.

I had Jimmy Slyde, one of the finest tap dancers of his generation, on a bill with singer Ada Lee one week. Jimmy, to my eternal embarrassment, got me up onstage to do a little shuffle with him. It happened like this: A few nights before, I was at the Pioneer Club, a Boston after-hours spot where the entertainers hung out. I was standing at the jukebox, talking to the famous jazz tapper Bunny Briggs. I had just booked him for a few concerts with his trumpet-playing pal, Roy Eldridge, and we were probably talking about that. A Basie record was playing, and I was shuffling my feet with the rhythm. Bunny looked down and said, "Man, you sand!"

And I said, "What do you mean?"

"That's what you're doing, they call that sand dancing. That's where the Basie song comes from." He was referring to a well-known tune the Count Basie band recorded in 1942, "It's Sand, Man."

I said, "You're kidding me. I always thought it had something to do with the sandman and sleep!"

"No, no," Bunny said. "It was dedicated to the dancers."

So then I was at Basin Street South, watching the show, and Jimmy Slyde was onstage. He must have talked to Bunny, because he called out, "My manager—he called me his manager even though I wasn't—is here, and he sands, and I'm gonna bring him up here." I'd had a few drinks, so I actually got up there, and I started doing a little shuffle with Jimmy, side by side. I was feeling good . . . and then I looked around and realized I was onstage at a busy nightclub. I said to myself, "What am I *doing*?" and I got off that stage in a hurry!

FIRST FORAY INTO FOLK AND POP

Even though I have a reputation as a jazz guy, most of my concert business at HT Productions was in the folk and pop worlds. I started with the Count Basie/Joe Bucci concert, but when I got serious about producing concerts early in my career, I presented folk artists. George Wein provided the spark.

George and Albert Grossman were business partners on some folk music ventures, including the Newport Folk Festival. Grossman was managing a roster of top folk artists, and he mentioned to George that he wanted them in Boston. He needed a local producer, and George sent him to me. So Ed Sarkesian, who managed Grossman's concert and tours business, called me, and he came at me with a big name right off the bat: Bob Dylan. This was mid-1964.

Ed Sarkesian was from Detroit, and before he met George and Albert, he had booked quite a bit of jazz. Through Ed, I ended up getting a lot of work from Albert Grossman, starting with Dylan. My role was producer. I prepared the budget, priced the tickets, rented the hall—and I got a good one, Symphony Hall—sent the newspapers photos and press releases, and bought newspaper ads. We quickly sold out Symphony Hall. And this was before Dylan had any commercial radio play. It was strictly because of his popularity on the folk circuit, the college campuses.

Grossman was pleased with the results of the Dylan concert, so Ed called me again and said he wanted to bring Peter, Paul and Mary to Boston. I ended up producing them not only in Boston but also in Providence and Worcester for several years. And after PP&M, Ed called again, this time with Gordon Lightfoot. I produced Lightfoot for five years in a row at Symphony Hall. In all, I must have worked with Ed for about 10 years.

Ed Sarkesian was a stickler for details. I had to provide a receipt for everything, no guesswork. I learned about expense reporting from Ed; he taught me the right way to do things, and he held me to it. I wasn't surprised—he had been an IRS auditor earlier in his career.

Oh, Peter, Paul and Mary enjoyed Worcester. After their concerts at the Memorial Auditorium, we'd go up the hill to Joe Aboody's restaurant, the original El Morocco. It wasn't a big place—back then it was still in the family home, a triple-decker on Wall Street. The restaurant was down in the basement. Al Coury from Capitol Records, a Worcester native himself, introduced us. Joe was a warm and welcoming host, and he loved music. Joe's dad played the doumbek, a Middle Eastern drum. He'd start with the Lebanese music he'd known all his life, and soon everybody would join in, singing and carrying on. And did we laugh! Those were unforgettable times.

So that's how it was in the 1960s, when I was finding my way in the music business. But it was all about to change when I got involved with Harold Buchhalter's Boylston Street clubs.

5

NIGHTCLUB OWNER

I've always said there were two VIPs in my early career. One was Joe Bucci, who started me in the music business, and the second was Harold Buchhalter, who started me in the nightclub business. I was a booking agent and artists' manager in 1963 when Harold tapped me to promote a club he was opening that September, the Jazz Workshop. One thing led to another, and three years later I owned it, and the one next to it, and the restaurant above it. Here's how it all happened.

HAROLD BUCHHALTER'S BOYLSTON STREET

Harold Buchhalter was a central figure in the development of nightlife in Boston's Back Bay. Without Harold, there would have been no Paul's Mall and no Jazz Workshop, and it would have been a very different scene on Boylston Street without him.

I met Harold at Lindy's, where Joe Bucci played in 1962, but I'd been in his clubs many times before without knowing it. Harold owned the Stable, one of my regular haunts in my Serta days. It was a basement bar on Huntington Avenue just outside Copley Square, across the street from Storyville. If Storyville was where the name bands worked, the Stable was where the top local musicians worked. It was the home of Herb Pomeroy's big band, and for someone like me, who loved the sound of Count Basie, Herb's band was the hottest thing in town. The guys in that band called the place the Jazz Workshop, a name they'd been using since the early '50s when some of them ran a little music school with that name.

Harold owned another club a few doors down on Huntington Avenue called the Showbar, a room with a vaudeville flavor where an ageless comedian named Freddie Hall was the emcee. It was across the street from Mechanics

Hall, a brick fortress of a building that served as Boston's first convention hall. They did everything at Mechanics Hall—boxing, boat shows, political rallies, everything. I worked furniture shows there for Serta. I used to build the displays for the booth myself.

Entertainment was only one of Harold's pursuits. He was investing heavily in real estate, around Kenmore Square and along Boylston Street in the Exeter Street area. There was a good reason for that.

When I met Harold in 1962, there wasn't much happening on Boylston Street west of Copley Square. As a matter of fact, it was a big construction site—the mammoth Prudential Center was being built on the old railroad yards. In 1962, it was mud and construction and traffic jams, but when "the Pru" opened in 1964, it would include a 52-story skyscraper, a Sheraton Hotel, three apartment towers, and retail space. In addition, the city of Boston was building the War Memorial Auditorium next door to the Pru, complete with a 4,500-seat auditorium. When all this was finally completed, it would be like opening a whole new part of the city along Boylston Street, with thousands of office workers, apartment dwellers, shoppers, and convention-goers looking for things to do and places to eat. Harold understood that and was one of the first to act on it.

Harold lost the Stable and the Showbar in 1962, when the state demolished their buildings to build a turnpike on-ramp. Even before the Stable closed, though, Harold was looking to relocate it to Boylston Street near the Pru. He was part owner of 733 Boylston, near the corner of Exeter Street, and in 1963, he opened the Inner Circle restaurant there. Next, he opened the Office Lounge at the corner of Boylston and Gloucester, two blocks away, and directly across from the auditorium then under construction. In September 1963, the Stable, reborn as the Jazz Workshop, opened downstairs below the Inner Circle.

He didn't stop there, either. He leased the basement space adjacent to the Jazz Workshop for another club, Paul's Mall, which opened in May 1964. It was different from the Workshop, more of a lounge, with comedy and music for dancing. The "Paul" in the club's name came from Paul Vallon, the club's first manager. As for the Mall, I was told that way back, there actually was a mall beneath the street, and it had something to do with automobiles, possibly serving as a showroom, but I never pieced together the whole story. In 1964, the "mall" was actually a wide corridor, and the club rooms were developed off it. We used it the way a theater uses its lobby.

Buchhalter opened one more place on Boylston Street in 1965, a seafood restaurant called the Half Shell, on the same block as the Inner Circle. It looked like a scene from the waterfront, with ships' lanterns and lengths of heavy chain strung between weathered beams reaching over the sidewalk.

Harold Buchhalter now owned three clubs and two restaurants, as well as a liquor store, within a few blocks of the Prudential Center and War Memorial Auditorium when they fully opened in May 1965. As he had predicted, there were thousands of people in the Back Bay who had never been there before, all looking for food, drink, and entertainment. There was foot traffic day and night along Boylston Street—there was never a better demonstration of the idea of "if you build it, they will come." Harold explained his business strategy to a newspaper reporter by saying, "Banks and that sort of thing don't draw people. Restaurants draw people, because they gotta eat three times a day. And a fella once told me that the only thing that spends money is people."

INTRODUCING MR. FACTS AND FIGURES

In the early '60s, I used to book bands at a popular club on Harvard Avenue in Allston called the Starlight Lounge. I booked my first act there in early 1961, my old friends the Jones Brothers, and they were a big success. That summer, I booked Joe Bucci there. I went out to listen to Joe, to see if the crowd there took to him the way they had at Jackie's Game Bar. I was happy to see everybody enjoying themselves. That's when I introduced myself to the club's owner, Tony Mauriello, who became my business partner for more than 20 years and a lifelong friend.

We hit it off. I liked Tony. He was an intelligent guy, and I enjoyed our conversations. Tony Mauriello wasn't just another guy running a tavern. Schooled at Bentley College, he had been the accountant at Samuel M. Gertman Company, a big restaurant supply firm, and after 10 years of that he wanted his own business. He bought the place in Allston in 1960.

I booked more acts at the Starlight Lounge. I booked the jazz pianist Sir Charles Thompson there with a singer named Betty Kenyon in 1962. Betty sang a bit like Anita O'Day, and I had to like her; she played the cocktail drum! She died very young, on the operating table—a tragic story. One night I brought Sir Charles and Betty into Raycraft and we recorded a few things like "Around the World in Eighty Days," and "The Ballad of All the Sad Young Men," which Anita had recorded around the same time. I still have that tape, and I cherish it.

Tony wanted to bring in bigger names, and to do that he needed to enlarge the Starlight and create more seating. He got the space by taking over the vacant shop next door and knocking down the dividing wall. I booked Ben E. King for the reopening and followed that with Bobby Hebb. Tony was doing well at the Starlight, but he told me that if a good opportunity came up to keep him in mind. That's when I introduced him to Harold, who was as impressed with Tony's business skills as I was. Tony had a head for business, and I called him "Mr. Facts and Figures."

Harold was developing a new club in Kenmore Square, with a small lounge fronting the street and a big main room behind it. The big room had a Grecian motif, with a fountain and murals of Mediterranean scenes. Harold made a deal with Tony to manage the place. He was going to call it the Forum, and he envisioned it as a discotheque. This was early 1964, and it would be the first upscale disco to open in Boston.

Discotheques were all the rage in 1964, and the most famous ones were in New York City. The high-class disco was Shepheard's in the Hotel Drake. Tony wanted to check out the operation firsthand, and he wanted Bill Hanley with him. Bill was the best sound man in the business. He'd installed the sound system for the Newport Jazz Festival, and in a few years he'd gain even more fame for installing the sound system at the Woodstock festival. Tony wanted great sound in his club, and that meant Bill. So the three of us drove to New York to look at Shepheard's and meet with Slim Hyatt, the top deejay in the city. After that trip Tony decided to do it, to open Boston's first high-end disco in the Forum. Bill Hanley installed the sound system. Tony hired a crew of college girls as waitresses and dressed them in billowy blue togas.

Actually, I think some of the club's ads referred to these young women as "toga-clad goddesses."

Tony had his disco, but there was that lounge in front, and he was having trouble coming up with a name. I suggested the What Ho Pub. That came from the 2,000 Year Old Man, who claimed to have seen Shakespeare's 38th and final play, *Queen Alexandra and Murray*, the bard's only flop. You didn't read this one in English class. There is a line, "What ho, Murray. What could it have been that I have seen?" and that inspired the name. It was a small bar with tables on one side and no real stage, and Tony hired guitarists from Berklee to play there. I also recall a few singing bartenders. The toga-clad goddesses were confined to the Forum.

THE NIGHT WHIRL OF ED MICHAELS

For years, newspaper advertising was the only sure way to reach a mass audience, and the papers' entertainment writers generated publicity with their interviews and reviews. Clubs couldn't have gotten along without them. There was one news hound, however, that I was especially fond of, and that was Ed Michaels of the *Boston Herald*, who was writing in the 1960s. You see, my friends, I was Ed Michaels!

It was 1963, and I was buying ads in the *Herald* whenever I booked an act in a club. That's how I met Ed Flanagan, who ran their advertising department. We were chatting about the ad business, and I told Ed I thought I could sell a lot of advertising if the paper created a Friday club page and put all the entertainment ads in one place. I knew the club owners around town would go for it. Ed not only set up the page, but he gave me a "What's Happening" column to write. We called it "Night Whirl," and the paper ran it every Friday. Somehow I found the time to write the column on top of everything else.

I wasn't the first person in town to write a column like this. The *Daily Record* had a big club listing on Mondays for years, with a column by Eddie Rugg plugging all the advertisers. The first edition of that one came out late Sunday night, along with all the lottery numbers and race results. But what I was doing at the *Herald* was a new approach. In Eddie's time, most of the clubs had seven-day bookings that started on Monday. That was his club page day. But we put our focus on Friday to catch the weekend trade, and the idea caught on, so we established that locally at the *Herald*.

With the page established, the advertising department took over booking the ads. I stayed with the column for years, but it got to be too much and I gave it up. It wasn't over for Ed, though, because I turned "Night Whirl" over to Jan Naples, and she carried on the tradition. But don't look for Ed Michaels in the Friday *Herald* this week. He surrendered his keyboard years ago.

OPENING PAUL'S MALL

In May 1964, Harold and Paul Vallon opened Paul's Mall, with Paul playing piano and his wife working as the hostess. The Mall was a lounge, geared for the singles crowd. Harold hired me to book the talent and handle promotion from day one. Part of my job as the promotions man was to invent a catch phrase for the club, and I came up with "Boston's only underground penthouse." Why? Because one wall was a diorama of a city skyline along its entire length—a skyline view like you'd see through a penthouse window. Don Aikens and George McQuade designed it, and it was quite novel. The lighting cycled through the whole day once per hour, from dawn to dusk and through the night and back to dawn again, so you could sit in one of the big armchairs and have your drink and watch the day go by. At night the buildings would shine with little twinkling lights. And it was three-dimensional, with a depth of about 2 feet. We installed a little fence to protect it. That diorama was in place until the day the club closed.

We carried the underground penthouse theme in our print ads, too, with an old-fashioned Beacon Hill streetlamp set against a bit of skyline. When the club opened, one columnist called it "sort of a gorgeous grotto."

Harold and Paul wanted some comedy, and I booked Henny Youngman for the grand opening. We had a house band too, the Penthouse Tenants, led by trumpeter Al Natale, for dancing.

I booked some great comics that first year at Paul's Mall: Professor Irwin Corey, Phil Foster, and George Carlin, who was on TV quite a bit and did well for us. He was still wearing a jacket and tie then and doing Al Sleet, the hippy-dippy weatherman. He actually had that job in Boston about five years before, when he read the news and weather on radio station WEZE. He was very funny, and he had great material. This was well before he changed his comedy to a more anti-establishment view and introduced us to the seven words he couldn't say on television. For a short time we hosted a talk show on WCOP-AM radio from the club, and the host, Tom Evans, interviewed our headliners.

In May 1965, Paul Vallon disappeared. Just disappeared. That was a real mystery at the time, and there were stories involving shady characters and gambling debts, but whatever the reason, Paul was gone. Harold asked me if I wanted to manage the club. I said yes, but not by myself. I wanted Tony to go in with me. Harold was comfortable with that. When I put it to Tony, he was all for it.

When we went to Harold's office to discuss terms, we were surprised to find another guy already there. It was Peter Lane, who was also interested in taking over Paul's Mall. That was the first time Tony and I met Peter, who was working as the function manager at a suburban country club.

When Harold was thinking, he'd hum. So there sat the three of us, and there's Harold—hmmm, hmmm, hmmm—and finally he said, "Why don't the three of you get together to operate it." Even though we didn't know each other, we decided to do it. The terms were very favorable. We were to pay Harold something like $500 a week over the life of the agreement, which was great from a cash flow standpoint, because we didn't have to come up with a small fortune to buy our way in. With Harold, you did business with a handshake. His word was his contract, and he never reneged on a deal. So we became comanagers of Paul's Mall, the three of us. That was on June 5, 1965.

We incorporated. It was very simple. There was probably a lawyer involved someplace, but as a general rule we tried to stay away from lawyers whenever possible. We formed MTL Incorporated—Mauriello, Taylor, and Lane, with offices at 739 Boylston Street, on the third floor. We divided the responsibilities according to our strengths and stayed out of each others' ways. I booked the entertainment and took care of the advertising and publicity.

Tony concentrated on the business side of the operation, and Peter was the floor man, supervising the staff and minding the cash register.

Peter was of Greek descent, and he was effusive and enthusiastic. Every day he'd greet you like a long-lost cousin: "Freddie, Freddie, you look good today. You feeling alright? Freddie, let me look at you, oh, you're looking good." And he loved to flatter women: "Oh, what a beautiful girl. Turn around, let me see you, oh, you look lovely." Peter seemed to know everyone in the Greek merchant marine; whenever a Greek vessel would call in Boston, its captain would visit Peter at Paul's Mall, and after every one of those visits, a new busboy would start upstairs in the Inner Circle—polite, hard-working, almost no English, never stayed around too long. I used to call it Peter's Greek Underground. I always wondered where those kids came from, but I didn't ask too many questions.

OPENING THE JAZZ WORKSHOP

The Paul's Mall prequel—its time before MTL came along—lasted just one year. The Jazz Workshop's was longer, going back a little more than a decade, and it's one of the great stories of Boston jazz.

The Jazz Workshop at 733 Boylston Street in Boston's Back Bay opened on September 13, 1963, but that wasn't the beginning of the story. For that, we have to go back to 1953. That's when a handful of Boston's jazz musicians got together and started a little school in an office building on Stuart Street called the Jazz Workshop.

A year later, the manager of the Stable, a nightclub on Huntington Avenue, dropped by the school to see if he could hire a band for his club. He hired pianist Ray Santisi, tenor saxophonist Varty Haroutunian, and drummer Peter Littman to play at the club. They called themselves the Jazz Workshop Trio and started playing in April 1954.

It didn't take long for the Jazz Workshop musicians to start cooking at the Stable, and more musicians started coming around. In late 1955, trumpeter Herb Pomeroy formed a big band that played two nights a week. Among the sax players was my old pal Serge Chaloff. Inspired by the bands of Count

Basie and Woody Herman, the Pomeroy Orchestra was a hard-swinging crew. I spent many, many nights at the Stable listening to that band.

The end came when the Commonwealth of Massachusetts took the property by eminent domain to make way for a turnpike on-ramp. The club closed in summer 1962, but that wasn't the end of the Jazz Workshop. Harold Buchhalter, who owned the Stable, promised the musicians a new Jazz Workshop in 1963, on Boylston Street, not far from the new Prudential Center. And as we've already noted, Harold knew that when the Pru opened, Boylston Street would become the most exciting place in Boston.

Harold transferred his liquor license from the Stable to his new room, and hired Varty Haroutunian, the Stablemate with the head for managing, to run the place. Like the Stable, the new room would be beneath the street, but it would seat about 175, double the occupancy of the old club. It would continue to be a haven for the top local musicians, but the new Jazz Workshop would book name bands too.

The time was right for a name-band jazz room in Boston in 1963. In fact, the only place in the city of Boston where you could consistently hear jazz players with any kind of national or regional reputation was at Connolly's, on Tremont Street in the South End. Connolly's had a house trio that would accompany touring guest artists—"singles," as they were called—during their engagement. Connolly's, though, was basically a neighborhood bar, a plain room that lacked a nightclub atmosphere. The Jazz Workshop would be a step up from that. And I have to say it: there were whites who weren't comfortable going to Connolly's, which was in a mainly black neighborhood.

By August, Harold's new Jazz Workshop was almost ready. The space was renovated, the manager hired, the musicians booked. What he needed was promotion, and for that he called me. Harold liked how I'd promoted Joe Bucci's engagement at Lindy's the year before, and he wanted that kind of print and radio advertising for the new club. The Jazz Workshop was my account from the day it opened—which happened to be on Friday the 13th, in September 1963. I still have the first press release I wrote for the new room, and here's a bit of it:

Jazz fans everywhere can rejoice, for the famed Jazz Workshop re-opens its doors this Friday, September 13, at a new address.

Formerly known as the Stable, located on Huntington Avenue, the club was torn down to make room for the New Boston. The new address, 733 Boylston Street, is directly across from the focal point of the All American City, the Prudential Center.

The smoke-filled Stable has been replaced by a room taste-fully done in chocolate brown, from the soft carpets to the walls. Illuminated photographs of the greats of jazz, taken by Boston's Lee Tanner, adorn the walls . . . many of them will appear on the stage of the new Jazz Workshop in the future. The "formal" informality of this club doesn't frown on casual dress but does require that the gentlemen wear jackets.

It's like a bit of time travel, isn't it? When the Prudential Center and Government Center were under construction, Boston's boosters were talking a lot about the "New Boston." And the All American City? Boston was awarded that designation in 1962 by the National Civic League because of all the "New Boston" activity. Those were the buzz words of the day. And how long has it been since gentlemen were required to wear a jacket at a jazz gig? At least we were "Friday casual" about it and didn't ask for a necktie too.

It's a pleasure to remember Lee Tanner, one of the great photographers of jazz. *Down Beat* and other magazines published his photos regularly. But photography wasn't his occupation—it was his passion. Lee was a scientist, a metallurgist, at a company in Cambridge, but he loved jazz, and he spent many nights at the Jazz Workshop and Connolly's taking pictures. It wasn't until I read this old press release, though, that I remembered Lee's photos hanging on the Workshop's walls.

Opening weekend was a shakedown cruise, three nights working out the kinks and confusion inevitable with the opening of a new place. Herb Pomeroy's sextet provided the music, and just for the record, the band on that opening weekend was Pomeroy, Santisi, bassist John Neves, trombonist Gene DiStasio, saxophonist Jimmy Mosher, and drummer Pete LaRoca.

The grand opening of the Jazz Workshop followed a few days later on Tuesday, September 17, when Stan Getz, one of the most popular saxophonists in jazz, opened a six-night stand. Landing a star as bright as Getz was a major coup for a new room. It was Getz's first Boston appearance in six years, and he was working as a single with Pomeroy's band.

Varty Haroutunian managed the Jazz Workshop for its first three years, and my role then was mainly in advertising and promotions. The bookings were Varty's though, and his schedule mixed local jazzmen, mostly veterans of the Stable, with nationally known artists. He brought in artists who stayed with the Jazz Workshop long after he departed, like Bill Evans, Mose Allison, and Mongo Santamaria. He also brought the legendary John Coltrane Quartet to the club.

AND THEN WE BOUGHT THE CLUBS

Now we circle around one more time, and bring both club stories back together in spring 1966. We heard a rumor that Harold wanted to sell the Inner Circle Restaurant, and that put us into a bit of a panic, because we didn't know what having a new owner would mean for our lease at Paul's Mall. We decided to make a move of our own—we went to Harold and offered to buy it. Then the discussion expanded to include Paul's Mall, and then it expanded again to include the Jazz Workshop. The discussions moved quickly. On June 5, the MTL partners were managers of a single nightclub. On June 6, we became owners of two clubs and a restaurant. It was one year and one day after we took over management at Paul's Mall.

Tony became the business manager for the whole operation, and Peter took over day-to-day management in the Inner Circle. (A few years later we closed the restaurant and converted the space into a small cinema, a story I'll get to in chapter 12.) Varty was still managing the Jazz Workshop. Then Tony heard that Varty was thinking of moving the jazz club to a new location, but Varty said no, there was nothing to it. After MTL became the owners of the Jazz Workshop, however, Varty went ahead with plans to move to the Hotel Bradford, in the Theater District. He opened his own place there in September 1966. He wanted to take the name "Jazz Workshop" with him, based on his long association with it, and he actually did call his new space the Jazz Workshop for a short time. We said no to that—Harold owned the club and he sold it to us. We ended up going to court over the rights to the name, and the decision went in our favor, and the name stayed with the club. Varty renamed his new place Varty's Jazz Room, and the Jazz Workshop remained on Boylston Street. I was now booking the entertainment in both rooms.

And that, my friends, is how I became a nightclub owner. We'll dive into those clubs in the chapters to come.

6

THE PAUL'S MALL STORY

Paul's Mall opened in 1964 (a story I told in chapter 5), and I was involved with the Mall from the day it opened until the day it closed in 1978. Name a role, and I filled it: publicist, talent buyer, manager, owner . . . not to mention sound and lighting technician, doorman, and occasional plumber. In June 1965, Harold asked Tony Mauriello, Peter Lane, and me to manage the Mall, and that's where we pick up the story in this chapter.

The Jazz Workshop presented the best in jazz and blues seven days a week for 14 years. Paul's Mall could not have been more different. It was a lounge for swinging singles, a cabaret, a comedy club, a nightclub for big-name headliners, and a showcase for emerging pop talents. Paul's Mall was all of these at one time or another.

The club changed as the audience changed. When Tony, Peter, and I came in, we aimed our entertainment at a downtown working crowd who were looking for a level of sophistication in their nightlife. These people were not diving headfirst into rock, even though there was a lot of it on the radio. We were more interested in the people going to work every day in the Prudential Center than the college students, who weren't old enough to buy a drink in Massachusetts anyway. But the rock wave was inevitable, and over time our audience got younger and wanted to hear more of it. In the 1960s, we presented Bobby Short and Jackie and Roy. In the 1970s, we presented Jimmy Buffett and Bob Marley.

You do what you have to do to survive in the nightclub business. You can change with the times, or you can close your doors. I myself resisted the move into contemporary acts for a time. I turned 40 in 1969, and yes, there was a generational thing at work. After all, I was a true-blue jazz fan and the

Count Basie Orchestra was my favorite band. But I've said many times that if I booked a nightclub strictly according to my personal taste, I'd be closed in three months. I had a choice at Paul's Mall. I could either make room for Kool & the Gang and Randy Newman, or I could go back to Serta Mattress.

I'm not knocking it. We had a mix of talent in the 1970s that no other club in the region could match. There was comedy, cabaret, soul, pop, jazz, oldies, folk, reggae, and blues. We had country-rock, folk-rock, jazz-rock, you-name-it-rock. It's a cliché, but I'll say it anyway: we had something for everybody. That's how we made it in the 1970s.

SWINGING '60S SINGERS

Truth be told, Paul's Mall wasn't doing too well when MTL took over in June 1965. The time wasn't right for a comedy club, and we needed something else to liven the place up and give people a reason to come down the stairs. Our first act in June 1965 was old friend Joe Bucci, still very popular, and with Joe swinging at the Hammond organ, the club had its best week in six months.

I went looking for singers. A good pop or jazz-pop singer was a reliable draw in 1965, and I found one in a downtown lounge called Chez Freddie's. Her name was Maggie Scott, and she played excellent piano to go with her singing. She worked as a duo with her bassist/husband, Eddie Stone. Maggie was a near-constant presence at the Mall in 1965–66, and today she's still teaching young singers how it's done at the Berklee College of Music.

I found a terrific group in Rhode Island that didn't have one singer; it had four. That was the Carey-Gee Four, fronted by a former big-band vocalist, Judy Carey. Speedy Gee, whose real name was Howard Garfin, played clarinet and all the saxes, Danny Skea played keyboards and did all the arranging, and John Davis was the drummer. They worked on the Four Freshmen's model, and all the guys sang as well as played. An engineer named Rik Tinory and I recorded the group live at the club in 1966, and we released an album titled *Zip-a-Dee-Doo-Dah* on our own label. It wasn't a hit record, though, and in 1967 the group moved on to Las Vegas and Lake Tahoe, where all the good lounge acts seemed to end up in those days.

The search for fresh faces took me to New York, where I found Marge Dodson, a singer with two Columbia albums to her credit. I first brought her to Paul's Mall in August 1965. She was just the *greatest* singer. She had it all— the sound, the timing, the phrasing. Marge returned for her second residence in February 1966, and by that time we had lined up a new house trio, led by pianist Dave Blume. His trio, with bassist Mel Nowell and drummer Wayne Waylett, was the house band at Paul's Mall for about a year. Dave was robbed of a recording career by a fateful accident. He was helping another musician move some equipment, and as they were moving across the sidewalk, Dave stepped into a trapdoor carelessly left open. He broke his wrist in the fall. Those were the days of hard plaster casts, and Blume had one—and he still figured out how to play credible piano with one hand. Unfortunately, the accident cost him a recording date with Verve Records.

Marge Dodson was just terrific with Dave Blume's trio, and I was anxious to get them on tape. Rik Tinory recorded them at Paul's Mall, and if I could have presented that music to a record company, I'm sure her career would have been quite different. Nothing seemed to click for her though, and eventually she dropped out of show business. She had another career to fall back on—she was newsman Harry Reasoner's secretary at ABC-TV.

Marge Dodson and Dave Blume both played at Paul's Mall for the last time in October 1968. I kept in touch with Marge after her performing days were over, and at one point I copied those tracks to a CD and gave it to her. I called her later to see what she thought of her younger self. She said, "Fred, I didn't know I sounded so good."

Another one of our New York singers had a different style completely, and that was Pola Chapelle, a *chanteuse* from the Greenwich Village clubs. She sang for the first time at the Mall in November 1965, backed by Keith Jarrett, who was playing dinner music upstairs at the Inner Circle at the time. She had a certain sophistication that appealed to me and a definite international flavor—she sang in French and Italian as well as English, and always included songs in those languages in her sets. There was a warmth, an intimacy, to her performance, and Paul's Mall had its most cabaret-like nights during Chapelle's engagements. She eventually gave up singing to make films.

BRIGHTER LIGHTS AND BIGGER STARS

Things were going well, and in November 1965 we decided to take a chance and book our first $1,000 act, the superlative duo of Jackie Cain and Roy Kral. They had been making music together for almost 20 years, and they had eight or nine albums to their credit. I *loved* Jackie and Roy's singing and had since I first heard them at Storyville in the mid-1950s. Even better, our customers loved it, and the duo played our club 11 times. But that first engagement in November 1965 was especially memorable for what stopped the show.

Jackie and Roy opened on Monday, November 8. On Tuesday I went to the office as usual, and late that afternoon I was on the phone with Noel Kramer, an agent with the Associated Booking Company in New York. I clearly remember what happened next. I glanced out the window and sort of pulled back in surprise from what I saw. Or didn't see. I said, "Noel, there's something funny here. I'm looking out my window and there are no lights in the city. And the office lights are out, too."

A few seconds passed, and he said, "What did you just say?"

I said, "I can't see any lights anywhere in the city."

He said, "I don't see any lights in New York either—we're dark." I got nervous, and I had a bit of a fright when I realized that this was much more than just a local power failure. Had the cold war just gotten hot? No, it was nothing like that: it was the first moments of the Great Northeast Blackout of 1965.

Our first $1,000 act, and we're in the dark.

What, and give up showbiz?

Jess Cain, the morning man on WHDH radio, often interviewed my artists on his program. Cain was an institution in Boston; he was on WHDH for more than 30 years. He was on the air when the Jazz Workshop opened in 1963, and he was still on the air when Scullers Jazz Club opened in 1989. He was the hot morning guy on Boston radio, and he had a huge, loyal audience. This was a natural promotion for us with Jackie and Roy—we could do "Cain Meets Cain."

Jackie and Roy always seemed to be having fun, even when they were answering interview questions they had heard countless times before. They knew the routine, and show hosts welcomed them because of their perpetually sunny dispositions. So there they were, cheerfully bantering with Jess and singing a few numbers. Jess wound up the segment with a typical close: "You can catch Jackie and Roy at Paul's Mall through Sunday night . . . and tell us Roy, where do you go from here?"

Roy looked at him, totally deadpan, and said, "Up. Straight up." And Jess Cain, a very witty guy who usually had a comeback for everything, had no answer for that.

A year later, we brought Bobby Short to Paul's Mall, our biggest act so far. He boosted the prestige of the club just by walking in the door, and we were lucky to have him.

Bobby had some bad luck in 1966, and that's what made him available to us. He had been part-owner of a place in New York called Le Caprice, which failed and drained all of his savings in the process. He needed work, and his agent heard about what we were doing at Paul's Mall. He had exactly the style and tone we wanted. We signed him for a return engagement before he even left town that first time.

Everyone remembers Bobby as the elegant star of the New York cabarets, but people forget what a great jazz pianist he was. He liked Nat Cole and Art Tatum, and you could hear both in his playing. Even in 1966, he was already one of the finer interpreters of the Great American Songbook. He was especially drawn to the songs of Cole Porter, and I'll bet he included at least one Porter tune in every set he played. Over a span of about two years, we booked Bobby a half-dozen times for a total of 14 weeks. Years later at Scullers he told me, "You kept me alive with that work at Paul's Mall." I was thrilled with that—it was a great compliment coming from a real gentleman.

GRECO MEETS DANGERFIELD

With Marge Dodson, Jackie and Roy, and Bobby Short, Paul's Mall was telling the world what kind of club it was. In December 1968, though, I was looking for something different, and I found it: José Greco and his 13 Spanish dancers.

From the mid-1940s to the mid-1970s, if you mentioned José Greco to most Americans, their heads would instantly fill with images of whirling flamenco dancers and the sounds of Spanish guitars. Greco *was* Spanish dance in those years, and even if he wasn't strictly authentic, he was hugely popular, constantly touring and appearing on television. He made an annual stop at Symphony Hall and regularly visited the local college campuses. He was not what you'd call a nightclub regular, but we found a way to bring his entourage to Paul's Mall.

The obvious question is, how do you stage a dance troupe in a nightclub? They needed room to move, and to provide it, we installed a basketball court. We removed the tables up front and extended the stage with a wood plank floor in order to show off the sight and sound of Greco's fancy footwork. We barely got the floor down in time—the carpenters were still working on it during the afternoon of the first show.

And it was worth it! You might think someone like me, with a lifelong love of the easy grace of tap dancing, wouldn't have much to say about Greco, but believe me, this was a case of shock and awe and I loved every minute of it. Greco up close, stamping his heels in imitation of galloping horses (one of his signature pieces), was truly something to see. And hear.

Greco was a courtly European gentleman of impeccable manners and demeanor. His character is central to a Paul's Mall story involving a well-known comedian and my friend Joe Aboody. I've mentioned Joe, whose family owned the El Morocco Restaurant in Worcester. Joe loved jazz—the El Morocco itself became a jazz club in the early 1980s—and he loved the Jazz Workshop. When he closed his place, he'd round up a car full of people and race down the turnpike to Boston to catch the last set. This particular night, he didn't race down the pike to see Greco, he came to see Miles Davis, who was next door at the Workshop. Joe and his crew arrived while Miles was on break, and they poked their noses into the Mall to see what was going on, but Greco had just finished for the night.

Now our comedian was a friend of Joe's and was working that night at the Surf in Revere. He met up with Joe at the Workshop. When Joe saw the empty Paul's Mall stage, he said, "Let my friend onstage to do a show." The room had emptied by then, but Joe's a friend, so I said okay. The guy started with some very blue material. Suddenly Greco came storming out of the dressing room, angry, and he was standing with his back ramrod straight and arms akimbo, more a matador than a flamenco dancer. He said, "*What is this filth that I am hearing?*" Everybody froze. Then Greco stomped out of the room, and the comedian shrank back into his seat, to be heard no more.

That comedian was Rodney Dangerfield, and he sure didn't get no respect from Greco, who later told me he took offense because he thought there were still ladies in the room who shouldn't have to hear Rodney's off-color material. And you know what? Maybe it's because I never got that image of a furious José Greco out of my head, but I never did hire Rodney to work at any of my clubs.

"WHAT BUSINESS ARE WE IN?"

In October 1969, we had the opportunity to bring in the jazz pianist Erroll Garner, which would have been a huge act for us, our biggest so far. Garner was a one of a kind, with a distinctive jazz style that crossed over to a wide popular music audience. Engaging him in a nightclub would be a major accomplishment for us. However, an artist of Garner's stature and reputation came at a cost. Up to that time, we had never spent more than $5,000 for an act at either the Mall or the Workshop. Mel Torme was $5,000, Miles Davis was $5,000, even José Greco and all his Spanish dancers were $5,000. Most acts were significantly less, and only a few topped $3,000 per week.

Erroll Garner was a $7,500 act. That would be over $53,000 today. Whoa! I sat down with Tony to talk over the numbers. Tony, the clear-headed businessman, had a better understanding of risk than I did, and he thought it was a great opportunity for us. He believed that a big act would draw a big audience, and that if people wanted to see a big act, they'd pay a little more for it. In those days, that meant a $3.50 ticket, which would be about $25 today. How times have changed!

Then Tony asked me, "Fred, what business are we in? Are we selling booze or are we selling entertainment? If we're selling entertainment, okay, then let's go all out." We booked Erroll Garner, and that opened the door.

Every agent and every manager in the country heard about it, and it moved us into the upper echelon of nightclubs, and we immediately began booking artists from the very top shelf. Within a matter of months, we presented pop, jazz, and comedy acts we couldn't touch before, including Hugh Masekela, Oscar Peterson, the Four Tops, George Shearing, David Frye, and David Steinberg.

After we made the decision that liquor sales were secondary to entertainment charges, we decided to start charging an admission at the door. It sounds funny to say it now, but in 1970, for a nightclub to charge an admission, like a movie theater, was unknown in Boston. Until then, we all added an entertainment charge to the guest check. Some places imposed a drink minimum, and we did that in our early years. The suburban supper clubs included the entertainment charge in the hefty price of the dinners. We decided to do away with all of that, because there was no way we could sell enough liquor to cover a $7,500 act.

Thus we began to sell tickets at the door, and it was an innovation at the time. It seemed like such a good idea that something had to go wrong with it, and for us, that came in the person of the chairman of the Boston Licensing Board, an old-time Boston Irish politician named Albert "Dapper" O'Neil, who opposed the idea of charging admission to a place that sold alcoholic beverages. He maintained it wasn't legal. He took it to the state senate, intent on making sure the law clearly stated that such an establishment could not charge an admission at the door.

You might ask, what's the big deal? The answer is tax revenue. There was no tax on entertainment, so no tax could be levied on an admission fee collected at the door. There was, however, a sales tax collected on meals and beverages. So I charge you $5 at the door, there's no tax. But if I add the $5 to your bar bill, it's taxable. A second tax, the club alcoholic beverages tax, was calculated as percentage of gross receipts—those bar bills again. So Dapper and the Department of Revenue had those two reasons for keeping things the way they were, with entertainment charges added to the check.

We went round for round with the revenue department on this, and a legislator who happened to be a club regular arranged a meeting with the state's tax commissioner, Nicholas Metaxas—a name I thought was particularly appropriate for someone in his line of work. I showed him contracts from the William Morris Agency that guarantee the performer a percentage of the admission. A theater owner can quickly calculate that amount, but I couldn't. Furthermore, this was interstate commerce, which was outside his jurisdiction. That was when he recognized that this was more than just a charge to the public, it was basic to a legally binding contract. Then I fed the fire a little more, noting that the Mall and the Workshop had the same liquor license as Symphony Hall and Fenway Park. If I couldn't charge an admission for my entertainment, they couldn't charge for theirs either.

"Think about that, Mr. Metaxas," I said. "Let's have free admission at Symphony Hall, but charge $10 for the program. Or let's have free admission at Fenway Park, along with $10 hot dogs and $20 beers. You could charge more when the Yankees were in town. Well, you're asking me to do the same thing. Let's have free admission to Erroll Garner with a six-drink minimum. For an act that's not as big as Garner? We'll have a three-drink minimum."

I made some points with him, to be sure, but things didn't change, and at one point the revenue department threatened to slap a lien on us because we weren't paying our taxes.

It didn't stop there, either. As I was digging through the fine print, I found language tacked onto a transportation bill that would establish a "general admission license." Any business that charged an admission at the door would have to obtain one. The fee for it would be $200 to $500. Well, when would it be $200, and when would it be $500? There were no explanations or qualifications, just those dollar amounts. Would the Orpheum Theater need this license? Would St. Margaret's church need one if they charged admission to their annual Christmas concert? I immediately saw the worst case—an inspector charging me $500, submitting $200 to meet the requirement, and pocketing the rest.

We finally took our protest to Governor Sargent. We bombarded the governor's office with telegrams, saying if he signed the bill, the state would immediately be sued by over 5,000 establishments that served alcohol. It stopped there. We finally had the ability to charge an admission fee.

My brush with the lawmakers was quite an experience, I'll tell you. But I was kind of feisty in those days and wasn't willing to lie down when the dispute was so important to our livelihood.

GARNER MEETS GARROWAY

One more Erroll Garner story, this one a little less taxing. Dave Garroway was already a big name in television when he came to WNAC in Boston with a new show, *Tempo Boston*, in 1969. But before WNAC he had been the host of NBC's *Today* show for 10 years, and before that he was one of the top jazz disc jockeys in Chicago. Garroway just loved jazz, and one guy he was crazy about was Erroll Garner.

I called WNAC and asked to talk to Garroway's producer. They put me through to her and I said, "I have Erroll Garner for Dave Garroway!" Nothing. She had no idea who Erroll Garner was. "Okay, just do me a favor, please find Dave Garroway, and ask him if he'd like to have Erroll Garner on the show." After a little more convincing, she went looking for him.

Ten minutes later, she was back: "How soon can you get here?" So I brought Erroll to the WNAC studio, and Dave did a short interview—and talked up Garner's appearance at Paul's Mall, bless him—and asked Erroll if he'd play a little. Of course he said yes, and he walked over to the piano, but there was no bench. Now Garner was a short man, just over 5 feet tall, and nicknamed "the Elf." He was known to sit on telephone directories to get the proper height at the piano.

Garroway said, "Oh, that's right, you need some height." So he signaled offstage, and in came a forklift with the piano bench. It pulled up to the piano, Erroll sat down, the operator adjusted the height, and Erroll played. That was Garroway at his best.

You can call that public relations, or promotion, or just a gimmick, but whatever you call it, people mentioned to me that they saw Erroll and the forklift as they were leaving Paul's Mall after enjoying the show. You don't think Garroway knew a few things about promotion? I thought it was a

shame that WNAC canceled the show after about nine months, and Dave
moved on.

HEY DAD, WHO IS THIS GUY GERSHWIN ANYWAY?

Even if there had been no battle with the taxing authority, 1970 wasn't a great
year for our nightclubs. The full impact of the rock revolution that began
with the Beatles was coming down hard on us. I can't say the audiences for
jazz and pop were shrinking, but they certainly weren't growing, and some
of our big acts in those areas were getting too expensive for us. Popular tastes
were changing, and the audience for rock and soul music was growing—and
it was getting younger.

This decline led us to experiment with a musical revue at Paul's Mall in
January 1971. We were looking for something that could build an audience,
go on an extended run, and help us put some money in the bank. Thus was
Hey Dad, Who Is This Guy Gershwin Anyway? born.

It started with Herb Hendler, a successful record producer and the former vice president of Beechwood Music, the music publishing subsidiary of
Capitol Records. He gave that up for the musical theater, and he ended up in
Boston, where our mutual friend Buck Spurr introduced us. Herb wanted to
produce a show, but not just any show, he wanted to produce a show based on
music that he loved, the music of George Gershwin. He talked Tony and me
into it—it fit our idea of presenting something capable of an extended run.
So Herb got to work writing the book and choosing the music. We hired the
musicians and had cast auditions at the club.

When the dust settled, we had ourselves a two-act show with 22 songs, a
singing and dancing cast of 10, and a crack band. We had entered the world
of cabaret theater.

The title was my idea. Here we were, presenting music to a generation
of listeners who didn't know much about Gershwin, and I pictured a puzzled
student-aged kid talking to his father, saying, "I've seen this show advertised,
but I don't know. . . . Hey dad, who *is* this guy Gershwin, anyway?"

Herb wanted to do a multimedia presentation, which was a far simpler thing to do in 1971 than today. We turned the wall behind the stage into a big screen by covering it with sheets of plywood painted white. We had three or four projectors in the sound booth, which was directly opposite the stage, and we projected images to fit each song—each song was produced like a scene, a little vignette. As a song would end, the lights would go down, and we'd project Gershwin-era images of photos or advertisements. I remember one, an ad from the *Saturday Evening Post,* pictured George Gershwin himself smoking a Chesterfield cigarette.

We had a good show band. Jeff "Skunk" Baxter was the guitarist, and he later went with Steely Dan and the Doobie Brothers. He was tagged with the nickname "Skunk" during the show, but I never did find out why. John Nagy, who became a successful recording engineer, was the music director, and pianist Jeff Lass wrote all the arrangements. Each one was done in the style of a contemporary group, so the Gershwin music had an updated, jazz-rock sound to it. One of our singers grew up singing in church, and he sang a swinging gospel version of "I Got Rhythm" that was just a killer. Lass also wrote arrangements of "Rhapsody in Blue" and "An American in Paris" to use as overtures. We had a lot of music—I think there were 22 Gershwin pieces altogether. It was great music, contemporary updates of the Gershwin song-book, but sadly, we never captured a good recording of it.

Hey Dad, Who Is This Guy Gershwin Anyway? ran for about six weeks starting on January 24, but it just didn't take hold, and we finally closed after the March 7 show. We lost money—not enough to sink us, but enough to leave us feeling some pain.

Buck Spurr loved the show. We sold him the rights to it, and he produced it in Cambridge a few years later with a different cast and a new title. The results were the same though, and that was the end of it.

We were a few years ahead of our time with *Hey Dad.* That concept, those kinds of revues, later became popular at dinner theaters, at places in the Boston suburbs like the Château de Ville in Framingham. I think if we mounted that show today, it would be a hit. Gershwin's music is timeless, and singers like Lady Gaga have shown a renewed interest in the Great American

Songbook. And multimedia shows are far more exciting now than they were in 1971. It's nice work if you can get it.

A YEAR OF TRANSITION

For Paul's Mall, 1970 was a milestone year, a year of highs and lows with some great, and some not so great, moments. It was an 18-month year, stretching from Erroll Garner's visit in October 1969 to *Hey Dad's* closing in March 1971. We learned a few things that year. With Garner, we learned we could bid for the top acts in the business, regardless of genre or style of entertainment. And after *Hey Dad*, we committed ourselves to contemporary acts and began working closely with the radio stations and record companies to promote them. The years of pop singers and "proper dress required" were behind us. Our younger audience was interested in comedy. We booked it, and with David Steinberg and David Frye, it had a heavy countercultural flavor.

We had no end of trouble that spring. It started in late March, when a snowstorm forced us to close one weekend night when Sarah Vaughan, one of our new and very expensive acts, was our feature attraction. That was serious revenue lost, and that was the only time she played the club. Then in April, Joan Rivers, at the height of her standup fame, disappeared after two nights. None of us knew where she was or what happened. We learned she had been hospitalized, an emergency brought about by a tubular pregnancy. In May, we booked the pop singer and heartthrob Bobby Vinton and hired an 11-piece band to back him, and after one night he decided he didn't like the club, or he wasn't feeling well or something, and he walked out. I got Jimmy Helms, a local singer who had just been on *The Merv Griffin Show*, to finish the week. Then two weeks after that, with Gary Puckett in the house, the sinks in the Half Shell restaurant backed up and their kitchen flooded. Clam juice leaked through our ceiling and dripped all over the bandstand, ruining the horn section's music. Puckett was furious. What a mess that was.

We got through all that, but right after Labor Day we had the Chuck Berry debacle. We booked Berry through the William Morris Agency. They signed a contract, we sent a deposit, all business as usual. A week before the engagement, Chuck called: "That's not enough money." I told him we had a contract. "Yeah I know, but I'm not coming in for that kind of money." I think he wanted $1,000 more, and I told William Morris we weren't paying it. Somehow they got it straightened out, and Berry came to town. The night of the date, he told me, "I want all my money in cash, right now." It was a lot of money, about $6,500.

I said, "Chuck, we've got to collect the money from the people coming in for the show to get the cash, and we won't get it all on a Monday night." Nope, he had to have all the money up front. So I went up and down Boylston Street, borrowing money from business owners I knew—the liquor store next door, the Half Shell, a few others—and I somehow managed to raise enough cash for him to go on. He finally took the stage at 10:30 p.m. I said then and there that I would never deal with him again. I told that to his agent at William Morris the next day in no uncertain terms. And I never did.

And then in November, we had Linda Ronstadt. Our contract that said she'd perform two 50-minute sets per night, and on Wednesday and Friday, she'd do three 35-minute sets. Things didn't go as planned. We got complaints—some people complained about her references to drug use and her "obscene" language, but more complained about being ripped off. Her sets ran short. Sometimes she'd sing three songs and that would be it. She missed one set on Saturday night—the band announced her, but she was still over at her hotel. What a handful she was! People complained about her lack of professionalism, and some demanded their money back. I hated to give refunds, but we didn't have much choice.

These were some of the rough edges we experienced as our club changed and our acts became more contemporary. Some of my friends in the media didn't like the transition one bit. Ken Mayer really unloaded on Ronstadt in his "Night Mayer" column in the *Herald*, recounting her 15-minute sets and her "dockside glossary of four-letter words." He concluded, "Linda Ronstadt owes Boston an apology and she owes herself a lot of growing up." None of this, however, was reflected in the writing of the younger, rock-oriented writers, who uniformly gushed over her. Typical is this, from the *Globe's* Linda von Getchell: "[Linda Ronstadt] is so professional, so relaxed, spontaneous, natural and engagingly flakey that if she couldn't sing a note you'd love her anyway."

The year ended on a triumphant note, though, when the Duke himself came to our club in December. His music was, of course, just the best, but let me just tell one story about Duke Ellington off the bandstand. WBZ-TV at the time had a live morning show, and they wanted Duke as a guest. Duke wasn't an early riser—he was known to stay up until all hours working on his music—but I asked him about it anyway: "Duke, there's a great morning TV show where we could do an interview, but it's early, we'd have to be there at something like 7:30. Would you do it?"

He said sure, he just wouldn't go to bed until after the program. He said, "There's just two things I need. Get me a coffee and a corn muffin."

"You got it," I said, knowing that a Howard Johnson's was right next door to WBZ, and strangely enough, they had great corn muffins.

So I brought Duke to WBZ, we met the host's producer, and the producer says, "Mr. Ellington, we'll talk first, have our interview, and then you go over to the piano and play."

And Duke says, "Oh, I don't play piano."

And I see what's happening, and I grab the host and tell her, "Get your producer away from him or we're going to lose this show. You don't tell him what to do."

She grabs the producer, and I run over to the restaurant for Duke's breakfast. I come back and everybody's ready to go. So she's asking questions and Duke's talking a little about his background. After a few minutes of that, he says "It's fine to look back, but it's more exciting to think about the future and what's coming up." Duke had just written some of the sacred music, and he talked about performing that and some other new projects. So the interview went great, and he did play piano for a few minutes—but it was his idea. I finally got him back to his hotel so he could get some sleep.

The key for me was his comment that it's okay to look back, but let's think about what's coming up. That has become part of my philosophy, that you gotta keep moving forward. It's what's next that's important. That Ellington interview rang a bell for me.

BREAKING ACTS: BOSTON'S POP SHOWCASE

During those transition years at the turn of the decade, we began working with the record companies and the radio stations to "break" (introduce) acts in the Boston market. For decades, theater critics regarded Boston as an important tryout town for Broadway-bound stage shows. By the same token, Boston was an important tryout town for new musicians, singers, and comedians trying to break out nationally. Paul's Mall served as a launching pad for pop and rock artists who became major stars in the 1970s. These included Earth, Wind & Fire, Bruce Springsteen, and the Pointer Sisters. Sometimes they came in as opening acts, sometimes in company-sponsored showcase sets. Those were early-evening sets we'd arrange for the writers and broadcasters. A well-received set could mean radio airplay, and being heard on the radio in Boston was crucial, given its market demographics.

Then there were the record industry promotion men, whose job was to get their labels' records played on the radio. My friend Al Coury had already left Boston for a West Coast job with Capitol Records, but I got to know two others quite well: Sal Ingemi with Columbia and Don DeLacy with RCA. If their artists were well received at Paul's Mall, they'd probably do well in other places.

WRKO-AM was the hot radio station in Boston in the early 1970s, when Paul's Mall got into the business of breaking acts. It was a Top 40 station, and if you wanted a hit record, it had to chart on WRKO. End of story.

WRKO was part of the RKO General radio network, and one of its most important member stations. The reason for that was Boston's huge youth market. If a record was popular here, it sent a signal to the rest of the network, and they'd give it airplay too. They had some great people working at WRKO, starting with Mel Phillips, the program director, who had the ear of the people at the RKO home office, and Harvey Mednick, the promotions director.

I got involved with WRKO in 1968, when Harvey wanted to start a new venture, a concert series called *WRKO Presents*. He asked me to handle the booking. Among the groups I produced in Boston for WRKO that year were Creedence Clearwater Revival and Blood, Sweat & Tears. These concerts were a milestone for the radio station, because up to that point, radio stations had not sponsored concerts. Now they do it all the time, of course, but these shows were a first for New England. And I liked working with Harvey; he had fresh ideas and could be very persuasive.

Mel Phillips always attended our showcase sets at Paul's Mall, and one group he heard was Seals & Crofts in 1972. They had a new single out, "Summer Breeze." Mel liked it, and WRKO put it in the rotation, and the song was on the charts in Boston before Warner Brothers even released their album. The song went nationwide and made *Billboard's* Top 10 that year.

Then along came WBCN-FM, and that was a different kind of radio station, very much in the spirit of the times. WRKO was a hits-driven station with programmed playlists, while WBCN had no scripts and no playlists. They started broadcasting live from Boylston Street in 1971, sometimes from the Jazz Workshop, sometimes from the Mall. We hit a nerve with the Mall broadcasts, and for groups that were unknown at the time, like Aerosmith and Tom Petty, the broadcasts provided major career boosts. WBCN was with us all through the 1970s, and they were there on the very last night at Paul's Mall in 1978, broadcasting B. B. King's last set.

The Emergence of Earth, Wind & Fire

I worked with the Ramsey Lewis Trio at Paul's Mall for the first time in July 1969. People loved the addictive, pulsing rhythm of his group—they were still loving it 40 years later at Scullers—and we had them back the following June. That week, his drummer told me he was leaving Ramsey and forming his own group. He asked me to bring him to the Mall if he got a record deal. I told him to call me when it happened.

In early 1971, he called. "We're signed with Warner Brothers. Can you bring us into Paul's Mall?" I had the week of Memorial Day open, so I booked them. That drummer was Maurice White, and his new group was Earth, Wind & Fire.

I was expecting good things, but nobody knew who they were, so we paired them up with a hot R&B band from Providence, Chubby and the Turnpikes. That's another band we nurtured at the Mall; they changed their name to Tavares and started climbing the charts. It was slow early in the week. But word of mouth got around, and by the weekend we were swinging. Saturday was big, and even Sunday, a normally slow night, was busy. We had a great week. Over the following months, though, White's group had trouble matching their Paul's Mall success.

Another year went by, and I got a call from Columbia Records saying they wanted a Boston showcase date for a group they just signed. "Who's the group?" I asked.

"They're called Earth, Wind & Fire." I had to bite my tongue, but I said, "Oh really . . . I think we can bring them in."

I remember telling Tony that if the people remembered their first gig, we should do really well. And people did remember, and we had a great turnout. That's when things really started taking off for Earth, Wind & Fire. It was a bonanza week for us. They were incredible.

I don't think Warner Brothers, their first record company, knew how to market a black group at that time. They didn't have much experience in that category, and not much happened. Then Columbia signed them, and Columbia knew how to promote. That week at Paul's Mall proved they had a good thing going.

In 2012, Earth, Wind & Fire played a concert in Boston, and they scheduled an appearance at a store on Boylston Street the next day. So I went down there and blended into the crowd. Three members of the band were talking and taking questions, and at one point Philip Bailey said, "You know, we love Boston, it's a little like home, because we got our start here at a club that was just down the street, Paul's Mall." So I raised my hand, and Philip saw me—"Fred Taylor, oh my God." The three of them came off the stage and there were hugs all around, and we had a nice little reunion.

It reminded me that there was something about the artists that we started in those days, that what we did at Paul's Mall meant something to them, something lasting. There was something about the club culture then, the way we interacted with artists. They played for a week, so it wasn't just a hit and run. You had a lot more interaction, and got to know them as people. And they didn't forget. That's the wonderful part of all of this, the relationships, and the warm feelings that little encounters like this bring back. I think the 1970s were an absolutely amazing period for music. Some of the greatest artists in popular music came along then, and they're still touring the country today and drawing good crowds.

First Sign of a Superstar: Bruce Springsteen

My favorite bit of Bruce Springsteen memorabilia is a copy of the *Boston Globe's* "Calendar" section, dated February 25, 1988. There's a photo of Springsteen on the cover, with a headline in big, bold type: "From Paul's Mall to the Centrum." He had long since become a superstar, and he was about to start a national tour with three nights at the Centrum in Worcester. The *Globe* gathered a group of writers and asked them for their favorite Springsteen stories. One of the writers was Nathan Cobb, and his favorite story was about Paul's Mall.

My Springsteen story starts in New York, in late 1972. I was meeting with Sam McKeith, who was my eyes and ears at the William Morris Agency. If something good for the clubs came up, Sam would let me know about it. So he said Columbia Records had sent him a demo of this guy Springsteen and they were thinking of signing him, and if Columbia signed him, then William Morris would too. Sam played it, and after about eight bars, I thought, "This sounds very good." Then I thought, "This is very Dylanesque." And it was—his original stuff had that Dylan folk-rock flavor.

Sam asked what I thought. I said, "If you sign him, I'll book him at the Mall." He called me a few weeks later and said that Columbia signed Springsteen, and so did William Morris, and they wanted to bring him to Boston. So I brought him to open for David Bromberg for a week in January 1973. We had him play an early evening showcase set for invited guests, at a reception sponsored by Columbia Records, and that's when Nathan Cobb first heard him. Nathan thought Springsteen was going to be the star of the future. So did I. So did everybody.

Springsteen played part of his sets solo and part with his band. They mostly played material from his *Greetings from Asbury Park* album. We did not have a WBCN broadcast scheduled during his week, but Bruce and the band did an on-air concert at the WBCN studio, and that helped get the word out. But this was his first time playing anywhere in Massachusetts, and people weren't really aware of him—even the *Boston Globe*, in their weekly events calendar, listed Bromberg's opening act as "Rick" Springsteen. And although the *Globe* reviewed Bromberg, the article failed to mention the opening act. But I'm telling you . . . people caught on fast. And he blew the place up. That debut made such an impression on Bruce that years later, when he first played in concert at Fenway Park, the first words out of his mouth were, "I love Boston. I got my start here at a little club called Paul's Mall." I felt pretty good about that.

A Humble Beginning for Barry Manilow

The Barry Manilow story actually starts with Bette Midler. A virtual unknown, she came to Paul's Mall in June 1970, as the opening act for impressionist David Frye. Manilow was her music director, and Bette encouraged him to go out on his own. It's not like Manilow needed the money. He had already made a small fortune writing jingles for television commercials. He sold hamburgers, soft drinks, insurance, cameras. He even won a Clio award for his Band-Aids jingle, and a Clio is to advertising what an Emmy is to television.

Manilow was represented by the William Morris Agency, and my guy there said they had this fellow Manilow who was working with Bette Midler but wanted to try performing. He'd released his first record, *Barry Manilow*, and they wanted a Paul's Mall date to promote it. But Manilow's schedule was tight, and they gave me a "take it or leave it" date in March 1974. I had to leave it, because I already had Freddie Hubbard booked for that week, and Freddie always did good business for us at the Mall. We usually brought in new acts to open for established ones, but I'd heard Manilow's record and couldn't see him opening for Freddie. It was like oil and water.

I thought that was the end of it, but they came back with, "We only want one day, March 4, and we've worked out the schedule, and we've got to have this day." I said, "Listen, I've already got Freddie Hubbard, and he's promoting his new album, *Keep Your Soul Together*. I can't help you." We kept going back and forth on this thing. Then they mentioned his manager was a lawyer named Miles Lourie. I perked up. I knew Miles Lourie. He was Freddie Hubbard's manager, too. So I called him and said, "Miles, do you realize they're trying to get Barry Manilow to open at Paul's Mall for Freddie Hubbard?"

"Yeah, but . . ."

"Miles," I said, "Do I gotta spell it out for you?"

"Yeah, I know, but . . ."

So I got Miles to call Freddie and tell him what was going on, and Freddie just said flat out that he wasn't going to go on after some guy who wrote jingles for television commercials.

Miles told me this, and I said, "Okay, how about this? We'll do two separate shows. The entire first set that night will be a showcase for Barry Manilow. No Freddie at all. Then Freddie will do the entire second set that night, no mention of Barry." Finally, we had something everybody could live with. All in a day's work. Barry came in with his trio, and even then he strung the piano with little lights, he had that going from the beginning. He sang "Mandy," his first giant hit, and that was the debut of that tune here.

Paul's Mall may have launched Barry Manilow, but he doesn't remember it fondly. He struggled to hold the audience's attention. He had a much better show when I presented him at the Harvard Stadium a few years later. Of course, he was a major star by then.

I should mention Melissa Manchester here. Melissa, like Barry Manilow, came from the Bette Midler orbit. She was one of the Harlettes, Midler's backup singers. She had just released her first album, *Home to Myself,* in early 1973, and she was on the promotional tour when I booked her as the opening act for David Steinberg in May. She was with the William Morris Agency, and they thought she was going to be the next Barbra Streisand. She was a fine piano player, on that borderline between pop and jazz, and her singing reminded me of Carole King. An interesting sidelight on that album: the composer of most of the songs on it was Carole Bayer Sager, a singer we showcased at Paul's Mall in 1977.

Manchester's manager and husband then was Larry Brezner, who later moved into the world of comedy as manager of both Robin Williams and Billy Crystal. I always chuckle when I think about Melissa and Larry. I took them to dinner the night of her first show, and at some point I dropped a Mel Brooks line, and they both looked at me with that "explain yourself" expression, and I said, "2,000 Year Old Man." And they were off and running, firing off Brooks and Reiner lines like true fans. The cult of the 2,000 Year Old Man was everywhere.

Yes We Can with the Pointer Sisters

The Pointer Sisters—what a lot of fun they were. It was a one-nighter, a Sunday, August 5, 1973.

First of all, they really are sisters, and this was the original group, with all four—Anita, Bonnie, June, and Ruth—in the house. Bonnie stopped performing a few years later. They were a gregarious group with a lot of spirit, and they sure seemed like they were having the time of their lives. They were touring to support the first album in 1973, the one with the big hit "Yes We Can, Can." It was their first tour on the East Coast. They were wearing their retro clothes with the feathered boas, and their music was a mix of R&B, jazz, gospel, and rock. It was high energy all the way. They sang with a lot of jazz feeling then, and when they sang the Jon Hendricks tune "Cloudburst," the place was up for grabs.

It was actually a funny weekend for the Pointers. They'd played at the Orpheum Theatre the night before, opening for a rock band, and the crowd was the rock band's crowd. So that performance didn't light any fires. At Paul's Mall, they had the stage to themselves and they made the most of it.

We had an early showcase set at the club, and after that night at Paul's Mall, they were in heavy rotation on WRKO. Mel Phillips liked it, so he put it on the radio here, and other RKO stations around the country picked it up. The music spread nationwide, and that first album went gold. Paul's Mall got a share of the credit for that, and that's how I came to have a plaque hanging in my office that's a certified gold record from Blue Thumb

Records. There's a facsimile of the Pointers Sisters album cover, and it says, "With deep appreciation to Fred Taylor from the Pointer Sisters." I brought the Sisters back to Boston in November 1973, for a sold-out concert at Symphony Hall.

We don't break acts that way anymore. A new group today would post a video on YouTube and promote it on social media. Radio doesn't have anything like the make-or-break power it once had.

By the way, a month before the Pointers came to Paul's Mall on that one-nighter, we had the New England debut of another artist of distinction, Joan Armatrading. She was already established in the UK and was launching her first US tour in July 1973. It was a club tour, and Paul's Mall was one of her first stops. She was the opening act for comedian Dick Gregory.

A Blackout for Billy Joel

Sal Ingeme, with 25 years at the company, was *the* great Columbia Records promotion man. One of the artists Sal brought me was Billy Joel. He told me, "Here's a kid who's gonna be enormous." On that recommendation, I booked him for a one-nighter in December 1974. Everything was going fine, and then, in a true "what, and give up showbiz" moment, the power went out in the middle of the show. Billy wanted to keep going, so we did. Now there are people who claim we put a candelabra on the piano and continued by candlelight, but I know for a fact there were no candelabras in our supply closet. What we had were flashlights. We stood those up on the piano, like torches, and that kid did some shtick. There was no band, just Billy at the piano. He did a little Ray Charles, a little Randy Newman, a takeoff of Mick Jagger, and of course his own songs. Billy had just released *Turnstiles*, with "New York State of Mind" on it, and he played most of that record at Paul's Mall. That was one of those shows that you never forget.

We had him back at the Mall in April 1976, and the house was full and the power stayed on. After that he was filling stadiums. When he came to Fenway Park in 2014, he greeted the crowd with, "I love Boston! I got my start here at Paul's Mall!"

Roses for Jane Olivor

In July 1976, Sal Ingeme told me he had another new singer releasing an album, Jane Olivor, sort of in the Streisand category, and he wanted to show-case her at the Mall. I listened to the record and told him that I didn't think Paul's Mall was the right room for her, because she was more of a cabaret singer. She would have been perfect for us back in the Bobby Short days, but our club and audience had changed since Bobby's last appearance eight years before. I suggested a few other rooms that might be better for her, but they didn't work out and Sal came back to me. Sal was a friend, so I said I'd find a spot for her.

We would normally introduce a new artist as an opening act, but the upcoming schedule wasn't doing any favors for a cabaret singer—we couldn't have her opening for Tower of Power or Gato Barbieri. I decided to schedule her on a Monday, by herself. We'd do an early evening showcase set to intro-duce her to the media, then a couple sets for the public. But we came up with an interesting hook. Actually, I think it was Sal's idea. We bought a few boxes of little bud vases and put a rose on every table. We dimmed the lights, and with our low ceiling, we were able to create an intimate cabaret atmosphere. And that's how we broke Jane Olivor in New England and got her album *First Night* airplay on the right radio stations.

The roses made the night at the Mall memorable, and the red rose be-came her trademark. Years later people were still telling me they were there that night for the roses.

I went on to present Jane in concert at Symphony Hall that October. When artists got "too big" for the nightclub, I could produce them in larger venues like Symphony Hall. I was doing a two-step, you might say—first in the club and then up a level. Not too many club owners were capable of mov-ing an artist like that, but doing so gave me an edge and it's one of the things that kept me in business.

Jane became an important artist in the late 1970s and early 1980s, but she was plagued by stage fright and stopped performing for many years. She wasn't alone in this—Barbra Streisand and Carly Simon, among others, suffer from stage fright. I produced a series of concerts around New England with

Carly Simon and she just did not want to be on stage—she was nervous, jumpy. Ella Fitzgerald always had a bad case of nerves before a show. And comedian Albert Brooks had the worst case of stage fright I've ever seen. I'll tell that story in chapter 9.

So that's the Paul's Mall story. We did it all there, from Bobby Short to José Greco to George Carlin to Erroll Garner and finally to a 1970s pop showcase. We introduced a generation of stars at Paul's Mall then, including Earth, Wind & Fire, the Pointer Sisters, and Bruce Springsteen. I'm not claiming that I "discovered" these stars, but I am claiming that I recognized their talents early, gave them critical support, and helped move their careers forward by breaking them in an important market.

Another one of those future stars was Jimmy Buffett. We played Buffett for the first time in 1973, as an opening act for Delaney Bramlett, and there were plenty of empty seats. It was a different story when we brought him back in February 1976—we turned people away at the door. He's never forgotten those days. When Buffett played at Fenway Park in 2018, I just had to smile when he stepped onstage and said, "I love Boston. I started here at this little club called Paul's Mall."

7

THE JAZZ WORKSHOP: THE SOUND OF BOSTON JAZZ

The Jazz Workshop was a basement room with a low ceiling, exposed pipes, a glorified broom closet for a dressing room, and seating for about 175. Despite its unpretentious environment, it was the focus of jazz activity in Boston for 15 years, and *everybody* played that room. I was there for all of it. Tony, Peter, and I bought out Harold's lease in June 1966 and became the owners of the Jazz Workshop. Varty remained as manager, but when he moved on in September, I took over the booking and became entertainment director. That's where we pick up the story.

Spending time at the Jazz Workshop was like taking a journey through the history of jazz, especially the history from "Salt Peanuts" forward—"modern jazz." It didn't stop there though. We had big bands, mainstream swing, fusion, Latin, blues, and a whole range of singers. At one end of the spectrum we had Coleman Hawkins, the most esteemed of the elder statesmen, while at the other we had George Benson and Larry Coryell, the trailblazing young lions. We presented every marquee name in jazz: Cannonball Adderley, Art Blakey, Miles Davis, Bill Evans, Charles Mingus, Thelonious Monk, and on and on.

The Jazz Workshop was more than a room for the established stars though. It was a hangout for students from Berklee and the New England Conservatory. They would be there, listening, sitting in, trying things out—learning. Some were hired right there at the club. When the Buddy Rich and Woody Herman big bands came through, they'd pick up guys to fill their vacant chairs by the carload, right from the Workshop. And the Jazz Workshop had a Sunday afternoon jam session until it closed. This was when the students and the headliners could really mix it up.

One more thing that made the Workshop different from the Mall. The Mall worked with the record companies to break acts locally, and the artists didn't stick around for more than two or three days. At the Workshop, though, bands came in for a whole week plus the Sunday session. They could dig in. They might sound a little rough on Monday but that was gone by Wednesday, and by Friday they'd be in top form. That's how we did it at the Workshop all the way to the end in 1978.

The Jazz Workshop did not break bands the same way Paul's Mall did. The situations were different. We did, however, have one significant first at the Workshop, and that was with Weather Report. I hired the new band for what was their first club date in July 1971. They were a groundbreaking group. Pianist Joe Zawinul had been with Cannonball Adderley before he got together with saxophonist Wayne Shorter, from Miles's band. I knew them both from those days, and that's how I got the call for that first Weather Report booking. Sometimes it's all about personal relationships in this business.

One quick story about Joe Zawinul. I had scheduled an interview for Joe on WBCN, and before we left for their studio, he stopped in the restroom. I'm waiting. And waiting. Finally I go looking for him. I asked, "Joe, what's the problem?" It was his zipper. It was stuck and wouldn't close. I knew there were pliers behind the bar, and maybe he could use those to yank the thing up. So I went to get them, and the look on the bartender's face was priceless when I said, "Gimme the pliers, quick. I gotta help Joe, he's in the bathroom." He got himself zipped up, and off we went to talk about the new album.

CHANGING OF THE GUARD

The Workshop did pretty well in our first few years. By 1969, though, jazz itself was struggling, and many of our established acts were losing their audience. When we brought them in, they didn't do well. To some degree, Paul's Mall subsidized the Jazz Workshop. Peter even proposed closing it and doing something else with the room. One of his ideas was to have belly dancers. I almost had a heart attack.

The people we knew from our early days were in their 30s and 40s—my age group. I turned 40 in 1969. That crowd was going out less often, moving

Jazz organist Joe Bucci in early 1963, playing the Hammond B-3 he nicknamed "The Monster." Fred became Joe's manager in 1960, marking his entry into the music business. *(Photo by Fred Taylor.)*

KIMBALL'S STARLIGHT BALLROOM
ROUTE 128 - EXIT 21 OR 21A LYNNFIELD
MONDAY AUG. 21 –8:15
CONCERT AND DANCE
★ PLUS — JOE BUCCI — Swinging New Jazz Organist
REG. ADM. $3.00 ADVANCE SALE TICKET **SPECIAL $2.50**
PRESENTED BY NORTH
SHORE CONCERTS

America's Incomparable Rhythmic Stylist

C♦unt basie
and his Internationally Famous Orchestra

ROULETTE RECORDS

THE MOST EXPLOSIVE FORCE IN JAZZ

Concert poster for the Count Basie Orchestra plus Joe Bucci at Kimball's in Lynnfield, MA, August 21, 1961. This was the first concert Fred produced. Rain forced this concert to an indoor location.

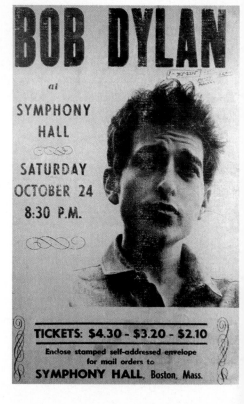

Poster for Bob Dylan concert at Symphony Hall, Boston, October 24, 1964. Fred produced this concert, Dylan's first at at this prestigious venue.

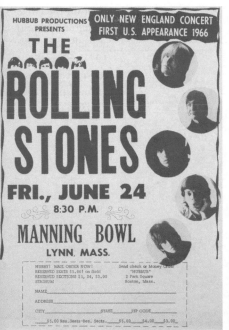

Concert flyer for the Rolling Stones at the Manning Bowl in Lynn, MA, June 24, 1965. Fred handled the promotion for this show— and got tear-gassed and stiffed for his efforts!

Flyer for Paul's Mall and the Jazz Workshop, Boston, April–May 1970. Joan Rivers, Bill Evans, George Shearing . . . just a typical month at the Boylston Street clubs.

Flyer for the Duke Ellington Orchestra at Paul's Mall, May 1971. It was the celebrated orchestra's second appearance at Paul's Mall.

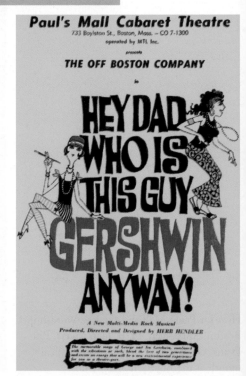

Concert poster for *Hey Dad, Who Is This Guy Gershwin Anyway?* at Paul's Mall, January 1971. This was the club's only venture into cabaret theater.

JUNE 14-20

3 Shows Nitely
9, 11, 1

"Erroll Garner is what jazz was all about in the first place." Leonard Feather, LOS ANGELES TIMES

STEREO
mercury

ERROLL GARNER

"Feeling Is Believing"

PAUL'S MALL   733 BOYLSTON ST., BOSTON   267-1300

Flyer for the Erroll Garner Trio at Paul's Mall, June 1971. When pianist Garner first played the Mall in 1969, he was the biggest act to play there up to that time.

Lily Tomlin may well be the finest and most influential comedienne to come along in twenty years.
—John L. Wasserman
San Francisco Chronicle

"And That's The Truth"

To Fred
with love + gratitude
for all these years
Lily 2008

IN PERSON AT SYMPHONY HALL
APRIL 6   8:30 P.M.

Lily Tomlin
records exclusively for

Concert poster for Lily Tomlin at Symphony Hall, Boston, April 6, 1972, inscribed by Lily to Fred in 2008. Fred introduced Lily to Boston in 1971.

Flyer for saxophonist Cannonball Adderley at Paul's Mall and pianist Herbie Hancock at the Jazz Workshop, May 1972. Without a doubt, Boylston Street was the place for jazz that week!

Fred in the whirlwind of the club office, October 1972. The original caption read, "A quiet day at the office: Taylor with ever-ringing phone, a snowstorm of paper." (Boston Globe *photo by Paul Connell.*)

Flyer for Charles Mingus at the Jazz Workshop and Dr. Hook & the Medicine Show at Paul's Mall, January 1973. The FCC was not pleased with Dr. Hook's colorful language during his WBCN broadcast.

Bluesman Muddy Waters performing at Paul's Mall on June 15, 1976, declared by Boston Mayor Kevin White to be "Muddy Waters Day" in the city. *(Photo by Duana LeMay.)*

Tony Mauriello, Boston Mayor Kevin White, and Fred. Mayor White announced that June 15, 1976 would be "Muddy Waters Day" in Boston in conjunction with his appearance at Paul's Mall. *(Photo courtesy City of Boston.)*

From left: John Cronin, Fred, and Tony Mauriello standing on Boylston Street in April 1978, when the Jazz Workshop and Paul's Mall closed their doors forever. (Boston Globe *photo by Charles Dixon.)*

to the suburbs, listening to less jazz, any number of things. All we knew was they weren't at the Jazz Workshop as often. Those mainstream jazz artists who were so popular earlier in the decade, the ones I heard at Storyville in the 1950s, like Dizzy Gillespie and Sonny Stitt, were falling off. And there were mainstream artists we tried once—just once—like Red Norvo and the World's Greatest Jazz Band, only to discover the audience just wasn't there.

I have to mention Dizzy Gillespie, because it was his "Salt Peanuts" that got me into all of this. I never had a focused conversation with Dizzy. He'd always be doing something else while we talked, like he might take off his ring and be fussing with that while I was talking to him. And then he'd interrupt and change the subject, "This ring comes from India," or that sort of thing. And off he'd go on that, and it would be fascinating, but I never had what you'd call a serious exchange with Dizzy. Serious or not, though, he was a great guy, and quite funny.

I remember the last time I booked Dizzy at the Workshop was in 1970, when we were having trouble doing good business with jazz artists like him. There were musicians like Diz who were established, great musicians, but they weren't drawing like they did in earlier days. But they still expected to be paid like they were. I had to explain to Diz that I couldn't afford to pay him what he was asking. We never had Dizzy back after 1970 because we couldn't come together on a price. But there's a funny thing that happens. If an artist lives and works long enough, he becomes a living legend. Then people say, "oh, he's a legend, you should bring him in." Then the business comes back. I've watched that happen to musicians who were elevated to legend status as the years have gone by. Joe Williams, Nancy Wilson, and Louie Bellson all fall into that category. They were struggling in 1970, but 25 years later they were big draws at Scullers.

In 1970, though, it was artists like Tony Williams, Gary Burton, George Benson, Herbie Hancock, Keith Jarrett, and Larry Coryell who were out front. These were the plugged-in bands who made sense to our rock-aware audience. We always asked our customers to fill out request cards to tell us who they wanted to see, and the younger crowd didn't want Erroll Garner or George Shearing. They wanted Pat Martino and Pharoah Sanders. My own tastes wouldn't have led me to these artists. Audience requests did. And we did well with them.

Radio helped us. The old Boston jazz clubs, like Storyville and the Hi-Hat, used remote broadcasts to promote their current attractions, and we did the same. At first, we had Bob Blumenthal hosting remotes over WHRB, the Harvard University radio station. Bob, a Workshop regular, became a great jazz journalist after his student years. In 1971, WBCN picked up the broadcasts. Sam Kopper, the station's engineer, would park his bus in the alley behind the club and drag the cables in. We would record the show, mix it in the bus, and send it by microwave to the tower—WBCN was in the Prudential Building at that time. We broadcast some great shows from the Workshop, for instance with Miles Davis, Chick Corea, Roland Kirk, and Betty Carter. Eric Jackson started hosting the broadcasts when he joined the station staff in 1972. Forty years later, Sam, Eric, and I did it all again from Scullers for WGBH radio. It was great to bring that live jazz sound back to the Boston airwaves.

PRESENTING THE LIVING HISTORY OF JAZZ

I could probably write a whole book on just the Jazz Workshop, and maybe I'll mention the idea to my publisher. There is just no way I can talk about all the great artists who played at the club, so I'll limit myself to some who made repeated visits over the years. And by the way, you won't find Miles Davis here—he stands on his own in chapter 10.

The Electric Jazz of Larry Coryell

Guitarist Larry Coryell went through many phases, and in the 1960s and '70s, people were saying that Larry was going to be the one to finally fuse jazz and rock. He sure tried. As a musician, I thought he was a genius. He absorbed everything he heard—classical, flamenco, the jazz masters, everything.

Larry came out of Gary Burton's group, one of the very first jazz-rock bands, and when we had them at the Workshop, the place was packed. Then Larry went on his own, and he became a Workshop regular. When he needed work, I'd bring him in. I'd have a cancellation and I'd call Larry to see if he could make the date. He played the Jazz Workshop 17 times. I remember he played in 1971 and 1972, those bands of his with Steve Marcus on saxophone, and I was just about the only guy over 30 in the place. He had tremendous appeal to the younger listeners, and that's what I was talking about when I said we either get younger or we close.

Larry's name is one of the first ones I think of when I think about jazz fusion. His band in 1974, the Eleventh House, more or less defined jazz fusion and what it was about. Trumpeter Randy Brecker was in it, and the blind pianist, Mike Mandel, whom I think Larry hired right out of the New England Conservatory. Great band.

Larry was married. His wife at the time was Julie, and they were struggling. There would be scenes at the Lenox . . . I just remember there was absolutely crazy stuff going on between them. And he had a drinking problem in the early '70s. So he went through all kinds of things. When I worked with him in recent years, he told me he cherished the things I did for him in those days.

Years later I brought Larry and his two sons, Murali and Julian, into Scullers. I knew those kids from before they could walk, and they both grew up to be guitarists. Murali sings as well as plays, and Julian is mostly a player. I think it was in the year 2000, the big millennium New Year's Eve, that I booked Larry at a restaurant on Huntington Avenue near Copley Square, some celebrity chef's place. The party rolled on at Scullers while I spent part of the evening there with just a handful of people and Larry with his trio.

That whole Y2K New Year's Eve thing was a fiasco. Promoters jacked up prices and the people weren't buying it. Entertainment-wise, it was a bust around the city. But we had a nice low-key thing going with Larry's group.

Bill Evans: The Headless Pianist

Pianist Bill Evans—what a brilliant improviser. His trio was outstanding, one of the best that ever played the club, and one of my very favorites. He played the Jazz Workshop 13 times, and every time his bassist was Eddie Gomez and they were amazing together. Gomez was a fine soloist himself, but his musical conversations with Evans just knocked me out. There's quiet and then there's

Quiet. The house was always hushed when they played—Bill Evans commanded your full attention. I'd call Bill's style unmistakable. His music was moody and intricate, and not a bit of sentimentality about it.

We called Bill the headless pianist, because he'd sit down to play and his head would droop lower and lower, closer and closer to the keyboard, until his nose would be about 2 inches above the keys. If you were sitting back in the audience, you couldn't see his head. It looked like everything above the shoulders was missing. But it was just Evans, concentrating on his playing. He got in his groove playing ballads and waltz-tempo pieces—he was the master of the jazz waltz—and always melodic. I'd just get lost in it. Sometimes people would criticize his sets, say that there wasn't enough variety in them. But I didn't feel that way. I'd be totally caught up.

Offstage, Bill was a very sweet, gentle guy. Tony Mauriello had a great relationship with him. Tony found out they shared an enthusiasm for greyhound racing, so Tony picked him up at his motel—Bill stayed at a motel out in the suburbs not far from the old Wonderland dog track—and they made a day of it at the races. They finally left for the club after the Daily Double—that's when you bet on the winning dog in two consecutive races, all or nothing. They walked in just in time for the first set. I remember Bill enjoyed the day, but neither of them won the Daily Double.

The One-Man Band of Rahsaan Roland Kirk

One of our biggest draws at the Workshop was Rahsaan Roland Kirk, the one-man band, who claimed he could play more than 50 instruments. I believed him. I might have even believed him if he'd said he could play all 50 at once. You just assumed that he'd play 2, and even 3, horns simultaneously, with a few percussion instruments thrown in. He developed a circular breathing technique that allowed him to play long passages without stopping for breath. He was a master of circular breathing.

Kirk mainly worked with the tenor saxophone, clarinet, and flute. But he played all the saxes, and a couple of reed instruments I'd never seen in any other hands—the stritch, a long, straight horn that sounds like an alto sax; and the manzello, which, as best as I could determine, was a customized soprano sax. He played the nose flute by blowing air through his nostrils. He could play trumpet and keyboards, every kind of percussion instrument, and even a few things he built himself. One was the trumpophone, which was a trumpet with a soprano saxophone mouthpiece. He claimed he could play bagpipes, but he never brought them to the Workshop.

Kirk would come clanking onto the stage wearing his harness with his horns dangling from it, and he'd start playing. He was inspired by Duke Ellington—he liked to play his tenor and clarinet together so he could sound like Duke's reed section—but also by gospel, blues, mainstream swing, avant-garde, everything. When he wasn't playing, he was at the microphone expounding on whatever topic was on his mind at the moment, a stream of consciousness that might cover a lot of ground. It was a part of his show.

Kirk suffered a stroke in 1975 but he came back from it despite his left arm being paralyzed. He just found other ways to prop things up. He played at the Workshop once or twice after the stroke, and I think the only difference was that he gave his sidemen more solo space—his energy level wasn't the same. He had a second stroke in 1977, and that one was fatal. He was only 42.

I never found Kirk particularly communicative, but he was easy to get along with. He'd just go about his business with very little fanfare. He was a dedicated musician, and he obviously loved the idea of finding multiple ways to make music. He could play three horns at once while blowing his nose flute and working different percussion things with his feet. He just loved putting all of it to work, using everything that could make a sound and adding it to his music. Kirk's antics could be pretty wild, but he was a masterful musician. He played our club an amazing 18 times. There was no one like him.

The Complex Charles Mingus

We booked bassist and bandleader Charles Mingus at the Jazz Workshop 10 times. Mingus was known for his quick temper, but I got along fine with him. I saw that temper in action though. One evening, the band got on stage and the sax player was obviously drunk. They started to play, and a few minutes into the set Mingus stopped the music and announced, "This quintet will now become a quartet." And he pointed at the sax player and said, "Get off." Booted him right off the stage. Mingus was deadly serious about his music, and you didn't fool around when you were playing it.

I was never a smoker, but Mingus loved cigars. He'd get offstage and light up a big whopping cheroot. I knew I'd be dropping off my coat at the dry cleaners the next day.

Tony had our best Mingus story, though, and I didn't know about it until after the fact. I don't remember what year it was, but it took an extended discussion to negotiate his fee. I think we settled on $2,500 for the week. And he did business for us. He started on Monday, and we had a good house all week. After the last set on Friday, Mingus stopped by the office, and Tony said something like, "Charles, the week has gone very well so far. And just to show you we're different from other club owners, I'm going to give you a bonus of $1,000." Mingus came in on Saturday, found Tony, and gave him two cigarette lighters from Shreve, Crump & Low, which happens to be the oldest jewelry store in America as well one of its most exclusive. "Take these," he said to Tony. "Maybe your wife smokes."

Mingus was a complex guy. He never said anything to either of us about appreciating what Tony did. He just came back the next day with that wonderful gift.

Noshing with Cannonball

I loved Cannonball Adderley, he had so much *soul*. He was outgoing, personable, and very audience-friendly. He got people smiling. He just wanted everybody to have a good time. The alto saxophonist played the Workshop eight times, and he could have played it eight more if he had lived.

I don't know how it started, but I got a food thing going with Cannonball. He loved to eat. Somebody told me that he liked salami, Al Coury from Capitol Records I think it was. So on one of Cannonball's early visits to the club, I brought him some of those hard salamis, the ones that look like hot dogs, a string of them. He got a kick out of that, so I brought more the next time, and after that it became a tradition. Whenever Cannonball came in, I'd bring him salami.

Some of the best Jazz Workshop experiences didn't actually happen at the Jazz Workshop, and so it was with Cannonball Adderley. In 1972, we organized a trip to the Montreux Jazz Festival, cosponsored by WBCN. My friend Bill Hokannen was in the travel business, and he arranged a charter flight and we took 120 people to the Montreux Jazz Festival for something like $199, which covered transportation, hotel and tickets. It was a great deal and a great trip! But back to Cannon.

We were staying at the Empire Hotel, which was up above the town on a mountainside, overlooking Montreux. There was another big hotel with a pool down below us, where the musicians were staying. I was down there saying my hellos, and I ran into Nat Adderley, Cannon's brother and the cornet player in their group. I asked after Cannonball, and Nat told me he was up in their room and gave me the room number. I told Nat, "If you see Cannon, don't tell him you saw me." Then I went all over town looking for salami but couldn't find any. Finally I bought some other kind of sausage, wrapped it up, and left it outside the door to Cannon's room. Then I went down to the pool.

Cannonball came down a little later and said to Nat, "You're not gonna believe this, but I found some salami outside my door!"

Then I popped around the corner and said, "Hey, Cannon!" He couldn't believe it. He got a big laugh out of my little stunt.

I had a wonderful personal relationship with the Adderley brothers, but we had a good business relationship too. In fact we booked Cannonball's final engagement in July 1975, at Milwaukee's Summerfest. He was driving back to New York when he suffered a stroke in Gary, Indiana. He never came out of his coma and he died a month later. He was only 46. A reporter asked me how I felt. Melancholy, I told him. Sometimes I still feel that way when I think about Cannonball.

Afro-Cuban Revolution with Mongo Santamaria

I first heard the sound of jazz-meets-Latin back in the late 1940s on Dizzy Gillespie records, and I loved the percussion. But Latin jazz wasn't a mainstream thing during the Jazz Workshop years. The music was certainly around, and there were groups like Tito Puente's that we would have brought in if there had been a big demand. But the one band everybody wanted to see was Mongo Santamaria's. Mongo played the congas, and he was the best. He appealed to a wide audience because he had a huge crossover hit with "Watermelon Man" in the mid-1960s. He kept mixing his Latin rhythms, jazz, funk, and R&B, and we kept bringing him in—13 times between 1968 and 1974.

Mongo was dynamic and exciting onstage, but the complete opposite off. He was quiet and polite, you'd never think he was capable of bringing a room full of people to a frenzy. He didn't talk to his audience when he was onstage, but he never stopped smiling.

He staged one show in November 1971 where I thought the walls were going to come down. He had a second conguero, Armando Peraza, who later played with Carlos Santana, and the two of them staged an incredible "battle of the congas" that wiped everybody out.

Other than Mongo, though, we didn't book too many Latin jazz groups. We had Willie Bobo, another percussionist with great crowd appeal. I liked Willie. When he got off the stage at the end of his sets, he'd always tell the audience, "We'll be white black." Willie also loved "Dindi," a tune written by Antonio Carlos Jobim. I think Willie included it on every album he recorded, and I think he played it every night he worked at the Jazz Workshop.

The music scene was different 25 years later at Scullers. We had a steady diet of Latin music there and a good-sized audience to enjoy it. By then, it was a thing. And when I brought it to the Tanglewood Jazz Festival as the opening night feature in 2002, we were very successful with it.

Don't Ride with Art Blakey!

Art Blakey, drummer and leader of the Jazz Messengers, was wonderful, a real crowd favorite. My best Art Blakey story starts with a frantic phone call I made to his agent, the legendary Jack Whittemore. In the days before mobile phones, Jack somehow managed to be at his phone 24 hours a day. I don't remember the year, but it was a Monday, and Blakey and the Messengers were due at the Jazz Workshop to start their week. In fact, they were overdue.

Nine o'clock and no Art. Nine-thirty and no Art. I called Whittemore: "Jack! Jack! Art's not here, do you know anything about Art?" No, he hadn't heard anything, but he told me to sit tight because Blakey was driving up from New York and would be arriving soon. Finally, it was almost 10:00, and Art and the band show up. I was frazzled, with a roomful of customers about to walk out. "Art, what happened?" I asked.

He replied: "Oh man, we were driving through Connecticut, and there was a flock of wild turkeys in the road, and I swerved and we went in the ditch!"

Wild turkeys . . . this story has passed into the lore of jazz, and there are still people who greet me at industry events and ask if I've seen any turkeys in the road lately. I'll tell you, Art could come up with stories! But he was as dedicated to jazz as anyone ever was, and so many great players came out of the Jazz Messengers. And Art's bands came to play, too. He pushed them hard, and they always put on a strong show. Real crowd pleasers.

When Terri Lyne Carrington was about 12, Sonny, her father, brought her to a Sunday matinee, and Art let her sit in with his group. That was the first time I ever heard Terri Lyne play, but certainly not the last—she's worked at Scullers numerous times. Terri Lyne is now one of the great drummers of our time. She's a composer, arranger, producer, and associate of great artists like Herbie Hancock, Joe Lovano, Esperanza Spalding, and Geri Allen. She's teaching at the Berklee College of Music. She's also an artist at the ping pong table. I've never been able to beat her at ping pong.

There Goes Freddie Mall!

I love the sound of a big band, and it's been that way since I was a kid, riding the trolley into town to hear them at the RKO Theatre. I had to bring the bands that were still active to Boylston Street. We couldn't fit 16 musicians on the Jazz Workshop stage, so I booked them at Paul's Mall, but in spirit, they belonged at the Workshop. And there were some great bands: Count Basie, Lionel Hampton, Woody Herman, Stan Kenton, Maynard Ferguson, Sun Ra. We had the master himself, Duke Ellington, twice.

The Buddy Rich Orchestra was probably the most popular big band in the country in the early 1970s, and they played for us three times. Buddy not only appealed to the jazz listeners, but he was a hit with the rock audience, too. Buddy was such a showman, and he had arrangements of rock tunes in his book, and the band just *cooked*. He called me "Freddie Mall." He had this thing with nicknames, pairing people and places. Maybe it was his little trick for remembering names.

Buddy was quite a personality. I've heard the stories about Buddy and his temper, but I never saw it. He was fun to be around, and you can be sure that he always told you what was on his mind. He was having serious back problems during one of his visits, and I referred him to an acupuncturist, who brought him a lot of relief. Buddy was very grateful, and he got back on the bandstand and thundered through the rest of the week.

In those days, along with everything else, I was also the club's sound and lights guy. During a rehearsal something needed fixing, and I was on my way to do that, and Buddy saw me from the bandstand and pointed with his sticks and announced, "There goes Freddie Mall!" which cracked everybody up.

Don Ellis led another exciting band that expanded the big band audience. He loved to experiment with different time signatures and different combinations of instruments. Whenever people would tell me the big bands were dead, I'd tell them to listen to Don Ellis. They came to the Mall in May 1971, flew into Boston from overseas, but half their instruments were on a different plane and went to New York instead. We drove all over Boston gathering instruments for the guys to play on opening night. We made it, though. I have many little stories like that, about dates when unexpected things happened, and you had to be creative. That's the thing about being a nightclub owner. You'd better have a sense of creativity, because let me tell you, you're going to be put to the test.

I managed a 10-piece band myself in the late 1960s called Brass '68, and there wasn't anything else like it in Boston. Trombonist Gene DiStasio organized it, a fabulous band, with two trombones, two trumpets, and a tenor sax up front. Then they had two electric guitars, bass, drums, and congas. No keyboards, and no singers. Brass '68—they later changed the name to the Brass Menagerie—was a very talented band, with great material, but they never broke through.

I'd known Gene for years. He played at the Stable with Herb Pomeroy's big band, and he was on the bandstand for opening night at the Jazz Workshop in 1963. And Gene . . . he had a day job . . . he was a dentist, an orthodontist! I used to wonder, would you want to be his first patient in the morning after he'd been out all night playing, and maybe had a few after?

Waiting for Freddie Hubbard

One of those Art Blakey alumni who made a splash at the Jazz Workshop was trumpeter Freddie Hubbard. Freddie played at the clubs a dozen times, all in the early 1970s, when he was recording for CTI and riding a wave of popularity. He was an exciting player, with great bands. Of course, Freddie's part of my Barry Manilow story, but I'll give you another one. I arranged for him to take part in an artist-in-residence program at Harvard, where he'd work with students and then play a big Saturday concert.

So it's the night of the concert, and at 9:00 there's no Freddie, at 9:15 no Freddie, and finally he shows up at 9:30. And he doesn't want to go on, starts in with some line of bull. I lost it and told him, "Freddie, there's an audience waiting, so cut the shit and get out there and play!" But my language was a little saltier than that.

And he says, "Oh man, you don't have to say anything like that, I'll get out there." And he did. Getting in his face brought him around. That was one of my more famous interactions.

And Freddie, every time I'd be backstage at some show and he'd be there, his opening line was always, "Get me a gig, man." Always. Then he was off the scene for a quite a while; he had a lot of trouble with his lip. It doesn't get any worse than that for a trumpet player. I heard he was trying to come back, so I brought him in as a special guest with David Weiss's group at Scullers, and it was painful to hear. I didn't want to have him back. He didn't have that Jazz Workshop magic anymore.

Nobody Compared to Les McCann

It might surprise you to learn that pianist Les McCann holds the record for most appearances at 733 Boylston. We started with Les in 1967, and we kept bringing him back right through 1978. He was with us 19 times, first in the Workshop and later in the Mall, usually for 7 days, but sometimes 10. Les McCann could really draw a crowd.

My outstanding memory of Les is his playing and singing on "Compared to What," that great number he recorded with Eddie Harris at Montreux. Each verse in that tune ends with the line, "Try to make it real, compared to what." Then there's a little pause, and the tune continues. And there were times when he'd sing "compared to what"—and a little pause—"*motherfucker!*" and then back to the tune. That's what he did nearly every time he played it, and everybody wanted to hear that tune. I'd always brace myself because I knew what was coming, and I do remember hoping that he wouldn't ad-lib it during one of our WBCN broadcasts. He didn't.

Even if you take away the piano, Les was something else, a terrific singer. Les could have been a first-class vocalist; his voice, his sound, was great. I loved his voice. It was soulful with a very pleasing timbre, a Bill Withers feeling and sound. You enjoyed hearing it. Les could have made some killer records as a singer, like George Benson did, but he chose not to. He would sing one or two things a set and let it go at that.

Les was a wonderful guy, but he was a torture for women. They had to be on their toes when he was around. You just could not leave him alone around the ladies. He was always chasing after them. Let's just say his behavior earned him a few slaps. No one would tolerate that kind of thing now. I shouldn't have tolerated it then, either, and I'm sorry I did.

Les was a smart guy, really sharp technically and a big camera buff. One thing he'd do at the end of a set is have his musicians stop playing one at a time and walk offstage, until he was the only one left. Then he would get up and leave, but his keyboard would keep playing. That was one of his programmed electronic tricks for ending a set. And people were never sure what to do—do you leave while the music's still playing? Do you wait for it to end? And what if you're hoping for an encore?

Down Home with Mose Allison

Mose Allison was at the Jazz Workshop 18 times, from our first days in 1966 through our last in 1978. And then at Scullers, I had him every year from 1993 to 2005, 12 more times. So that's 30 engagements in total, and no other artist I've ever worked with can match that.

We never lost money on Mose Allison. He was consistent, and he never tried to jack up his price. And it was always a fair price, and so I could keep a fair ticket. People loved him. He wasn't just up there playing; he was telling his life story in tunes like "Young Man Blues," "V-8 Ford Blues," and "Your Mind Is on Vacation," the one that became his signature song.

Mose was an interesting guy. He was a Mississippi country boy who came to the big city, and his songs had that sadder-but-wiser attitude. He sang his blues like a Southerner, but his piano playing was straight from New York. And he was a sharp guy socially and politically too. The songs that he wrote had some bite. He had definite opinions about things. It was satire with a bluesy feel. And he had something I prize: a sense of humor. You've got to smile when you hear a man sing, "If silence was golden, you couldn't raise a dime. Because your mind is on vacation and your mouth is working overtime."

I tried to talk Mose into composing a tune about automated phone systems, with their decision trees and endless choices, and how painful it can be to reach a real person on the phone. It's worse now than when we talked about it. I thought Mose could do the subject justice, and I even had a name for it: "I Got the Press-or-Say-Two Blues." I really wish he'd written it. I'm sure it would have become an instant classic.

Breezin' with Benson

George Benson—now there's a story. George first attracted attention as the guitarist in Jack McDuff's organ group. I started with George in March 1967, when he first went out on his own, and I basically kept him going in his early years. We brought him back twice a year, all the way through 1975. Sixteen times in all, one of our top draws. That first group, in 1967, was the one with organist Lonnie Smith and saxophonist Ronnie Cuber. Later I booked *their* groups too. George built a base in this market at the Workshop, and when his record *Breezin'* became a big pop hit, he easily sold out concerts here because he had that base. The hit record just added to it. Boston always was good to George.

George was such a great guitar player. He really knew the history of the jazz guitar, but it was for something else that he stole the show at our Christmas party in 1968. We always threw a Christmas party for our staff, and we'd have it at Paul's Mall, and whoever was at the Workshop would come over and play. George Benson was there—he was on a double bill with Freddie McCoy—and he got up onstage and started doing impersonations and singing, and that was the first time we had a clue that he could sing. In all of his appearances at the Workshop, with Jack or on his own, he had never, ever sung. It was strictly instrumental. He revealed his singing talent at that Christmas party and knocked us all out.

We worked with George for eight years, through 1975, and then the next year he made *Breezin'*. We couldn't afford him after that. But I always liked working with him. He was always very affable, very friendly. He had a sunny disposition, and you can hear it in his singing.

Muddy Waters and the Everlasting Blues

Muddy Waters was the first bluesman we booked after taking over the Jazz Workshop. That was in January 1967. But we began a steady parade of blues groups in 1969, when our audience was getting younger. So we brought in Muddy but also Willie Dixon and his Chicago Blues All-Stars, Junior Wells and Buddy Guy, John Lee Hooker, James Cotton, and Willie Mae "Big Mama" Thornton.

Muddy Waters was the audience favorite, the living link between acoustic delta blues and electric rock. Everybody from folk-blues fans to hard rockers found something to like in his no-frills approach. He played our clubs a total of 17 times. We loved Muddy, and Muddy loved us.

We had a few special events for Muddy that I remember well. One was his 60th birthday celebration in 1975. Muddy made an annual stop at the Workshop in the spring, and his birthday was April 4, so we'd celebrate whenever he got to town. (Muddy at various times reported his year of birth as 1913, 1914, and 1915. We played Muddy in April 1973, 1974, and 1975, so we were ready for any 60th birthday year he liked.) In 1975, he arrived on April 21. The next night, he was the guest of honor at a surprise 60th birthday jam session. All the best local blues and R&B musicians were there, from the J. Geils Band to Duke and the Drivers to the James Montgomery band. Guitarist Jeff Beck was in town for his own show, and he came by with guitar in hand. The Associated Press put photos of that session on the wire, and papers everywhere printed it.

My fondest Muddy memory is from a night in 1977. He was well into his second set. It was close to midnight, and in strolled B. B. King, who had finished his own gig somewhere else and decided to stop by to say hello. He didn't have his guitar, but he grabbed a chair and sat with Muddy onstage, and they started reminiscing, talking about long-gone juke joints, old-time guitar players, and places where a road-weary musician could get some home cookin'. Just talking about this and that, as old friends do. They finally did sing a few duets, with Muddy playing his guitar. I don't recall the tunes, some slow blues I think, or something from church that they'd known all their lives. We were in the presence of greatness. And me without my tape recorder! Moments like that are the gems of life.

Our biggest day for Muddy was June 15, 1976, which was proclaimed Muddy Waters Day in the city of Boston by Mayor Kevin White. Muddy's first set that night was broadcast live on WBCN, and Reggie Johnson, from the Mayor's Office of Cultural Affairs, read the proclamation honoring Muddy for 40 years of sharing his music, and for "his closeness to Boston through the Summerthing program and his appearances at Paul's Mall and the Jazz Workshop since 1965."

Muddy's thank-you remarks to the capacity crowd were typically humble, but there was no doubting that he was absolutely thrilled by the recognition—his hometown of Chicago hadn't honored him this way, nor had the Mississippi town where he was born. We had a giant cake and plenty of champagne, and everybody came together—the room was full of joy that night. Then Muddy's band played a second set that almost burned down the house.

Maybe it was Muddy's guiding hand at work, but the sound of the Chicago blues was very popular with the Workshop crowd. We presented James Cotton eight times, and James himself was a former member of Muddy's band. I continued to book James all the way to 2016, at Scullers.

Finally, there was the King of the Blues, B. B. King. The first time he stepped into my club was the night he dropped in to visit Muddy. I think he liked the vibe that night, because after years of trying, I was finally able to bring B. B. to Paul's Mall in 1977, and he drew a crowd of about 3,200 for the week—we sold every seat for every show for seven days. That's a testament to how popular King was at that time. And of course he played the last show at Paul's Mall in April 1978.

I didn't confine my blues shows to Boylston Street. In one venture, I even crossed the state line into Rhode Island. That was for the New England Blues Festival, a one-day affair that took place on July 7, 1975. I got together with Dean Saglio from Providence to stage it. I booked the talent, and Dean, with his local connections, found the ideal spot for an outdoor festival— the Stepping Stone Ranch in Escoheag, down the road from Providence. We had Muddy Waters, Paul Butterfield, Taj Mahal, Koko Taylor, and Freddie King—great bands all day long. It was a beautiful place for a festival, too, in a park-like wooded area. We had good weather and terrific turnout, well over 20,000 people. Unfortunately, only about 7,000 of them bought tickets. The others discovered that if they walked a little way through the woods, they'd find the holes that had been cut in the fence. They simply strolled right in all afternoon long.

Because of all those "music should be free" types, we took a beating on that festival. I didn't have a dollar in my pocket when I headed home that night. It's a good thing I didn't have to stop for gas.

A THREAD IN THE FABRIC OF BOSTON

I have a picture with Mayor Kevin White presenting me with a silver Revere bowl. The date was August 21, 1972, and it was a big day for Tony Mauriello, the Jazz Workshop, and me. It was the day of the city's tribute to our club. The city recognized the Workshop as being more than just a place where people went to hear some music. It was a part of the texture of the city, a piece of the patchwork that made up the community. It was a place that brought people together, a gathering place for all kinds of people, and it played an important part in the cultural life of the city. We were humbled to be honored like that, and I'm still very proud of what we accomplished there, and what we meant to the people who came through the door. This is the inscription on the bowl:

To the Jazz Workshop

In recognition of its significant contribution to the preservation of jazz music in Boston

Presented on August 21, 1972 by the mayor's office of cultural affairs

City of Boston

Kevin H. White Mayor

8

ROCK, REGGAE, AND ROLLING STONES

I was so busy with jazz, folk, and comedy that I didn't pay much attention to rock music until the mid-1960s. I didn't have time for it. But I was always aware of the trends, and those were good years to tune into rock. That's when it started getting interesting, what with the Beatles and the Rolling Stones and Dylan going electric and the rest of it.

I started working with rock bands in 1965, encountered the Stones in 1966, and went on from there. Here are a few faces I met along the way.

THE LOST WERE FOUND . . . ON CAPITOL

I became good friends with Al Coury, the Capitol Records promotions man, when we worked on Joe Bucci's *Wild About Basie!* album. Al was always a man in motion, and if you were with him at any time, you became part of the party. I vividly recall an afternoon when he stormed into our office on Boylston Street, said "Come on, Fred, we've got to get going!" and hustled me out the door and down the stairs. I had no idea what was going on. He was parked right out front. We jumped into his car and Al swung out into traffic. At the first light, he glanced over at me and asked, "Where are we going?" It still cracks me up.

One night we squeezed into the back room of the Rat—the Rathskeller—a Kenmore Square dive bar popular with the college students, to catch a band called the Lost. Al liked them, and he signed them to Capitol. They released their first single in late summer 1965. It was "Maybe More Than You," backed with "Back Door Blues." Al worked hard for that band, but that was his trademark. He only signed you if he believed in you, and if he believed in you, he worked his butt off for you. Al took that record to every radio

station in the region and made the station manager listen to it. Al could be
persuasive, if not downright intimidating, and the song got airplay. "Maybe
More Than You" became a regional hit. Al landed opening appearances with
the Supremes and Sonny & Cher, and his big coup was to get the Lost on a
college tour with the Beach Boys in 1966.

It must have been Al who got me started with managing and publicizing
the band, and we introduced the group and their record to the local press in
mid-October. I applied a little bit of press agentry to the situation, placing
an ad in the classifieds in the Boston papers on October 1—in the Lost and
Found category, naturally—notifying the world that "Coming on Capitol
Records: The Lost is found."

I was managing Paul's Mall by then, and I had Joe Bucci all that month
and he was doing business for us, so I couldn't toss him out for a rock band.
Instead, we went to Tony Mauriello's Kenmore Square club, the Forum, for
the local debut. We had a meet and greet with the writers, and one set by the
band. I introduced them with what became my standard line: "Ladies and
gentlemen . . . the Lost have been found!" I'd vary this as necessary: "The Lost
have been found at college!" (when they opened for the Supremes at Brandeis
University); "The Lost have been found at church!" (when they played for
a Lenten service at an Episcopal Church); and my favorite, "The Lost have
been found at the Cheetah!" (when they played two weeks at that Manhattan
disco). I lost count of the number of times I found those guys.

I met Ernie Santosuosso of the *Boston Globe* that day at the Forum.
He was new to the entertainment beat, and he thought I was with Capitol
Records. I had to call him the next day to tell him I was actually representing
the band. Ernie and I became the best of friends, and I could always count on
him to plug my shows in his weekly column.

Just before Christmas 1965, we had an opportunity that was a publicist's dream. On December 18, the Lost played a debutante party for Debbie
Fiedler at the Longwood Cricket Club in Chestnut Hill. Her father was
Arthur Fiedler, the conductor of the Boston Pops. Maestro Fiedler's birthday
had been the previous day. The leading society band in Boston then was
the Ruby Newman Orchestra, and Ruby had been at it for a long time—he

played at the weddings of two of Franklin and Eleanor Roosevelt's children. I've always believed that Mr. and Mrs. Fiedler picked the Newman Orchestra for this party, and Debbie picked the Lost. Arthur, let it be said, was a notorious publicity hound, and he wasted no time getting out on the dance floor when the Lost started to play. A photo of Arthur doing the frug, or whatever dance it was, ran in *Billboard* a few weeks later.

Anyway, here I was, a jazz guy promoting a rock group that we hoped was going to be an American version of the Rolling Stones, and I confess I wrote some pretty corny press material. I had one brochure hyping the Capitol recording that said, "The company that gave you the Kingston Trio . . . the Beach Boys . . . the Beatles . . . Now have found THE LOST." We never brought the group to quite those heights, although they did have their moments in the New England/New York area.

The Lost disbanded in early 1967. They fell apart for various reasons— tepid support from Capitol, "artistic differences," a little of this and that. I never knew the whole story. But they were good fun and wrote some great tunes, and I couldn't imagine a livelier way to enter the rock world in 1965.

THE STONES WERE A GAS, GAS, GAS

The big music news in Boston in spring 1966 involved the Rolling Stones. The Stones announced that their third tour of the United States would start with a concert in Lynn on June 24, playing outdoors in the Manning Bowl. It would be the only Massachusetts stop on the tour. Danny Kessell, the tour's producer, hired me to handle show publicity.

The Stones had a new album out, *Aftermath*, and they'd be pushing it on this North American tour. The featured single getting all the airplay was "Paint It Black," and it hit number one on both the *Cashbox* and *Billboard* charts two weeks before the Lynn concert.

Lynn was going to be a big show, almost three hours of music, with local and national groups scheduled to play. The McCoys would be there to play their big hit "Hang on Sloopy," and the Standells would take us down to the banks of the River Charles with *their* big hit, "Dirty Water." The Trade Winds, from Providence, Rhode Island, were also on the program. On top of all that talent, the Mods, the winner of the New England Battle of the Bands competition, would open.

You could get into the Manning Bowl for three bucks. Three! Today you can barely afford a download of "Paint It Black" for that.

I worked it. I sent press releases every other day to every newspaper from Providence to Portland. I bought radio spots on stations throughout New England, paying special attention to Boston. My go-to guys were Arnie Ginsburg at WMEX, who would emcee the show, and Bruce Bradley at WBZ. That station has been all news for so long that people are surprised to learn it was once one of the top rock stations in the region, and "Juicy Brucie" Bradley was their prime-time deejay.

Not everyone in the media approved of a dyed-in-the-wool jazz guy like me fraternizing with the rock 'n' rollers. I gave tickets to all the newspaper columnists, and one of them, my buddy Kenny Mayer from the *Herald*, thanked me by writing: "We have two tickets for the Rolling Stones concert in the Manning Bowl June 24. Who wants them, and why?" At least he wasn't complaining about young people with long hair.

The Stones themselves made my publicist's job easier. They were rock's bad boys in 1966—the *Globe* even ran an article contrasting the "goodies"— the very polished Dave Clark Five, who were playing in town at the same time—and the "baddies," the more sinister Rolling Stones. The Lynn police were taking no chances with these supposed hooligans, and they called in all off-duty officers as well as extra cops from out of town.

It rained on the day of the show, and the Stones's plane was late because of heavy fog at the airport. But the show started on schedule. At about 11:00 p.m., with the Stones still playing, the rain started again and the police stopped the show. Of course the crowd was disappointed, but that was as far as it went. They surged forward but did not storm the stage. I thought they just wanted to get a closer look at Mick Jagger and the band. But the police panicked. They fired tear gas into the crowd, and we all hit the ground, looking for air but sucking in dirt. It was bad. *Then* people got angry. The band jumped into their limos and headed for the exit, with some of the crowd chasing after them, hoping for autographs or perhaps the shirts off their backs.

The police later claimed the crowd was "angry," but that's not what I remember. It wasn't like they were hauling people to the police station by the busload. Five of the 15,000 or so fans in attendance were arrested for being drunk or disorderly. I certainly saw no disturbance requiring the use of tear gas!

I picked myself up from the wet ground and went looking for Danny Kessell. My contract stated that I was to be paid in full on the night of the concert, and I was even making jokes about asking for a bonus for combat duty. Kessell, however, was not to be found on the grounds of the Manning Bowl. He had slipped away and left town as quickly as the band.

So what was my reward for my hard work? First I got tear gassed, and then I got stiffed.

What, and give up showbiz?

I didn't put too much effort into finding Kessell—no one knew where he went, and I was too busy for a wild goose chase like that in June 1966. We had just bought the clubs, and I had more than enough to do. Some ten years later he showed up as the road manager for some group at Paul's Mall. That was awkward, and I didn't have to say very much before he launched into some crazy story about Lynn. But by then I had written the whole thing off.

FOXBORO IN THE FALL

Tony and I had a pretty good track record, but one of our projects that flopped was the Fall Music Festival at Foxboro Raceway in October 1969. We were approached by a Foxboro businessman who asked if we could get Crosby, Stills & Nash for a concert there. There was no stadium then—there wasn't a football team then either—but he knew about the Foxboro Raceway, a harness track, and thought he could stage concerts there. He put up the money, and Tony and I booked the bands and ran the events. We agreed to split the profits 50/50. We were optimists.

CS&N were not available, so instead we recommended Neil Diamond, then an up-and-comer with a few hit records but little, if any, concert exposure in the region. Then we filled out the program with British bluesman John Mayall, a one-hit-wonder Canadian band called Motherlode, and a folk-rock group, the Holy Modal Rounders, who had the playwright Sam Shepard as their drummer. It was an unusual lineup of talent.

Then we changed gears and went country and western for the second half of the festival the following weekend. We brought in Jeannie C. Riley, who had a huge hit the year before with "Harper Valley PTA," and the guitarist and singer Roy Clark, who was hosting a country-themed variety show called *Hee Haw* on CBS television. That double bill looked good. Never mind that country wasn't big in this area at that time.

Well, neither of these weekends pulled in a crowd. We lost money. We learned a valuable lesson in Foxboro: if you are going into a venue that has never been used before, you have a "newness" problem that can overshadow your attraction. Unless you have the Rolling Stones coming in, it's tough to get people to go to a place they don't know. We were presenting good acts that were on the rise, but going into a totally new venue created a problem that I never saw coming. I didn't make that mistake again.

You can file this one under "problem venues." But I couldn't go back anyway, because the Foxboro Raceway was demolished to make way for Gillette Stadium, the home of the New England Patriots.

A FEW WORDS FROM DR. HOOK

A week or two after Bruce Springsteen played at Paul's Mall in January 1973, Dr. Hook and the Medicine Show came to town. Theirs was one WBCN live broadcast from the Mall that I will *never* forget. That band almost got WBCN knocked off the air. Dr. Hook—Ray Sawyer, the lead singer—was a gregarious guy with a patch over one eye and an outrageous sense of humor. He also liked to use one of George Carlin's seven forbidden words, and he used it as a noun, verb, and adjective. And you'll have to forgive me but I have to tell it like it was—the word was *fuck*. And he didn't just sprinkle it into his speech here and there, he ladled it in profusely. Nice guy, and he wasn't trying to be disrespectful or aggressive, it was just the way he fuckin' talked.

There was no such thing then as a 5-second delay, and the engineer wasn't going to be able to bleep out anything. As we approached broadcast time, we implored him: "Ray, we're going live now. Please be careful on the air."

"Sure, sure," he said. He tried to watch his tongue, but he did slip, more than once, and I was in the back of the room covering my ears with my hands. It was definitely one of those "oops" situations. Sure enough, the next day WBCN got a call from the Federal Communications Commission. In fact, the FCC was threatening action against the station. The manager at WBCN begged: "It was late night. There were no kids listening. Nobody's complained." There was a lengthy discussion, and in the end there may have been a fine, but WBCN came through it without any other penalties. I explained the situation to Ray.

You can probably guess what he said.

FIRST TIME AROUND WITH AEROSMITH

I presented Aerosmith at Paul's Mall twice when they were getting started in 1973, and the guy who made it happen was Frank Connolly. Frank was a local legend among us showbiz types—he had the knack for recognizing a hit show or a hit act before any of the rest of us. One example: In the 1960s he ran the Carousel Theater in suburban Framingham, and in 1965 he hired these two guys named Simon & Garfunkel and the rest of us said, "Simon who?" I think he paid them 200 bucks. I first worked with Frank as publicist on *Jesus Christ Superstar*. He brought the first production of that show to Boston Garden, in 1971. For some reason, he was slow to pay me. My partner Tony said I should go after Connolly for the money, but I decided confrontation wasn't going to get me anywhere, so I told Frank to pay me when he had the money, and in the meantime I'd leave him alone. Frank was the type of guy you didn't bug. And eventually he paid me. Then he repaid the favor.

He told me he had signed a new rock band from Boston, some Rolling Stones wannabes with huge potential, and when the time was right he'd get them a great record deal. A little later he said it was time to get this band some exposure and asked for a date at Paul's Mall. The band was Aerosmith, and he had indeed landed a great deal for them on Columbia Records.

We brought them into Paul's Mall for four nights in March 1973, with a radio broadcast on WBCN. Then we brought them back in April. Those appearances, and that broadcast, helped kick their career into high gear. Frank Connolly wanted exposure for the band, and Paul's Mall delivered.

A few months later, I booked Aerosmith to open for Sha-Na-Na at the Suffolk Downs racetrack. Attendance topped 40,000, by far their biggest crowd, and that day Aerosmith broke into the big time. No more dates at Paul's Mall! Unfortunately, that concert left a bad taste in my mouth. It was marred by a few troublemakers climbing on the sound equipment and throwing cans of beer at the musicians on stage. But no rowdy crowd could slow them down. Aerosmith was on their way.

We played an important part in the early days of Aerosmith. I was honored when the band members were among the first contributors to the Fred Taylor Scholarship Fund at the Berklee College of Music when it was announced in September 2017.

THIS IS REGGAE MUSIC

Bob Marley and the Wailers first came to Paul's Mall in July 1973. Those were early days for the whole Jamaican reggae scene in this country. It was our first reggae band, and speaking for myself, it was my first encounter with the Rastafarian religion and culture. Boston was the first stop on their first US tour, the "Catch a Fire" tour. They were virtual unknowns, and I looked forward to meeting them.

They arrived on Monday but I didn't have a chance to meet them that afternoon, which I normally tried to do on an act's opening day. I finally arrived at the club about a half hour before the show, and went down to the dressing room. I opened the door—and walked into a dense cloud of marijuana smoke. I caught quite a buzz just standing there. They were smoking joints, and we aren't talking any pencil-thin kind of thing—these were the size of a big cigar. The band was full of energy and excited to play, and they took the stage and did a great show. That was the original Wailers, with Peter Tosh in the group. We did a WBCN broadcast that week, and an air check of that broadcast came out years later on CD.

Over the years, various artists have written into their contracts that we supply all kinds of food, drink, and other amenities. I'll never forget the stipulation written in by the Wailers. They wanted hotel rooms with kitchens, complete with a full complement of utensils. They liked to prepare their own meals—it was the only way they could get Jamaican home cooking. We usually put our artists in the Lenox Hotel, across the street from the club, but they didn't rent rooms with kitchenettes. The closest place we could find was on Beacon Street in Brookline.

Bob Marley and the Wailers owed their fast start here to a movie. In 1972, Jimmy Cliff starred in *The Harder They Come*, a movie about a Jamaican outlaw that featured a reggae soundtrack. For many in the US, it was their introduction to the reggae sound. It arrived at the Orson Welles, a popular theater in Cambridge, in April 1973.

Someone at WBCN learned that the Welles was going to screen the film, and they approached the advertising agency handling the film's promotion in Boston. Movies were almost exclusively promoted in newspaper ads back then. WBCN said that *Harder* was a film about music—music with a particular appeal to their audience, and they could promote it on radio more effectively than any print ad could. The agency went along with it, and WBCN did a hell of a job with the promotion. *The Harder They Come* eventually ran at the Orson Welles for more than a year as a midnight movie.

I was already advertising on WBCN and I knew how effective it could be, so when the opportunity to book Marley and the Wailers came up, I immediately thought of WBCN. I went to them looking for a tie-in. So we had the movie showing at the Orson Welles, and the band performing at Paul's Mall, and a live broadcast from the club over WBCN. And the band put on one of their best shows in Boston that night.

The Wailers came to Paul's Mall two more times, in November 1973 and June 1975. The November date was a two-nighter, a Saturday and Sunday, and I was lucky to get them—I had a cancellation and the Wailers just happened to be available. The June 1975 engagement was for a full week, and by that time Bob Marley and the Wailers, and all of reggae for that matter, were well established in the pop mainstream. We drew over 3,900 people that week. We sold every seat for every set, with SRO patrons lining the walls. It was a full house and we turned people away.

My last event with Bob Marley and the Wailers was a concert at the Music Hall in April 1976. They tell me the band was great that night but I don't remember anything about the show, because all my memories are about some behind-the-scenes drama that happened earlier in the day. I had some tough guys from the Teamsters Union get in my face. They didn't have a contract with the Music Hall, but they tried to intimidate me and get me to hire their guys to unload Bob Marley's equipment truck. I told their business manager no, and said if he kept pressuring me, I was going to file a claim with the National Labor Relations Board. I knew there would be trouble, so I hired my own security people—and they were armed—to guard the truck while it was at the theater's loading dock.

The Teamsters showed up on the day of the show anyway and threatened the guy driving Marley's truck while he was still out in the street. I had the Boston police escort the truck to the dock, but then, bingo, there were the Teamsters, six of them, converging on the truck.

I said, "Gentlemen, I talked to your business agent and told him your services weren't required, and I warned him that if the teamsters tried to interfere with this truck, I would file a complaint with the National Labor Relations Board, and that could cause a lot of trouble. Also, if you'll notice, there's a gentleman standing over to your left with his hand in his pocket and he is not feeling himself up, either. And there's another gentleman on your right. And I would advise you not to get near this truck."

And they hesitated. One guy did sneak up on the truck and tried to get under the hood. We stopped that. We finally got the equipment inside and the concert started as scheduled. Like I said, I'm told it was a good show.

I went to the NLRB the next day. And I got a judge to issue an injunction against the Teamsters Union, ordering them to stay away from me and any place where I was doing business. There was an NLRB hearing, and the Teamsters agreed to leave me alone, but the bigger issue, of the Teamsters pressuring promoters and venues to hire unneeded union help, was not resolved. You still hear about these cases popping up in the news.

THE PATTI SMITH PHENOMENON

Donald Byrd and the Blackbyrds were always a good draw for us, so we booked them into Paul's Mall in January 1976. That was our policy—the more popular act went into the bigger room, and the lesser-known act played the smaller room. That's how Patti Smith ended up in the Jazz Workshop for four nights early that month. The Blackbyrds did well, as always. But Patti Smith . . . we were not prepared for the crowd wanting to see and hear her. We could have easily packed Paul's Mall. We could have torn down the wall between the two clubs and filled the whole place, too. We probably could have piped the sound into the movie theater upstairs, and with audio only, sold that out, too. The demand for tickets was that great. She was hotter than hot, and my friend Ernie Santosuosso at the *Globe* knew it: "When the media finishes with this singular poet-singer," he wrote the day before she opened, "you'll reappraise the Springsteen hype as a mere whispering campaign."

I was not listening to much punk rock myself in those days, but she was creating a lot of buzz. Smith, with her band led by guitarist Lenny Kaye, had released their first album, *Horses*, in December. Wrote one of the local papers, "Brace yourselves: The colorful Patti Smith opens next Thursday at the Jazz Workshop. She makes Janis Joplin sound like a daughter of the American Revolution."

I don't remember if John Cale, who produced *Horses* and was traveling with the group, sat in on bass every night, but he did on the night of our WBCN broadcast. He joined them for the encore, a thundering cover of the Who's "My Generation." Well, we were in a basement with a low ceiling, and Cale got into the music, and he punched a hole in the dropped ceiling with the neck of his electric bass. It was a good thing that it was the finale, because we had to stop the show to keep somebody from getting hurt. What a wild night that was!

We were mobbed. We added an extra show for Smith's last three nights, and we sold every seat for every show and the phone was ringing off the hook. There had never been such a demand for tickets. We turned away more people for Patti Smith than for any artist at either club up to that point. We had more than 1,900 people in four nights. Then we closed for two nights to fix the ceiling and get ready for Ron Carter's opening on the 14th.

It turns out that the mayor of Boston, the Hon. Marty Walsh, is a Smith fan. He declared October 10, 2015, as Patti Smith Day in Boston, noting in his proclamation that she "earned the love of Bostonians beginning with her earliest shows at the Jazz Workshop." He didn't mention the hole in the ceiling.

9

TICKLING BOSTON'S FUNNY BONE

Humor has been a part of my life, as much as music, as long as I can remember. As a kid in the 1940s, I could indulge in both by listening to the radio, which was my window on the world.

All the best bands were on the radio back then, and so were the funniest people. I'd listen to George Burns and Gracie Allen, Abbott and Costello, Jack Benny—my favorite, I wouldn't miss him—and Spike Jones, who mixed comedy and music better than anybody. Radio comedy was fast paced and performed live for a studio audience, or at least it sounded live. It was happening *right now,* while I listened, and I liked that. I wanted to be there, to be part of it somehow. Maybe someday I could even be telling the jokes!

I got my chance when I was a student at Boston University in the late 1940s, when I made music with the Don Creighton Orchestra and did some comedy at my fraternity, Tau Epsilon Phi. Eventually I became the frat's entertainment director. My greatest triumph was hosting the classical pianist and humorist Victor Borge at the house, which was on Beacon Street. I loved Victor Borge, the "Clown Prince of Denmark," who was a master when it came to mixing music and humor. He was so funny that people would forget what an accomplished pianist he was. Even Madame Chaloff admired him. Anyway, he was in Boston for a concert and I arranged to bring him to the fraternity house afterwards. He told the jokes on that occasion, but on other nights it was my turn. I emceed our events and did monologues. It was stand-up comedy, and that's the show I took on the road that summer at the Strawberry Hill Inn. Sometimes I'd sing. Murray Liverman was my partner, and we'd sing things like the R&B novelty tune "Shorty's Got to Go:" "He took my hat, that dirty rat. Has anyone here seen Shorty? Shorty's got to go!"

I enjoyed making my fellow students laugh. I became known on campus as a guy who could produce music-and-comedy variety shows, and I put together a few things, including an infamous pep rally at the Boston Arena that ended with a cast member taking a tumble and breaking his arm.

After college came Serta Mattress, and after that came the music business. I never thought that music would lead me back to comedy, the other love of my life, but it did. It couldn't have worked out better.

YOUR NIGHT AT NICK'S

When I started booking music, I became a regular at Nick's, a popular restaurant and lounge on Warrenton Street favored by publicists, agency people, and other creative types. The Shubert Theater's stage door was across the street, and the performers would drop by after their shows. Dottie Dean was a fixture at Nick's, playing at the piano bar, and I swear she knew every Broadway tune ever written. She'd play, and the Shubert crowd would sing. Every so often I'd bring my cocktail drum and play along with her.

George Campbell, who ran one of the ad agencies, started something called "Your Night at Nick's." If it was your night, the club would host a party and you'd be the guest of honor, and the other regulars would tell stories about you, none of which were true. The best thing, though, was the cigarette lighter. George presented you with a silver Zippo lighter, inscribed with "Your Night at Nick's" and your name. I was dubiously honored with one of those nights, and I still have the lighter.

I once impersonated a doctor at Nick's, but it wasn't my idea. That was the night I became known as Doctor Fred. There was a group of doctors in the lounge, conventioneers; and Nick Polley, the owner, wanted me to meet them for some reason. We were walking over to their table, and he said, "I'm going to introduce you as a doctor." And before I could say, "*What?*" I was sitting at a table surrounded by doctors who of course thought I was one of them. I have no idea how I bluffed my way through it, but I did, and from then on, people at Nick's called me Doctor Fred. My souvenir lighter actually says, "Your Night at Nick's—Doctor Fred."

Toward the end of my time as a Nick's regular—you work too many nights in the music business to be a regular anyplace, unless you run your own joint—I discovered the 2,000 Year Old Man. This was not long after Mel Brooks created the character and made the album *2,000 Years with Carl Reiner and Mel Brooks*. I instantly became, and still remain, a fan. I listened to that record so often I wore it out. And I'd go to Nick's and spontaneously start doing bits from it and everybody liked it. I'd be saying, "No, no, I didn't write this stuff, it's Mel Brooks, it's the 2,000 Year Old Man!"

The Old Man's record was on Capitol, and I called my buddy Al Coury and had him send me a box of records that I could sell at Nick's. It was my entry into the cult of the 2,000 Year Old Man, and to this day I'll meet someone who will drop a Brooks line, and I'll answer with a Brooks line, and then we're off. You never know who will be revealed as a member of the cult. I remember swapping lines with Melissa Manchester when she played Paul's Mall. And I very proudly take credit for introducing Lily Tomlin to the old gent.

That brings me to Paul's Mall. When Paul Vallon opened the club in May 1964, he wanted to try some comedy. I was handling the booking, and the first guy we booked for the grand opening canceled at the last minute. There was a mad scramble, mostly by me, to line up a replacement. I needed somebody with a name who could get to Boston in a hurry. I called Henny Youngman, he said he'd do it, and our grand opening was saved.

From then on, it was one pratfall after another at Paul's Mall. Ten years before the comedy club craze hit the nation, we did more comedy than anybody else around Boston. And it was a fascinating time, because it was when Henny Youngman's "Take my wife, please" style of comedy gave way to a new approach, in which the comedians told stories about situations and events. Comedy was becoming more than just a stand-up comic firing jokes at an audience, and Paul's Mall presented the men and women who were making it happen.

What a lineup we had at Paul's Mall! There were old-school comics like Lenny Kent and Timmie Rogers. We had George Carlin in 1964, when he was telling jokes about the Hippy-Dippy Weatherman, and again in 1968, when he took his act to the Supreme Court. We had improv groups, like the Proposition and my favorite, the Ace Trucking Company. We had Pat Paulsen, a presidential candidate, and David Frye, a presidential imperson-ator. We had comedy teams, like Proctor and Bergman and Cheech & Chong, who recorded their album *Big Bambu* at Paul's Mall in 1972. Our last come-dian was Franklin Ajaye, and I remember Franklin because his manager was Wally Amos, the "Amos" of Famous Amos cookies. We had big names and rising stars and complete unknowns. I'm telling you, if comedy had a home in Boston between 1964 and 1977, it was Paul's Mall.

Of course, certain performers stand out, and they're waiting in the wings for their turn at the microphone. So without any further introduction, please welcome to the Paul's Mall stage 10 of the funniest people you could ever hope to meet.

THE SILLY SEMINARS OF PROFESSOR IRWIN COREY

I booked my second comedian on the heels of Henny Youngman, and it was none other that the World's Foremost Authority, Irwin Corey. Irwin, in his battered tuxedo jacket and worn sneakers—he claimed his wardrobe was condemned—wasn't really a stand-up comic. He was an educator, and he conducted seminars on stage, or as he called them in his born-in-Brooklyn accent, "seminahs." "This," he would announce to his Paul's Mall audience, "is a seminah, and at the end, we're going to ask questions." Then he'd launch into a baffling monologue on some topic or other.

Irwin didn't open his show by bouncing onstage and announcing "Good evening ladies and gentlemen." No, he'd make his way slowly, apparently deep in thought. He'd face the audience and be about to speak—but then he'd lapse back into deep thought. Then he'd nod, as if he were ready—but he still wasn't ready. Then he'd turn all his pockets inside out, like he was looking for his notes. This could go on for a couple minutes. Finally, he'd enter with, "Howevah!" And off he'd go.

Doing standup in nightclubs was only part of Irwin's act though. He'd been in movies, on television, and on the stage—he played the grave digger in

Hamlet, and he was in *The Prisoner of Second Avenue* in 1974, when he saved my ass one Saturday night, but we'll get to that story a little later.

Corey was an incomparable character and an audience favorite, and I brought him back a half-dozen times. Offstage, we'd have some serious, or at least semi-normal, conversations. Irwin was very political—oh boy, did he have opinions! And he was always interested in a deal. There was a travel company in our building that was about to go public, and Tony and I made a small investment in it. This was about 1966. I mentioned it to Irwin and he wanted in, so we got him in. When it went belly-up a couple of years later, Irwin, shall we say, let us know the extent of his unhappiness with our investment advice.

We never had Irwin on a radio broadcast, but WBCN, which sponsored a team in a softball league, recruited him to umpire one of their games on the Boston Common. That was just hilarious. Ball or strike? Fair ball or foul? These were not split-second decisions for Irwin, these were the subjects of lengthy discourse. I have no idea if they finished that game. They were still playing, and Irwin was still umpiring, when I left to go to work.

In 2004, I had my last zany experience with Irwin, and it was so typical of him. He came to town with *Sly Fox*, a play starring Richard Dreyfus, and Irwin was the Court Clerk. It was opening at the Shubert Theater on a Monday, and Lennie Sogoloff, who also was a fan of Irwin's, and I met him the night before. We went to Chinatown looking for dinner. We found a place, up on the second floor, and almost all the customers were of Asian descent. Not only that, but we learned that almost all of them were there for a gathering of people who shared the same last name.

Now this place was on two levels: you entered on the upper level and walked down into a bigger lower level, which was crowded with the people with the same name. We were walking through the place on the upper level, overlooking the crowd of diners. So Irwin turned to them, got their attention, and announced: "Everybody who's here, raise your hand!" People were obviously confused by this, but many of them raised their hands. "Excellent!" he said, and walked on, oblivious to the confusion he left behind. That was

Irwin. He had no hesitation about injecting himself into situations like that to see what would happen. You could never tell what he might do next.

Irwin visited Scullers while he was in town with *Sly Fox*, but he didn't attempt to befuddle the audience. The harmonica virtuoso Toots Thielemans was playing that night, and Toots, a Belgian, was a Corey fan and insisted I take their picture together. Irwin had fans all over the world. What else can I say about Professor Irwin Corey, who was my friend for so many years? He was just a very memorable guy.

WHAT YOU SEE IS WHAT YOU GET WITH FLIP WILSON

I was in New York City scouting for acts in 1966, and I went to Birdland on 52nd Street, where there were two saxophonists that I wanted to hear, Cannonball Adderley and King Curtis. I hired them both eventually but not that night. Meanwhile, performing between their sets was a comedian I didn't know, Flip Wilson.

King Curtis finished his set, and out came Wilson, who sat on a stool, lit a cigarette, and started telling stories. I thought he was hilarious. When he finished, I found him backstage and introduced myself, gave him my spiel, and asked him if he'd ever been to Boston. He said no, so I asked him if he was interested in that, and he said yes, so I asked who was managing him. That turned out to be Monte Kay.

Monte was a near-legend in the business, and I knew him as manager of the Modern Jazz Quartet. I called Kay and arranged to bring Flip to Boston. John Sdoucos and I were still doing some concert work, and John by then was quite active in the college market. We put Flip on a show with Herbie Mann at Boston University to get some local exposure. I saw Flip in a jazz context, so then I brought him into the Jazz Workshop. That was September 1966. I had Ray Santisi's trio as an opening act. There were only a handful of people in the audience—he was still an unknown—but they were falling over backwards laughing. I told myself, this guy is gonna hit, and we've got to keep working at it. I booked Flip again for a week in January 1967, this time at Paul's Mall.

When I arranged that first club booking with Monte Kay, I told him something along the lines of, "Monte, you have a great act on your hands—Wilson is unique among the comedians, he doesn't tell jokes, he tells stories that are incredibly funny, and his delivery is great. But you're not paying enough attention to him. You've got to get to get him some exposure." I really pushed. And Monte got him on the Ed Sullivan Show in November, and that was when doing well on Sullivan was like being handed the keys to the kingdom.

Wilson was on the Sullivan show for the second time on January 8, 1967, and that pushed the doors wide open for him. He opened at Paul's Mall the next night, and it was near chaos on Boylston Street, all week long. Everybody wanted to see him. It was showbiz . . . a complete sellout. And he was terrific.

Guy Livingston reviewed Flip at the Mall for *Variety*, the entertainment weekly, and it was Flip's first review in that magazine, a must-read for people in the business.

I think Flip started to see a bit of his future that week in Boston. I was bringing him around to the stations for interviews, and we stopped at a restaurant on Soldiers Field Road for lunch. All the waitresses recognized him and asked for an autograph, and as we were leaving more people recognized him, and we finally got outside and he said, "Man, you know, everybody's on you when you get popular." He was facing up to that side of fame—the interruptions, the strangers wanting to talk—he was coming to terms with it. He wanted to protect his privacy somehow. He was a very thoughtful guy.

Wilson played my clubs three times, a week each time, and after every show, he would sit in the dressing room and make notes—about which lines got a good response and which ones didn't—and he kept editing and refining his stories. After every show, he would analyze himself and the audience reaction, always trying to get better, and that impressed me.

By 1968 Wilson had outgrown Paul's Mall and was on to bigger things, like his weekly series on NBC TV. He once told me he had a five-year plan for success, and maybe he achieved it, because he walked away from his TV show in the mid-1970s when it was still quite popular. I never saw him again.

CAN WE TALK ABOUT JOAN RIVERS?

There weren't too many women working in comedy in the late 1960s. One was Phyllis Diller. I never booked her, but I once spent an afternoon chauffeuring her around the area, from the western suburbs to a restaurant in the North End. No one could be further from her onstage character than Phyllis, who was sharp and perceptive. And then there was Joan Rivers, who was well known because it seemed like she was on *The Tonight Show* every other week. Joan bombed on her first visit to Boston, at the Show Bar in the early '60s, and she was in no hurry to make a return trip. We finally brought Joan to Paul's Mall in April 1970, and she worked Monday and Tuesday and business was good. With Bill Evans next door at the Workshop, we were looking forward to a big week. Wednesday, showtime, no Joan. In fact, no Joan at all that night, and it made me angry to have to refund customers' money because my act let me down.

We found out the next day that Joan was in Beth Israel Hospital—she had been admitted with the severe symptoms of what turned out to be a tubal pregnancy. Thankfully, she was alright, and of course any thought of performing was out of the question. The story was kept quiet, she took a little time off, and Joan was back as guest host of *The Tonight Show* a month later. We never rescheduled our booking. In fact, she didn't perform in the area again until the early 1980s, after I was out of the nightclub business. I don't think most people, even Joan's fans, know that little story, even now.

BOSTON LOVES LILY, AND THAT'S THE TRUTH!

In January 1971, I got a call from an agent at William Morris, talking up one of their new signings, Lily Tomlin. Of course I knew her; she had been on television with *Laugh-In* for a year and had just released an album, *This Is a Recording*. Lily had been performing in small comedy cellars in New York for some time, but she hadn't been out on tour, and Morris was trying to set up her out-of-town debut. They were offering me one of the first nightclub dates on the tour. I jumped at the chance to bring Lily Tomlin to Boston for the first time.

Since Lily was already known, I first tried to book her into a big room. I called Caesar's Monticello, a supper club in suburban Framingham that featured name entertainers, mainly middle-of-the-road types. They weren't interested. Okay, I decided, I'll present Lily myself at Paul's Mall. We booked her for four nights during the first week in April, Thursday through Sunday. The sensational jazz organist Jimmy Smith was down the hall at the Jazz Workshop, so the week was shaping up quite nicely.

Lily had left *Laugh-In* by then, but her album had created a bit of buzz, and when she opened on April Fool's Day 1971, we had a line of people waiting to see her going up the stairs and out the door. We said, *wow!* We hit the jackpot. And she was just wonderful, onstage and off. Just delightful.

What a breath of fresh air Lily was in the comedy world! Lily was a storyteller, and she created a cast of characters that people just loved—Edith Ann, the five-year-old; the Fast Talker, who never finished her sentences (I could relate to that, I've been known to do it myself), and especially Ernestine, the nasal-voiced telephone operator and the "star" of *This Is a Recording*, asking "Have I reached the party to whom I am speaking?"

Phone company employees loved Lily and turned out in force for her shows, and not just at the Mall, but wherever she performed. They were Ernestine's people. Lily often invited them to sit up front, and she asked us to save some tables for them. She told me that Bell Telephone offered her money—quite a bit of money—to do their TV commercials, but she figured it would ruin the character and declined.

Lily insisted on doing a Sunday matinee, but there was a catch. It was for kids. Admission was 50 cents, and anyone over the age of 12 had to be accompanied by a child to be admitted. That drove the college students nuts, but that was the rule and the room was packed with families. It might have been the only show in the history of Paul's Mall where we had a run on ginger ale.

I liked Lily, and we established a good rapport. A year later, she was way too big for the Mall and I presented her in concert at Symphony Hall. My friend Ernie Santosuosso, who covered nightlife for the *Globe*, wanted to interview her, so I brought him backstage and made the introductions. Ernie is like me, a fan of the 2,000 Year Old Man, and as it turned out, Lily didn't know about him. Something set us off, and we launched into a Brooks and Reiner routine, back and forth, until I came to and said, "Wait a minute! Wait a minute! *She's* the act, Ernie, you gotta interview *her!*" And he had a great interview.

Fast forward about 10 years, and Lily came to Boston, to the Wilbur Theatre, for her one-woman show, *The Search for Signs of Intelligent Life in the Universe*, and I saw it and thought it was a *tour de force*. I wanted to go backstage afterward to offer congratulations, and back then the only way to get there was to go outside and down a service alley to the stage door. I knocked and told the guy who opened it who I was, and asked to see Lily. "You wait here," he said, and closed the door. So I'm outside, in the rain, waiting for this guy to come back.

Finally he opened the door, and there was Lily, and the first thing she said was "Fred, I got the Mel Brooks album!" Here it was, years later, and she remembered that exchange with Ernie and me. Lily isn't a star with a big ego. She remembers people.

In 2008 I brought Lily to the Hanover Theatre in Worcester, and Ernie went with me to the show. We went backstage afterwards. Lily greeted us like long-lost friends, and we posed for photos, and Lily was the same open, genuine person who played Paul's Mall in 1971, the one who wanted the telephone operators sitting ringside and who insisted on doing a show for the kids. It was almost 40 years later, and we still had that great rapport.

THE UNFORTUNATE FEARS OF ALBERT BROOKS

Albert Brooks, now he's a story. His father, Harry Einstein, was also a comedian, and Albert changed his name because he couldn't see going through life known as Albert Einstein.

Brooks came to Paul's Mall in March 1974, and I thought his material was just brilliant, very inventive. In one sketch, he was a nature photographer who lost his slide show and tried to re-create it with a box of stuffed animals. In another, he was a guy who just received a Dear John letter, and while a recorded voice read the angry letter, we watched him sitting on a stool and reacting to it. I liked his material. I thought it was unique and very creative.

At the end of the first night, Albert was sweating profusely, saying, "I don't know, I don't know."

"Don't know what?" I asked.

And he said, "I don't know. But I've got to change my hotel room."

So we changed his hotel room.

Then the second night he finished his act and started with "I don't know" again, and he was in pain and suffering anxiety attacks. We called a doctor and finally got him settled down. At the end of the third night, he was on the phone with his psychiatrist in LA. His shows were great and the audiences loved him, but he was coming unglued. Albert was a nervous wreck.

Day 4 was Saturday, and we were opening up when we learned that Brooks had caught a flight back to LA that morning. Here it was, Saturday night, biggest night of the week, and Brooks blew town! The reviews had been good and we were looking forward to a full house. We had an opening act, a pop singer named Leo Sayer, but he wasn't going to replace Albert Brooks. The prospects for the evening could not have been worse.

What, and give up show business?

I needed to come up with a plan B in a hurry, and I hit upon one looking at the newspaper. I noticed that *The Prisoner of Second Avenue* was playing at the Shubert Theater, and an old friend, none other than Irwin Corey, was playing the taxi driver. So I rushed down to the Shubert as the matinee was getting out, and I found Irwin, and I said, "Irwin, can you help me? Albert Brooks just flew the coop. We have a show tonight and nobody to star in it."

He said, "Yeah, but maybe you noticed, I'm doing a show here."

I asked, "What time to do you get through?"

He said, "We're done at ten."

I begged. "I can hold the show. I'll rush you over at one minute after ten. I'll get a police escort if I have to."

He agreed to do it.

We kept Leo singing until 5 minutes after 10, and then Irwin Corey waltzed in to do the Saturday night show. I have no idea where he found a tuxedo jacket—he must have raided the wardrobe department at the Shubert. Talk about luck: it was unbelievable, and he outdid himself that night. I owed Irwin, big time. That turned out to be the last time he performed at Paul's Mall, and I'll never forget it.

By the way, the reason for Albert's anxiety goes back to his father. When Albert was a little boy, his father Harry was taking part in a roast at the Friars Club in LA. He had just finished his monologue and was taking his seat when he slumped over. The audience laughed; they thought it was part of his act, but he had suffered a heart attack and died on the spot. Albert feared a similar fate, and it drove him from the comedy stage. He went into film and had success on both sides of the camera, but he never did standup again. After Paul's Mall, he called it quits.

THE WIZ: RICHARD PRYOR

We announced Richard Pryor was coming to Paul's Mall in April 1974, and we had the joint sold out from the get-go. He played for four days, eight sets, and sold every seat. Nevertheless, people were coming to the door and trying to buy tickets.

"We're sold out."

So they'd say, "There's room out in the hallway."

We'd say, "You can't be there, that's the fire exit."

Or they'd say, "I'll pay just to stand where I can hear him."

And no matter how many people we turned away, there were always more coming down the stairs. Richard Pryor was a crowd magnet.

Maybe you have a mental image of Richard Pryor as the high-energy, profane comedian. I saw a different Richard our very first night. After the first show, I went into his dressing room to see how he was doing, and right away he asked me, "Is it alright?"

I said, "Richard, it's better than alright, it's fabulous."

And he was so *pleased* with that. He was sincere and honest. He wanted to know if he was doing everything we wanted, and I was so knocked out, he was such a straightforward guy. I just never forgot that first encounter. My friend at the *Boston Globe*, Ernie Santosuosso, had the same reaction to

Pryor, who was soft-spoken, thoughtful, and relaxed throughout their long interview session.

In 1978, Richard made the movie *The Wiz*. Actually, he *was* the wiz in *The Wiz*. And he was out on a concert tour, and I managed to book him for two nights at the Music Hall, on the same weekend that *The Wiz* opened in Boston theaters. Of course we had a big Richard Pryor promotion, and had the mayor declare October 26–27 as Richard Pryor Weekend. I thought it would be nice to have the deputy mayor—Clarence "Jeep" Jones, who was of African American descent—present Richard with the mayor's proclamation.

So Jeep came to the dressing room before the show, and I made the introductions and explained to Richard what it was all about. We asked if he'd like to accept the proclamation onstage. And Richard thought about it for a few seconds. Then, completely deadpan, he asked Jeep, "Tell me one thing. Do they let niggers go to school around here?" I don't remember what Jeep said. I myself almost fell over. There was no such thing as a moment Richard could not turn upside down, and he certainly upended the seriousness of his mayoral proclamation. I honestly can't remember if Richard accepted his proclamation on the stage or not.

That was the last time I saw Richard. Like so much else about him, it certainly was memorable.

SUPER SHOW!

John Kerry had a distinguished career in politics, representing Massachusetts in the US senate, running for president in 2004, and later serving as secretary of state. But before all that, he was the lieutenant governor of Massachusetts. It was his first elective office, and when he launched his campaign, I produced a big fundraiser for him at the Hynes Auditorium. We called it the Super Show, and it was! The date was April 17, 1982. The entertainers were all long associated with liberal causes: Peter, Paul and Mary provided the music, and Chevy Chase and Robin Williams provided the comedy.

I met Robin only once, on the night of this show. We were trying to get into his dressing room, but the door was locked, so the two of us were standing there, waiting for someone to bring the key. Robin turned this situation into a standup performance for one—me. He started talking to that door: "We know you're in there! You can't stop us! We're comin' in!" He was going at it like he was on stage. Then we got into the room, and he wasn't "on" anymore. He turned it "off" and became a different person. I don't remember what we talked about, but he was a warm, friendly guy, somebody I wanted to get to know. But the public didn't see a lot of that side of him. What we saw was intensity. In his shows, he was on from start to finish, all high energy, no letdown.

His death really saddened me. I thought there was some inner frustration in him, that he was unable to get out all that was in him. It was tragic. Funny outside, tortured inside. And a really nice guy.

SOCIAL STUDIES

We certainly had our share of satirists and comedians who based their humor on the events of the day and the world we lived in. Here are a handful who found their humor in politics and society.

Mort Sahl was a stream-of-consciousness satirist. I remembered Mort from Storyville in the '50s, and I was excited to bring him to Paul's Mall in April 1969. But the public's tastes had changed since then. Long story short: Mort Sahl bombed, and it was very embarrassing. It's not that he was an old hat kind of guy—his material was always as fresh as the morning paper—but his approach had become *passé*. He wasn't quite right for Paul's Mall in 1969.

We had no such problem with Dick Gregory, whose humor, like Sahl's, was always informed by current events—and always controversial. He was totally committed to activism and civil rights. When he first came to the club in July 1972, though, he was already incorporating "lifestyle humor" into his monologues. He hadn't eaten solid food in 16 months and had lost an amazing amount of weight. So he talked about that, and about running the Boston Marathon a few months before. Dick's humor always had a message, and that time it was "health."

Regardless of lifestyle, though, Dick was a wicked satirist. We used to send postcards to our mailing list, and on the cards for Gregory's shows, we'd sprinkle in a few of his observations. For example: "If a nine-year-old kid can find a drug dealer, why can't the FBI?" and "If you're going to shoot all the looters, make it retroactive and give the Indian a gun."

Dick came back a year later, in July 1973, and announced from the stage that this was his final nightclub engagement; that with all the smoke and drink, clubs were unhealthy, and he was exiting the club scene to concentrate on the concert hall. It didn't last. He returned to the clubs, including mine, in 1976.

We had David Steinberg in 1970, who did monologues he called "sermons." Well, he had been studying to be a rabbi before he discovered comedy. He was another one who had a strong countercultural bent, and he reminded me of Woody Allen, only edgier and more political. We had him back in 1973 and again in 1974, and he was about as antiestablishment and anti-Nixon as you could get. The college students absolutely loved him.

David did great standup, but he really found his place writing and directing in television. He worked on *Friends* and *Seinfeld*, and has directed *Curb Your Enthusiasm* since its beginnings.

If there is a tragic character in my comedy story, it's David Frye. Frye was an impressionist, the best I ever saw, and he didn't bother with the Broadway and Hollywood stars that the other impressionists featured. David specialized in politicians. He did a brilliant Lyndon Johnson, but he was an unforgettable Richard Nixon. He didn't just imitate Nixon, he somehow channeled him, capturing his dark and brooding character. But David had an inferiority complex, and he would always introduce himself as "David Frye, the comedian," in case we had forgotten. And it wasn't just part of his act. David wanted to be more than just a Nixon impersonator; he wanted to be recognized as a comedian in his own right. The creative comedians, the ones who write and perform their own material, are at the top of the ladder, and that's where Frye wanted to be. He struggled to find material that was his own, but on his own he wasn't very funny. It became an obsession with him, wanting to be recognized as a great comedian.

Frye played Paul's Mall three times, and the singer who opened for him in June 1970 didn't find that much humor in the situation. She was a relative unknown named Bette Midler, who once told Jay Leno on *The Tonight Show* that she spent the week fending off Frye's amorous advances, although she put it a bit more colorfully than that.

I started this chapter by saying that humor is as dear to my heart as music, and always has been. People have asked, if that's true, why didn't I present comedy at Scullers? It was a straightforward business decision, and not a hard one either. The Comedy Connection opened in 1978, just about the time I closed Paul's Mall, and that opened the floodgates to what seemed like a dozen comedy clubs. Even after the comedy club boom of the 1980s passed, there were always multiple venues presenting comedy in Boston and Cambridge. There still are. I saw no point in going up against well-established locations that were already competing for the better comedians and bigger shares of the same audience. I like a good laugh as much as anybody, but I decided to let Scullers be a music venue, and I never regretted it.

10

MILES DAVIS: HIPPER THAN YOU

Sometimes when I talk about Miles Davis, I assume that because he was a first-rate jazz trumpet player and a musical genius and a celebrity and a superstar, everybody knows all about him. But then I catch myself and remember that of course it isn't true. I just *think* it should be true. So allow me to introduce you to Miles Dewey Davis, a man who was my friend for more than 20 years.

WELCOME TO THE JAZZ WORKSHOP, MR. DAVIS

I met Miles in 1967 and knew him for the rest of his life. But even if he had stopped making music in 1967, he had already contributed enough to jazz to be placed in its highest ranks. He played bop with Charlie Parker in the postwar years, led the "birth of the cool" sessions in 1949, and formed his first great quintet with John Coltrane in the 1950s. He ended that decade recording the album *Kind of Blue* with Coltrane and another friend of mine, Cannonball Adderley. That album has become the greatest-selling jazz record of all time, far in excess of two million copies. Then came another landmark album, *Sketches of Spain*, his collaboration with Gil Evans. He launched his second great quintet in 1964, with Wayne Shorter and Herbie Hancock. You can't overstate the impact of Miles and these two quintets.

That's where things stood when I first presented Miles Davis at the Jazz Workshop in 1967. I was approached that summer by his agent, a top-notch guy named Jack Whittemore, who asked if we wanted Miles for the Jazz Workshop. Columbia Records was about to release a new Davis album called *Sorcerer*, and Jack thought the time was right for a trip to Boston. Tony and I were definitely interested. We booked him for Thanksgiving week in

November, seven nights, with a late Sunday afternoon matinee. We thought we'd do well even over the normally slow holiday weekend.

I was looking forward to meeting Miles, but I was a little nervous too, because Miles had the reputation of being aloof and uncommunicative. He was known to ignore his audience during shows and play with his back to them. In fact, there was a Miles joke making the rounds at the time: "Have you heard about the Miles Davis doll? You wind it up and it turns its back on you."

When I came downstairs to the Jazz Workshop on that opening Monday, I found him sitting at the bar, and I introduced myself. I said, "Hi Miles, I'm Fred Taylor." I might as well have been talking to the wall. I tried again. I said, "How do you like to run your sets?"

He turned to me and said in that raspy voice of his, "I came here to play, man."

Okay, I thought, he wants to be all business, I'll be all business. I looked at him and said, "We start at nine, we close at two, and you're in charge." And I walked away.

Miles had that band onstage and he hit at nine sharp. He played his set, took a break, got back up and played his second set, and finished at two.

As we were closing up, Miles asked me, "What did you think of the band?"

I thought it sounded a little rough, and I told him so. I said, "It sounds good, but I bet you'll sound better by Wednesday."

And he replied, "You know, you're right."

I was excited to be bringing Miles to Boston, and it turned out there were plenty of local jazz fans who were excited about it too. On those weekend nights when we didn't think we'd do well, people were lining up outside, from our door on Boylston Street down to the corner of Exeter, then around the corner and all the way down the block to Newbury Street. It was standing room only at the Jazz Workshop!

The band on that first engagement was a quartet, not the usual quintet. Herbie Hancock was absent for whatever reason, and the group worked without a piano. Tenor saxophonist Wayne Shorter was on the front line with Miles. Bassist Ron Carter was back in New York, but Jack Whittemore found a terrific substitute, the great Eddie Gomez, on loan from the Bill Evans Trio. The drummer was Tony Williams—who, by the way, was a Bostonian, and all of 21 at the time. Five years before, Tony had been skipping school so he could practice his drums all day, and now he was turning heads everywhere with his approach to jazz drumming. Every one of those musicians played at the Jazz Workshop numerous times.

You can never predict how a first impression goes over, but apparently I made a good impression on Miles, and we got along fine after that. Our opening-night exchanges created an understanding between us, and I'll tell you why. Miles didn't like flattery or backslapping or chit-chat. He would always cut right to the chase. No small talk. He had no time for bullshit and I understood that, because I didn't either, and he appreciated my directness. He hit me and I hit him right back, and he loved that. From then on, I became his go-to guy in New England. Every time he put together a new band, I'd get a call. It might be at 3:00 in the morning, but I'd get a call. There would be that voice: "I got a great new band. Bring me in." So I'd scramble to find a date and I'd bring him in. We had Miles Davis at the Jazz Workshop or Paul's Mall 11 times between 1967 and 1975.

Miles was a big boxing fan, and there was a time when he liked to work out in the ring. It must have been a great way to work off frustrations. He was in our office one day and ragging on my partner Tony about something. Miles mentioned boxing, and finally Tony had had enough. He stood up and told Miles, "I'm ready to go when you are," and they kind of glared at each other, and that was the end of it.

Tony told me later, "Of course I knew he would have knocked the stuffing out of me. But I had to let him know I'd heard enough." Everything was fine between them after that. But that's what I mean about getting along with Miles. He hit you, and you hit back.

JAZZMAN OF THE DECADE

Miles was already one of the biggest names in jazz in 1967, and we watched his stature just keep growing through 1975. We moved him from the Jazz Workshop into Paul's Mall because we needed those additional seats. In January 1970, we had more lines around the block. *Down Beat* magazine had just named Miles Jazzman of the Year and *Filles de Kilimanjaro* the Jazz Album of the Year, and the magazine's readers voted him the top trumpeter and his band the top group in their annual poll. Everybody wanted to see this group, and what they heard was the music on *Bitches Brew*, an early milestone in jazz fusion. Miles Davis was setting the pace in jazz once again. Wayne Shorter, Chick Corea, and John McLaughlin were in that band that week, and the groups they formed after leaving Miles defined jazz in the 1970s.

The biggest crowds and the longest lines around the block came in July 1974, when we had Miles at Paul's Mall for eight nights and drew more than 3,800 people. I remember talking to students who hitchhiked from western Massachusetts just to stand in line and hope they'd get in. We sold out 16 shows and were filled to capacity every night. A ticket cost $4.50, which, in 2018, is about $23. Miles earned about $9,200 on that engagement, which equals about $47,000 in 2018. I can tell you with absolute certainty that you would never lure a superstar into a nightclub right now for eight nights, two shows per night, for $47,000. I'd say you were dreaming. But back then, we could do things like that.

Then it was over, because Miles just wore out. He had pain in his joints and a bleeding ulcer, and he was still suffering the effects of a 1972 auto accident. He quit the scene in 1976 and stayed out of sight for five years.

"I NEED A DATE"

In early 1981 I heard that Miles had picked up his horn again, and that he'd been in Columbia studios in New York with a new band. I didn't make too much of it though, because we had heard rumors like that the whole time Miles was absent. Then in May, I got one of those late-night calls: "I need a date." Miles was planning an "official" comeback concert in New York during the Kool Jazz Festival in early July, but he wanted to tune up in front of an audience with his new band before that. And for that, he called me.

In late May we started working out the details with Miles's manager, Mark Rothbaum. They were looking at late June, meaning we had a month at the most to get ready, which didn't leave much time.

I had been out of the club business for three years, but I always kept an eye on what was happening on the local scene. I knew of a place that might be available, a shuttered nightclub near Kenmore Square called Kix, down an alley off Commonwealth Avenue. The building was an old parking garage, which in the '60s housed a rock club called the Psychedelic Supermarket. Kix shared the building with a disco. With about 400 seats, I thought Kix might work well for what we had in mind.

Bob Epstein, a real estate developer—he's now a part owner of the Boston Celtics basketball team—owned Kix, and I knew he was a big jazz fan. I called him. "Bob," I asked, "Can I bring an act into your club?"

"Who's the act?" he asked.

I said, "Miles Davis."

I could almost see Bob jumping out of his chair. "Miles Davis!" he exclaimed. "My God, yes!" So the biggest logistical problem was resolved: we had our venue.

Next, I was going to need help with publicity and media relations. Just taking care of all the press people who would descend on Boston when news of the Miles dates got out would be a challenge. I approached Sue Auclair, a former jazz singer who did publicity work for clients in the arts. At the time, she was the public relations director for the organization that sponsored Boston's First Night celebration on New Year's Eve. I asked if she might be interested in handling the publicity for an act I had coming to Boston at the end of June. Just like Bob, she asked, "Who's the act?"

And I said, "Miles Davis."

"Miles Davis!" she said, and she jumped right in.

That's how Sue and I started working together, and she's still my first-call publicist today.

Our first press release ran in the Boston newspapers on June 17 with the news that Miles Davis was emerging from his self-imposed retirement, appearing live at Kix in Boston for eight shows—two shows a night for four nights, Friday through Monday, June 26–29. I think the ticket price was $12.

And speaking of tickets, we still used the paper kind in 1981, and ours were being printed by an out-of-town company and shipped to us by air. But with four days to go and a lot of those tickets already sold, we were still waiting for the goods to arrive, and getting more and more nervous. Finally, a day before the first show, we got word that the tickets were in Boston. That was the good news. The bad news was that they were somewhere in the airline's cargo hanger at Logan Airport, and if we wanted the tickets right away, we'd have to go there and find them ourselves.

So Sue and I went to Logan and hunted for our package, sorting through what seemed like mountains of boxes. Finally we found them, and after we got out of there, we had to race around distributing the tickets to our sales outlets.

SHOWTIME AT KIX

The big day, June 26, finally arrived. Miles was staying in a hotel that was very close to Kix, and all he had to do was cross Commonwealth Avenue. But Miles wanted it to be an event, so he drove to work every night. I can still see Miles and Cecily Tyson, whom he would marry later that year, wheeling down the alley in his yellow Ferrari. After five years of waiting, there he was, and it was a madhouse. News of this engagement had sounded like a thunderclap across the entertainment world, and there were press people from France, Belgium, Japan, the UK. It was unbelievable. The alley was full of people shouting and cheering. We took Miles in through the disco, which had a side door into Kix. When he came through that door people just gasped—"There's Miles!"—and we hustled him down to the dressing room.

In spite of all the hubbub, Miles was very quiet, a man with a purpose. He walked directly to the dressing room, no stops to wave to the cameras or shake hands. He was subdued—aware of everything but a bit tentative. My God, he had to be nervous, even if he wouldn't admit it. The band members, on the other hand, were ready to go; they had a "let's do this!" kind of attitude. They came to play, and if Miles was a bit subdued, the band was almost rowdy by comparison.

When the band finally took the stage, we had Oscar Jackson, a deejay on WGBH, present Miles with a proclamation from Mayor Kevin White, declaring it to be Miles Davis Week in Boston. Then the music started, and the crowd just loved it. Miles's playing was not strong; like his mood, his playing the first night was tentative, but the band was together and it was fabulous.

This marked the debut performance for this new band, and even with the rough edges, I thought they shined. Bill Evans was the sax player, Mike Stern played guitar, Marcus Miller played bass, Al Foster was on drums, and Mino Cinelu was the percussionist. I knew Mike; he studied at Berklee and worked around Boston in the mid-1970s. He was one of those guys who hung around at the Jazz Workshop. And Al Foster had worked many of the Workshop dates with Miles.

Columbia Records sent their sound truck to Boston, and Teo Macero, Miles's producer since the *Kind of Blues* days, was at the controls. I didn't realize it at the time, but they recorded everything. It did not result in an actual "Live at Kix" record, but some of the music was released on the album *We Want Miles*, which came out in 1982.

To mark the event, Miki Boni, an artist friend of mine, designed a commemorative T-shirt. It was very simple, a black T-shirt with white lettering, just the word *Miles* written in cursive script, with the *i* looping through the *l* and emerging as a horn. We gave one to everybody in the band. In 2015, I found a few in the bottom of a box and gave one to Mike Stern when his group came through Boston.

All in all, it was a sensational event, simply unforgettable. And I know it sounds like a cliché, but in this case it was true: the atmosphere in that room was electric. Miles was back. His health was still a little shaky, but he was back.

People have asked over the years why Miles chose to stage this gig in Boston. He answered the question himself. I had arranged a one-on-one interview with Miles for the *Boston Globe's* Ernie Santosuosso, and Ernie asked Miles why he picked Boston for his tune-up.

"Why Boston? 'Cause I love Boston. I just happen to have a thing with Boston. Every time I have a new band and a good band, I just come to Boston. Also, I wouldn't do it for anybody else but Freddie Taylor. I like Boston people. It isn't a question of how many jazz clubs you have here. It's the attitude of the students. The students are thinking, you know what I mean? They are not afraid to look beyond today's music or anything else."

Believe me, I was very pleased that Miles mentioned me, but it was also a testament to Boston and its audience.

LATER CONCERTS AND FINALE

Kix was a high point, but it wasn't the end of my working with Miles on concerts. We brought him into the ballroom at the Hotel Bradford with the same band in November 1981, and again in April 1982. They had been touring and playing constantly since Kix, and the critics said that the band was better on their return visits. I thought so too. For that November show, Sue Auclair arranged for Adrienne Hawkins, the director of the Impulse Dance Company, to lead a group of dancers in staging a welcome for Miles in the lobby of his hotel, and later to dance to Miles's opening number that night at the Bradford. Miles didn't say much about it, and I don't think he was too impressed.

In September 1987 I brought Miles to Boston for a concert at the Opera House on Washington Street. At that time, I was suffering—*suffering*—from degenerative osteoarthritis in both hips, and that meant that I could barely walk. I had tried everything and was in terrible pain, and I finally accepted that I needed both hips replaced. In fact, this concert was about the last thing I did before I closed my office prior to the surgery and recovery. I knew Miles had gone through this, and after that concert I quizzed him about his experiences and how the recovery went.

Fast-forward to June 1989, when I produced "An Evening with Miles Davis," a concert to benefit the Boston Jazz Society as part of the Boston Globe Jazz Festival. We were again at the Opera House. I'd had my surgery, and I was feeling like a million bucks. I went to the airport to meet Miles, and we were walking back to my car. I said "Miles, there's something I gotta tell you."

"Yeah?"

"And it's taken me a lifetime to be able to say this."

At this point, he was really giving me some strange looks.

I said, "Miles . . . I am now hipper than you. I got two. Count 'em, baby—two."

He threw his arms around me, and rasped that term of endearment I knew so well: "You *motherfucker*."

That was our last concert together, and the last time I saw him.

Miles died in 1991 and it hit me hard. The funeral was at St. Peter's in New York, and it was packed. I remember I sat next to Roy Haynes. Mayor David Dinkins spoke, and Jesse Jackson, and various dignitaries. At the very end, they projected an image on the wall, a huge image, of Miles standing at the door of an airplane at the top of the boarding stairs, and he was waving. Maybe it was at Montreux. The music from *Kind of Blue* was playing in the background, and it was like he was saying farewell. It was so emotional. And that was the end of the funeral. People filed into the reception hall, and there was total silence. It was probably five minutes before conversation started.

That's still such a powerful memory for me—his wave, that farewell wave.

Not everyone knows that in his last 10 or so years, Miles became quite an artist, with a fascinating sense of color. He was serious about it, as serious as he was about music. A book of his paintings and sketches was published in 2013. About a year or so after his death, someone with the estate took some of his artwork and made a series of neckties to show it, and those of us who worked closely with him received one. I'm not much for neckties anymore, but I make it a point to wear mine on very special occasions.

Behind the public pose, Miles was intense, direct, and highly creative, and I always enjoyed working with him. He was a no-nonsense guy, but he had a sense of humor and I liked to tweak it occasionally. There will never be another like him, and I'm proud to have called Miles Davis a friend.

11

LIGHTS OUT

You hear it said so often: all good things come to an end. I don't know if that's a universal truth, but it was true for Paul's Mall, the Jazz Workshop, and Cinema 733. For us, the lights went out at the close of business on April 9, 1978—or to be more accurate, in the early morning hours of April 10. It was a major milestone in my life, and I still talk in terms of "before we closed" and "after we closed." Tony and I almost saved the whole operation too. We were *this close* to relocating to the nearby Paris Cinema building, and if it had come through, we might still be in business there today. But it was not to be.

About a week before the end, we held a press conference at the Jazz Workshop to officially announce the closing. Channel 5 even sent a camera crew. "I'll be back!" I told the reporters. "As an act!" That got them thinking.

WATER, WATER, EVERYWHERE

In late 1976, Tony and I faced up to reality: our time was running out at 733 Boylston. Paul's Mall and the Jazz Workshop were basement spaces in an older building that had its share of physical problems. By 1977, they simply could not be ignored. We were looking more than a bit dilapidated. We had never done an end-to-end makeover, and you can't have thousands of people going through a place every week without leaving it a little beat up. We needed paint, carpeting, new furniture. We needed to gut and replace the restrooms—ours were nearing the end of their useful lives.

Our worst problem, however, was water, the bane of almost all Back Bay buildings. Whenever there was a heavy rainfall, the drainage pipes that ran under the alley behind our building couldn't handle it. There was always water backing up in the alley and trying to get in. Then there was the water that was already in. We were at the bottom of a five-story building, and everything funneled down to a single sewer line. So if there was any kind of blockage, our toilets would back up, and the floors would be covered with an inch or two of water. Then we'd be frantically sucking up the water with vacuums so we could open on time. That was a recurring problem. We might have canceled a Sunday matinee or two because of the wet floors, but we never canceled an evening show. We'd call the city water department and they'd come with their giant roto-rooter and clean out the sewer line, and that would fix the flooding problem for a while, but that wasn't our only water problem. We had water coming through the ceiling, too.

The Half Shell restaurant threw fish skins, lobster shells, everything into the kitchen sink, which would clog, and if they weren't on it right away, it would overflow. Their kitchen floor would be covered with clam juice, and inevitably some of it would find its way into the Paul's Mall ceiling, and then it would drip onto the bandstand. It could become a real mess, as for instance when Gary Puckett and the Union Gap were at the Mall, and clam juice rained all over the horn section's music stands. The band made it through the engagement without the horn parts, but Puckett was quite upset and insisted that we replace the music, which we did. The Half Shell never did clean up their act. We always had to keep one eye on the ceiling.

WHEN A FULL HOUSE ISN'T ENOUGH

So we had the plumbing and wear-and-tear issues, and perhaps we could have taken care of those things and given the clubs a reboot. But we hesitated, because even if we fixed every physical problem and made the rooms all shiny and new, we still had a problem that was even greater: our space was obsolete, too small, and there was no way to expand it. That structural wall between the rooms, 4 feet thick, was as permanent as the Rock of Gibraltar. Our seating capacity was fixed, and it wouldn't produce enough revenue to keep us in business much longer. We had to move—or close.

The changes in the live music business in the 1970s seemed to come at lightning speed. When we bought the clubs in 1966, we'd book an act, and on the day of the first show, three or four guys would roll up in a station wagon and unload a drum kit, a bass, maybe a small amp, and a few horn cases.

They'd carry their own gear downstairs and set it up. We'd test a few microphones and be ready to go. Ah, for the simple life! Then, starting in the '70s, a truck would pull up and two roadies would start hauling in equipment. Even in jazz, much of the music had gone electric, so there was more equipment, sometimes lots more. More equipment meant longer sound checks. Bands started traveling with their own sound technicians.

The record companies were changing how they did business at the same time. If an artist had a new release, the company wanted them introducing it in as many places as possible. They didn't want an artist in one city for a week. All of a sudden, there were many acts we couldn't get for a week; we could only get them for two or three nights. That was a far cry from 1967, when we booked Bobby Short in Paul's Mall for three weeks at a time! By 1974, it was three days of this and two days of that, and I was spending all my time on the phone, patching together a schedule for a pair of seven-nights-per-week clubs.

When groups were playing for only a night or two, they dispensed with the truck and the equipment completely. They would specify in their contract what equipment they wanted—what we call "backline"—and we'd rent it and have it ready to go. The artist would roll in from the airport in time to hit at 8:00.

I should add that all these scheduling and logistics considerations were more of an issue at the Mall, where our bookings had moved into contemporary rock and pop. There was more stability at the Jazz Workshop. We were still booking acts there for seven-night stands, and thank God for that, because I would have been on the phone 24 hours a day otherwise.

Other costs were rising too. Inflation picked up, especially after the oil embargo in 1973, which led to price hikes of about a third in lodging and transportation. And don't forget rent, utilities, insurance, housekeeping—all going up. This all had to be factored into the price of admission. These costs were hurting us, but they weren't the budget-busters.

What was killing us was the cost of the entertainment. It was driving clubs like ours out of business. You'd pay an artist $3,000 for a week, and then their record would start selling, and they'd want $15,000 for a week. If the record hit big, they'd want $15,000 a night. Of course we couldn't pay that, and that act was lost to us. I'm not exaggerating with these numbers. When we started with George Benson in 1967, we hired his quartet for a week at the Workshop for $1,000. In 1976, when *Breezin'* became a best seller, he wanted $15,000 a night. Believe me, this wasn't a unique situation. The biggest draws had become too expensive for us.

And to think I was worried about paying Erroll Garner $7,500 for a week in 1970. Little did we know what was coming in just a few years.

Against this backdrop of price increases, we had our two clubs with their set number of seats. We had reached the point where we couldn't raise the price of admission to offset our lack of capacity. We were being squeezed. There's a break point where your admission charge gets too high for the room you have. We saw that coming in early 1977 and began planning a move to a larger space.

We set a target date for closing on Boylston Street that was just over a year away. We were booking months in advance, so we couldn't just close abruptly. We decided on April 9, 1978, and made no commitments beyond that date. The search for a new place went into high gear.

THE PARIS CINEMA STORY

We had our eyes on the Paris Cinema, a single-screen theater on the next block of Boylston Street, between Fairfield and Gloucester. We'd heard it was closing. We toured the theater and got very excited—we thought it could be a fabulous place in a great location, where we could combine Mall and Workshop into a single venue. We liked it so much, we struck a deal with Arthur Baron, the building owner, to lease the theater for $20,000. That was Tony, Mr. Facts and Figures, at work again. He knew we wouldn't make any money on this lease, but we would control the location while we firmed up a long-term deal. Tony set it up so we could terminate the lease at any time. That was more smart thinking on Tony's part.

We were still talking in March 1977 when we hired an architectural design firm, Cambridge Seven Associates, to draw up preliminary plans for a renovation that would turn a movie theater into a concert club. The results were spectacular—seating for 650, a lobby lounge, dressing rooms off the side of the stage, a marquee on Boylston Street, and an L-shaped balcony. That would have really been something, because the Paris didn't have a balcony; we'd be creating it in the new design. We were high as kites thinking about the possibilities.

Naturally, we started running into problems. We learned that although Arthur Baron owned the building, a New York company owned the land, and they leased it to him. It was a two-owner thing, and we had to negotiate with both. The negotiations stalled when we couldn't get a long-term lease. We had to have that. If we were going to spend more than $400,000 on the renovation, we couldn't accept a two-year lease. There was no sense going in if we couldn't stay long enough to recoup our investment.

Then the city of Boston got involved. The building inspection department took a look at our plan and told us an occupancy of 650 was too high. They set a limit of about 350, and that was a no-go. All that would do was transfer our capacity problem to a new address.

With the owners unwilling to give us long-term contracts and the city limiting the maximum occupancy to 350, we couldn't make it work. We had to walk away from the Paris, and that was a shame. That's one of my biggest regrets. We thought we had a hell of a deal with the Paris Cinema. And I tell you, to this day I believe that if we had been able to do it, I think we would still be there, and we would probably have one of the great, great rooms in the country. The location was ideal. The capacity would have been right in the sweet spot, even for today, 650 seats. In this business, 600 seats in your own club equals about 1,500 seats in a theater. The jump in expenses in going from club to concert hall is that significant.

There was no plan B. We looked at the Harvard Square Theatre in Cambridge, but we had already realized that wasn't the right place for the Mall/Workshop. We kept looking, but properties like the Paris Cinema only rarely became available. We resigned ourselves to the idea that we would be closing.

IT ALL ENDS APRIL 9TH

That's what it said on our last ads and flyers: 15 years of bringing great artists to a great city ends on April 9, 1978. On the one hand, I was dreading this day, and on the other I couldn't wait for it to get here and be done. It was the end of the line, and as much as I didn't want to reach the end, I was anxious to have the whole business finished. If we're gonna close, let's get it over with. There were things I knew I had to do but wished I didn't, like say, "so long and good luck" to our 30 employees. Some, like our floor manager Dick Stasium, had been with us for years.

It became kind of a grind toward the end. Scheduling problems started in late 1977. We'd book a band for three days, then be closed for two. Sometimes I brought in local bands to fill out the schedule. In early 1978, there were more complications. Muddy Waters was ill and canceled. Then came the infamous Blizzard of '78, and we shut the whole place down for three days. We reopened on February 9 with Les McCann in the house, one of our biggest draws. We had 32 customers.

There were still big nights in our last month. Sonny Rollins, McCoy Tyner, and Stanley Turrentine all drew well. My jazz guys were in there punching until the end! Then it was April, and closing night was a week away. Believe it or not, we were still introducing new acts to our audiences. Our second-last artist at the Jazz Workshop was the exciting South African pianist Dollar Brand, who would soon change his name to Abdullah Ibrahim. How new was he? New enough for the *Globe's* newspaper ad to identify him as "Dollar Brano." It might have been the last week, but the little things, like fixing the print ads, still needed to be done. Like they say in the theater, the show must go on.

During those last weeks, people, our regulars, kept stopping by to say how sorry they were that the clubs were closing. And they asked questions, like where were they going to go to hear their music? And where were the acts who couldn't fill a concert hall going to play? There weren't too many places that I could recommend. The Merry-Go-Round presented jazz and pop singers, including old friends like Mae Arnette and Jackie and Roy. Lulu White's had just opened in the South End, but it featured Dixieland. After we closed, Lulu's started booking jazz acts that were typically "ours," like pianist Dorothy Donegan and drummer Roy Haynes. But these were only slices—no venue anywhere could offer the whole pie.

People asked a similar question upstairs too. Cinema 733, the little theater we opened after we closed the Inner Circle restaurant, was the last of the second run/revival houses in the Back Bay. The Kenmore Square and Park Square Theaters had already closed. I'd tell people, if you wanted a midnight movie on Saturday night, there was always television.

That last week, we had the great blues guitarist and singer B. B. King at Paul's Mall, with the young jazz singer Dee Dee Bridgewater opening. The line started early for B. B. on April 9, and Paul's Mall was packed as showtime approached. The audience weren't all big fans of B. B. King. I'm sure a fair share of them just wanted to be part of history, wanted to be able to say they were there for the last night.

Next door, the vibraphonist Milt Jackson was closing the Jazz Workshop, and we were pleased to have him. Milt revolutionized the role of the vibes in jazz, and starred as the featured soloist in the Modern Jazz Quartet from its first day to its last. We didn't have a house band anymore by 1978, but whenever the Jazz Workshop brought in a single, I'd hire local musicians to fill out the band. So it was on this last engagement. We had Ray Santisi's trio to accompany Milt. This was truly coming full circle. Ray had been part of the first Jazz Workshop at the Stable, and he played with Stan Getz at the grand opening of this Jazz Workshop in 1963. Here he was, taciturn on the bandstand as always, playing piano on the last night, 15 years later.

Fate did not allow us to exit without a last-minute problem. For one last time, the kitchen sink upstairs in the Half Shell backed up and water came dripping through the ceiling. We had to rope off three or four tables to the left of the stage. That was bad enough, but we were broadcasting our last night on WBCN, and the cables snaking down from the truck were just inches away from a puddle. I had somebody keeping an eye on that all night.

People told me I was surprisingly calm that night, but I think I was just numb. It was a lot to take in. Tony and I decided to go out in a business-as-usual way, with a minimum of fuss. We didn't have a crowd of musicians coming down to sit in on the last night, although James Montgomery brought his harmonica and sat in with B. B. When the music ended, the people went up those stairs one last time, and they all said something along the lines of "Thank you for all the great music and we're really going to miss this place." I appreciated that at the time, and I've appreciated it more as the years went on.

Even that night, though, I was aware of what Boston was losing. It wasn't just all the talent that we presented week after week. The clubs were a cross-roads. We welcomed everybody, from bankers to Berklee students. Boston went through some very tense times during the club years, but it didn't matter if you were black or white, young or old, jazz fan or rocker, you could come to our clubs and relax, have a drink, and listen to great music. If we closed, that would be gone. No one else was stepping up to take our place. And we knew it.

There was an after-party. The writers, deejays, record company promo men, musicians, agents—all the usual suspects—hung around after closing time with Tony and me and the rest of our crew, drinking up the booze and serenading us with "Auld Lange Syne."

I don't remember who locked up for the last time. I stumbled home and fell into bed. When I woke up the next day, I was just a guy who used to own a couple of music clubs.

12

MOVIE MOGUL

So Tony and I closed the Boylston Street clubs, but we didn't have much time to think about it, because we had another business that needed our attention. During the last year of the clubs' operation, we also managed the Harvard Square Theatre! The clubs were exciting, no doubt about it, but we had another venture upstairs on Boylston Street, and that was our little movie house, Cinema 733. It was the forerunner to our time at the Harvard Square. I'll tell all our celluloid stories in this chapter.

GOODBYE INNER CIRCLE, HELLO CINEMA 733

I got into the theater business because I owned a failing restaurant.

The restaurant was the Inner Circle, which was Harold Buchhalter's first venture at 733 Boylston, and we took it over when we took control of the clubs. The food was okay, but the dinner music was great. We hired pianists to play through the dinner hour. Meredith D'Ambrosio was one, but she just called herself Meredith then. Sometimes I'd bring out my cocktail drum and join her. Meredith went on to a long career as a jazz singer, and I brought her to Scullers numerous times. Our most famous dinner pianist, though, was Keith Jarrett, who played at the Inner Circle in 1965 when he was a student at Berklee. We brought him downstairs to Paul's Mall to accompany some of our singers. One night he sat in with Charles Lloyd at the Jazz Workshop, and Lloyd hired him and off he went to start an amazing career. So those were two major talents we had playing dinner music at the Inner Circle back in their salad days.

By 1970, the Inner Circle was not doing well at all. Peter Lane was running it, but he was running it straight into the ground. He was always finding ways to cut costs, and you can only go so far with that before the quality starts to suffer. I'd talk to him, and he'd say he was doing the right thing, but he wasn't, and the numbers showed it. It upset me. It was getting harder and harder to work with Peter. And Tony wasn't Peter's biggest fan, either. Peter was a partner, and we couldn't just fire him, but somehow we had to get him out the door. We thought putting a different kind of business in the Inner Circle space might be the way to do it.

Times were changing in 1970, and Peter was becoming the odd man out. He wasn't on the same wavelength as Tony and me, and he wasn't happy with how the operation was evolving. He wanted things the way they were in 1967, and those days weren't ever coming back. Tony and I started talking, and the idea to buy out Peter took shape. We approached him, and he wanted a lot of money, $100,000, but we had it, and so we bought him out. MTL Inc. would move ahead without Peter Lane. And our first order of business was to do something different with the Inner Circle space. We had an idea: movies.

In 1970, mini-cinemas were a thing. Jerry Lewis was backing a mini-cinema franchise operation, and Tony and I considered going with that and opening one of his turnkey operations. Then we could hire someone who knew that business to manage it. And that's what we did, but we decided to remain independent. A good thing, too, because that venture ended badly for Lewis and forced him into bankruptcy. We found our manager when we met Neil Evans, who was looking for a space where he could run a theater to show foreign films. We made a deal with him.

We closed the restaurant. Our last day of business was September 13, 1970, which, coincidentally, was seven years to the day after the opening of the Jazz Workshop. We never talked about it, but I'll bet Tony planned it that way.

With that taken care of, we leased the space to Neil, and he set to work on the renovations. He needed seating, a projection booth, a ticket counter, a refreshment stand, everything. Neil, though, got bogged down in the details, so we jumped in to help him get the place finished. The end result was a small auditorium with about 180 seats. We named it Cinema 733. It opened on Christmas Day in 1970, and the first picture was by the French director Claude Chabrol: *This Man Must Die.* For Neil, this film was right in the pocket. He planned a policy of first-run, mainly foreign fare, and this was a good start.

Despite the good buzz from the opening, though, Neil stumbled. It turned out he knew a lot about film but not so much about operating a theater. Tony and I had to step in, and we ended up taking over Cinema 733.

Neither Tony nor I had ever run a theater, but Tony took to it, and he was the one who went looking for movies. It was hard at first. He'd make the rounds at the film distributors but had trouble making bookings—they were skeptical: "What do you guys know about the business?" Then Tony met Arthur Friedman, a distributor for United Artists, and Arthur helped us. Arthur called Tony and said he had a picture that he thought might do business for us. It was *The Hospital* with George C. Scott, and Arthur thought its black humor would appeal to our Boylston Street crowd. And it did pretty well for us. Then Arthur found us a few more films, like *Straw Dogs* and *Putney Swope.* Things were looking up.

Then in September 1972 we developed what became our claim to fame—our double feature program. We called it "Tomorrow's Classics Today." We concocted a mix of second-run films, cult favorites, revived classics, you name it, and we paired them in double features that we changed three times a week. It was an immediate hit. Two dollars for admission—a dollar for the matinee! We had the theater operating in the black a month after we started the double features. Then we had a separate midnight show on the weekends. *Woodstock* was one of the popular midnight movies.

We continued the double features until the day we closed, in April 1978. Our last one was *Chinatown* and *Looking for Mr. Goodbar,* two movies in which the leading lady meets a tragic end. A bit like the Cinema 733 itself.

A NEW VENTURE: THE HARVARD SQUARE THEATRE

Our Boylston Street operation was winding down when we got wind of an opportunity on Harvard Square in Cambridge. We were actively looking for a new location that would give us more seating in a single room and allow us to merge Paul's Mall and the Jazz Workshop under a single roof. That's the plan we talked about in chapter 11, with the Paris Theatre. The Harvard Square Theatre offered a similar situation. It was a classic 1920s movie palace, bigger than the Paris, with a proscenium stage and seating for about 1,900. Like the Paris, it had only one screen, but it was big, and wide enough to show 70 mm movies. Of course we were interested.

Arthur Friedman told us that the operator of the Harvard Square Theatre was struggling. He thought Tony and I should try to lease it, and if we did, he could supply us with films. By then he had left United Artists and gone into partnership with Roger Lockwood in a film distribution company—Lockwood-Friedman. And they wanted to get their foot in the door on Harvard Square.

Tony and I met with Ed Mank, who owned the theater building, in early 1976. We talked to Ed, but Ed was managing a realty trust, and he had an office full of people to consult—partners and attorneys and whomever else. They were dragging their feet, and we were getting nowhere.

Finally we set up a meeting with Ed, minus his team. We asked him, "Ed, do you want to lease the place?" He did. We said we'd assume the current lease and negotiate a longer term. Then of course we asked about money. We knew he was leasing the theater for $80,000 a year.

I asked, "What's it gonna take?"

He said $100,000 a year.

"How come it's $100,000 for us when the guy in there now is paying 80?" Ed said it should be 100 now, but he couldn't raise the rent because the revenue wasn't there.

Tony and I stepped outside to talk strategy. Tony said, "Fred, if it's worth 80, it's worth 100. $20,000 shouldn't make a difference, because if it does, we don't want the theater." And we decided to do it. But now here comes Tony, Mr. Facts and Figures, and he knew exactly where he wanted this deal to go. Tony said we'd give him the $100,000, but in return we wanted an option to buy the property.

So we went back to Ed and made our proposal. He agreed—but added that if we wanted the option to buy the theater, he wanted $700,000 for it. We thought maybe half a million dollars would do it, but he said if we did well, the theater would be worth more to him. "A little extra juice for me," I recall him saying. So we settled on a five-year lease, from 1977 to 1982, with the option to purchase. Finally we had a deal. Then we called in the lawyers to finish the paperwork.

LIVE SHOWS, DAILY DOUBLES, AND ROCKY HORROR

Now we had a theater in Cambridge with a history of live entertainment. The Harvard Square had dramas, musicals, concerts—Bruce Springsteen played a concert in 1974, a year after we presented him at Paul's Mall. With 1,900 seats, the theater certainly had the capacity for concerts.

We presented some shows in the theater after we got in. We had Roy Buchanan and Hall & Oates in 1976 and Iggy Pop in March 1977, with David Bowie as a sideman. In 1979, we had the Clash in their first US concert. We also had other producers bringing in a few stage shows. One was *The Best Little Whorehouse in Texas*. And then there was *Oh Calcutta!* Oh my. There was a little nudity in that one, and the producer brought it to Cambridge to sidestep the Boston city censor. All the permits were in order, but about a week before we started hearing rumbles that the city council might cancel it. They didn't, but all the talk kept our box office very busy all week.

Over time, we realized that it was a better movie theater than concert hall. We ruled out the Harvard Square as the successor to Paul's Mall, and by 1978 we were doing mostly movies, but if an outstanding event came along, we'd break from the film schedule for it. I think Tom Waits in 1979 was the last of those shows.

What we did instead, with the closing of Cinema 733, was import our double feature program, but with a twist. We brought in a new double feature *every day*. We called it the Daily Double. When you think about it, over the course of a year, that's a lot of movies, and there was an art to programming them. You had to know a lot about movies, of course, but the logistics of it were demanding. There were films coming into and going out of the office every day, and somebody was always on the phone trying to keep track of them. The tricky part was working out the timing for the schedule, and Tony and Arthur did that; it was amazing. Then we'd print a three-month schedule on legal-sized paper and flood Harvard Square with them. And just like at the 733, the double features were profitable after the first month, and we never looked back.

I laugh whenever I think about those Daily Doubles. We had fun with them. There was always a connection between the two films. It could be anything, like two Alfred Hitchcock pictures, or a pair of Monty Pythons, or spaghetti westerns, or haunted houses . . . anything. I believe you can never have too many films by Mel Brooks, so I had Tony schedule *Blazing Saddles* and *The Producers*, and then I ducked out of work so I could sit in my own theater and watch them.

Our double feature program might have been the only one of its kind in the country. Other theaters had double feature programs, but ours changed *every day*. And it ran for years like that. It was a great little operation. Even when the theater began showing first-run films almost exclusively—they were the big moneymakers—we didn't want to give up the double features. We knew that home video and cable were cutting into the audience, but we still wanted to have a place to show them. We bought a small single-screen theater on the other side of the square called the Janus Cinema, and we ran our Daily Double over there. We were still running it when we sold the Janus in the same deal as the Harvard Square Theatre.

We also brought our weekend midnight movies to Cambridge, and that brings me to the *Rocky Horror Picture Show*. We picked it up in 1984 when the Exeter Theatre in the Back Bay closed down. And unlike the Exeter, we added a live revue on the stage, with the cast doing whatever the cast in the film was doing.

Rocky Horror has a status that goes far beyond mere cult movie. It is a total audience participation event. The patrons dress in costume, bring props, recite the actors' lines in unison, sing along. Hundreds of people would turn out, every Saturday at midnight. The new owners kept it going after we left. And after the Harvard Square Theatre closed its doors in 2012, another Boston theater picked up *Rocky Horror* and it still carries on today there and in theaters around the world. Amazing.

CHANGING THE THEATER

I had one role at the Harvard Square Theatre that was the same as Boylston Street: promotion and public relations. There was all the usual business of press releases and interviews and advertising. The theater didn't put as many demands on my time as it did on Tony. He was more deeply involved in the operation of the place. But I did take on a second role, as the manager of our construction and renovation projects. We had two big ones—in 1982, when we converted the balcony into twin cinemas and relocated the theater's entrance; and in 1985, when we added two more theaters in the rear of the building on what had been the theater's original stage.

In 1982, we bought the theater from Ed Mank, but we didn't do it alone. We brought in a few other investors. Arthur Friedman, our film supplier who had been with us since Cinema 733, was one, along with his partner Roger Lockwood and Harold Blank, who worked with them at Lockwood-Friedman. Arthur became the film buyer, and he was great at it.

We knew that to make the theater profitable, we needed additional screens, and we needed to show first-run films. Now that the theater was ours, we could go to work on installing two more screens. We went to Harvard Trust, the bank next door, to ask for a loan. We had all the numbers that showed we had been increasing our business by more than 20 percent per year, which they liked, but I also had to use the deed to my apartment as collateral and promise the bank everything up to and including my first-born before we got the money.

We used the balcony to create two new theaters. We walled up the open end of it and then divided the space in half. This created two theaters, each with about 225 seats. Then we built a new projection booth for the main auditorium, since the original projection booth was on the other side of the new wall.

The other part of this project was to move our theater entrance. We did not own our front door, which was on Massachusetts Avenue, opposite the news stand. The street door opened into the lobby, which was just a glorified hallway leading into the theater building. That was a right of way, and we were going to have to pay to keep it. It made more sense for us to own the access to our building, so we built a new entrance and ticket window around the corner on Church Street, opening up what had been a long expanse of blank wall. Our new address was 10 Church Street.

The second part of our plan was to begin showing first-run movies. This was not so easy, because other theaters in the area, like the big multiplex in Somerville at Assembly Square, opposed it. They claimed it would infringe on their territory. Theater territories were very important then. Film distributors didn't want their films in theaters that were close together. Somerville saw us as pulling away their customers.

That's how it stood when Woody Allen came along with a new film, *Zelig*, and he told the distributor, "I want Harvard Square." Perhaps he knew about our success with his films on the Daily Double—I think we even showed a few Allen triple features, which were perennial favorites and always well attended. So when Allen said give them *Zelig*, we got it, and we ended up running it longer than the Boston theater that had it, and doing a better gross. So that broke us into first-run films.

By 1984 we were doing great business. We decided to add a couple more theaters in the big empty space above the stage. We weren't using the stage for live shows anymore. In fact, we weren't using it for anything. And it had great height, it was open all the way to the roof. So we built two more theaters in the stage area, stacked one on top of the other, along with a new corridor along the outer wall to reach them. We also expanded the lobby by taking a little space from the main auditorium and added a new refreshment stand. We worked around the construction to keep the theater open, and we had everything ready to go in March 1985. We now had five theaters, with the main auditorium seating about 700 and the other four seating about 225 each. On one of our brand-new screens we showed Woody Allen's latest, *The Purple Rose of Cairo*. And we had first-run films on all five of our screens.

Fred surrounded by present and former staffers of WBCN-FM at their 20th anniversary party, Concord, MA, March 1988. *(Photo by Dan Beach.)*

Fred Taylor, the man of all musical genres, at the WBCN 20th anniversary party at the home of Dan Beach, Concord, MA, March 1988.
(Photo by Dan Beach.)

Left: Miles Davis at the Opera House, Boston, June 1989. Fred first presented Miles at the Jazz Workshop in 1967, and staged his 1981 comeback at Kix. This was the last Davis concert Fred produced, as well as Miles's last concert in Boston. *(Photo by Sue Auclair.)*

Bottom: Fred with vocalist Melba Moore and Mark Fallon, general manager of the Guest Quarters Hotel, the home of Scullers Jazz Club, at the club's third anniversary party, October 1992. *(Photo by Leo Gozbekian.)*

Blix Street Records presented this gold record for Eva Cassidy's recording Songbird to Fred in November 2001, honoring Fred for his efforts to publicize and promote Cassidy's music. The singer died of cancer at age 33 in 1996.

Trumpeter and vocalist Chris Botti, saxophonist Grace Kelly, and Fred at Scullers Jazz Club, 2006. Fred was a strong supporter of both artists early in their careers. *(Photo by Bob Kelly.)*

Fred with flugelhornist and trumpeter Chuck Mangione at Scullers Jazz Club, October 2008. *(Photo by Don West.)*

Fred with saxophonist Grace Kelly, pianist and jazz icon Dave Brubeck, and Newport Jazz Festival founder George Wein at the 2010 edition of that event. *(Photo by Bob Kelly.)*

Top: Jazz vocalist, pianist and composer Bob Dorough, singer Jaime Cullum, and Fred at the Newport Jazz Festival, 2010. *(Photo by Bob Kelly.)*

Right: Fred and 1994 NEA (National Endowment for the Arts) Jazz Master Ahmad Jamal at the 30th NEA Jazz Masters ceremony in 2012. Fred first brought pianist Jamal to the Jazz Workshop in 1967. *(Photo by Bob Kelly.)*

Left: Esperanza Spalding at Scullers Jazz Club, 2014. Fred was among the first to recognize the talent of this extraordinary bassist and singer. *(Photo by Fred Taylor.)*

Bottom: WGBH radio's Eric Jackson, Fred, saxophonist David Sanborn, and Sam Kopper, producer of the "Live from Scullers Jazz Club" broadcast on WGBH-FM, November 23, 2015. *(Photo by Sam Kopper.)*

Right: Fred with pianist and singer Harry Connick Jr. in New York, on the set of Connick's television program, *Harry*, in 2017. Fred first presented Connick as an unknown 19-year-old as an opening act for singer Al Jarreau at the 1986 Great Woods Jazz & Blues Festival. *(Photo by Bob Kelly.)*

Bottom: Fred Taylor Scholarship Benefit Concert Artists at Berklee Performance Center, Boston, September 12, 2017. From left: Jason Palmer, Catherine Russell, John Patitucci, Danilo Pérez, Terri Lyne Carrington, Pat Metheny, Monty Alexander, Grace Kelly, James Montgomery, Fred Taylor, Bo Winiker, Robin Young, Kat Edmonson, Mark Walker, Bill Winiker, Tim Ray, James Dale. *(Photo by Sam Kopper.)*

At the after-party following the Fred Taylor Scholarship Benefit Concert at the Berklee Performance Center, September 12, 2017. From left: Irene Chang, Grace Kelly, Fred Taylor and Bob Kelly. *(Photo by Kofi Poku.)*

Berklee College of Music president Roger Brown with Fred at Fred's "20th anniversary of his 70th birthday" party, Dover, MA, June 2019. *(Photo by Kofi Poku.)*

AND THEN WE SOLD IT

I think it was early in 1985 that we first heard from someone who wanted to buy the theater. We were approached by USA Cinemas, which was the new name of a well-established Boston theater chain, Sack Theaters. There were major changes going on in the movie business, mergers and acquisitions going on right and left, and the chains were courting independents like us. USA Cinemas was growing and thinking about going public. They came to us wanting to buy the theater. Alan Friedberg, their president, thought Harvard Square would be a good anchor for them. We said we weren't interested in selling. They came back still wanting to buy it, and we'd say, "But we don't want to sell it." It kept going on like that for about a year.

Finally, in the summer of 1986, they asked us, "What's it gonna take to get you out?" For better or worse, it was decision time.

Tony and I didn't want to sell though. The theater made us a good living. It was a wonderful cash-based business, and we knew how to run it. I think our last year there we grossed 3 million dollars. But Arthur, Roger, and Harold all had plans to do other things, and they were pushing to sell. Finally, we had a meeting at Locke-Ober with Alan Friedberg and his controller. Friedberg was determined to buy the theater. We told him we wanted 10 million dollars. He came back almost immediately and offered us 9.5 million. Deal.

This was probably the worst business decision we ever made. Sure we made money on the deal, and I invested my share in the stock market and in land on Nantucket Island. Well, the market crashed in 1987 and I took a beating. So did Tony. It was a painful time. On some of those dark days, and I had many, I wished I'd never had the money.

That's what happened with the Harvard Square Theater. We were very successful there, but success is a fleeting thing. First came the windfall, then came the crash—and I was broke.

And that time, I almost *did* give up showbiz.

13

THE ONE-STOP CONCERT SHOP

My clubs usually get most of the attention when people ask about my musical past. But I was producing concerts before I ever stepped into a club, and I'm still producing them now that I've stepped out again. And that is because my company, HT Productions, is what's known in the concert business as a one-stop.

You can be one-dimensional in this business and do one thing, like rent equipment or handle publicity. Or you can be like HT Productions and offer promoters and artists' managers a longer menu. I'd ask them, "What do you need?" and regardless of what they wanted—well, as long as it was legal and aboveboard—I'd provide it. I've booked halls, priced tickets, rented equipment, installed lights and sound, bought advertising, arranged media events, set up interviews, provided transportation and hospitality, and completed financial settlements after the show. With one call to HT, a promoter could schedule a show, or multiple shows, anywhere in New England.

You prosper as a one-stop because of what you know. A promoter might only need help finding the right venue, and I know every one from Worcester to Portland to Providence by number of seats and how they sound. It's the kind of accumulated wisdom that makes me unique. I tell people I'm a craftsman, not a conglomerate.

You do this for a while and you earn a reputation among the promoters as a can-do guy. And promoters talk: "Who do you work with in Boston?" So back in the beginning I did a good job for George Wein and that led to a call from Albert Grossman and Ed Sarkesian. I did a good job for them, and that led to a call from Irving Granz. And from him to Lou Robin. And so on down the line of agents and promoters. That's how I got the calls to produce

Sarah Vaughan, Johnny Cash, Carly Simon, and the rest. And that's how I built HT Productions into a business that's survived since the 1960s. So with that, let's go to some shows.

BOSTON GLOBE JAZZ FESTIVAL AND MUSIC FAIR

The Boston Globe Jazz Festival got its start in 1966 at what was then called the War Memorial Auditorium, later renamed the Hynes Auditorium, and ran until 1970. Then it took a break. When the paper decided to revive the festival in 1976, they asked me to plan and produce it. They set the date for the Thanksgiving holiday weekend in November.

I wanted to do something a little different with the festival idea, so I proposed a two-track program. First was the "expected" jazz festival, with name bands playing concerts at the Hynes Auditorium. Second was a music fair in the adjoining exhibition hall. This had a bit of everything, with performances by local jazz groups plus workshops, clinics, product displays, and panel discussions. If it was about music, we wanted it at the music fair. As far as I know, it was the first time anyone tried coupling a concert series with a trade show.

We had some great concerts. It was like the Jazz Workshop's Greatest Hits, with Sonny Rollins, Herbie Hancock, Freddie Hubbard, Buddy Rich, Grover Washington Jr., and others. Our Saturday night was something special. Norman Granz, of Jazz at the Philharmonic fame, was then managing many of the top artists in mainstream jazz and recording them on his Pablo Records label. I approached Granz with the idea of presenting a whole evening of Pablo artists as the centerpiece of our festival. Granz loved the idea and put together a package with Ella Fitzgerald, the Count Basie Orchestra, pianist Oscar Peterson, and guitarist Joe Pass. I had presented each of these artists before, but to get them all together on one night made for an outstanding a show.

Just one Joe Pass story. The year before, I booked Oscar and Joe together at Symphony Hall. I don't remember where Oscar was coming from, but because of bad weather his plane couldn't take off and he missed the concert. Joe Pass did it solo, and he was brilliant. And I mean *brilliant*. He brought down the house. He had just released a magnificent album of solo guitar called *Virtuoso*, and he proved to be every bit a virtuoso that night. But when he came off the stage, he looked almost miserable. "Joe," I said, "Why the long face? Listen to them out there, they loved you!"

He looked at me mournfully. "How am I ever gonna top that?" he replied.

I loved Joe, he had such a big heart. He told hilarious stories, and I can still hear him ending them with an emphatic "*Ma*-ma, *Mi*-a!"

If the festival main stage was for the likes of Joe Pass and Buddy Rich, the Music Fair stage hosted some great local jazz. Tony Cennamo, the WBUR deejay, helped us with programming, and we had Billy Thompson's Alto Summit, Baird Hersey's big band, Paul Fontaine's Sextet, and Stanton Davis and Ghetto Mysticism. You could hang around the fair all day and hear a different group every hour.

The dates were November 25–28, the Thanksgiving holiday weekend, and that was both good and bad for the Music Fair. Good because people had their days free and could attend. Bad because so many potential vendors were otherwise booked for the start of the holiday sales season. People turned us down, saying, "Great idea, we'd love to do this, but not on these dates."

Although I received a nice letter from Tom Winship, the editor of the *Boston Globe*, thanking me for my efforts to revive the festival—he called it a "musical smasheroo"—the *Globe* was unhappy with the overall results. The festival concerts did well at the box office, but the Music Fair lost just enough money to end the idea of sponsoring a second one.

WILD AND CRAZY WITH STEVE MARTIN

Lou Robin was an influential concert promoter on the West Coast, and he'd call me when he had clients with East Coast dates. One was Johnny Cash, and I started producing his concerts for Lou in 1972. The Cash shows were always in the Boston Garden, so that was the local venue that Lou knew.

In 1978, Lou called me about his current hot property, the comedian Steve Martin. Martin was well known because of his television work, and he was big box office in 1978, having just released his album *A Wild and Crazy Guy*. Lou wanted to stage a show at the Boston Garden.

I said to him, "Lou, a standup comic in the Boston Garden? Give me a break. Or let me have the binoculars concession." I explained that what worked for the Johnny Cash show wouldn't work for a guy doing standup, and Lou got that. He asked for a suggestion.

"I'll tell you what. If Steve will do two shows that night, we'll make as much money at the Hynes Auditorium." The Hynes was smaller, with 4,500 seats—the Garden could seat three times as many—but it had a better stage and seating, and it wasn't built for sporting events. And the costs were lower at the Hynes. I ran the numbers, and Lou said okay, and we booked Martin for October 8, the Saturday of the Columbus Day holiday weekend.

We sold out the two Saturday shows almost immediately. Steve was big! I called Lou, asked if Steve would be open to doing a Sunday matinee. He said okay. We put the Sunday matinee on sale and it sold out. I called Lou again, and asked if Steve would do a second show on Sunday. He said okay. We put the Sunday evening show on sale and it sold out. We had sold 18,000 tickets. I called Lou again. "Lou," I said, "It's crazy here. I've got more Martin fans than tickets. Here's an idea. Monday is a holiday, people won't be going to work. What if we add a late show on Sunday?" He said okay. We put that third show on sale, and you guessed it, it sold out.

When you're hot, you're hot. Every producer and promoter everywhere prays for a weekend like that.

I don't know how Steve Martin managed it, but he did five shows in two days and never lost his edge or ran out of energy. Now *that's* a wild and crazy guy! Boston turned out to be the highest grossing city on the tour. And it wouldn't have happened if I hadn't talked Lou Robin out of doing that one big show at the Boston Garden. But that's the advantage of knowing your market.

ON THE COLLEGE CIRCUIT WITH IMPULSE JAZZ

I've worked with many record company people over the years, but only a few stand out in my mind. One of those special ones was Steve Backer. At a time when there was a lot of "jazz is dead" talk going around, Steve worked tirelessly to record deserving jazz artists and get their records into the stores. He did well for his companies and his artists in what was a tough climate for the music. In my opinion, Steve was successful because he was always willing to try something new, and planning something new is what brought us together in 1972.

Steve was the director of national promotions for Impulse Records, a label famous for its recordings of John Coltrane and the musicians who worked with him. Steve believed that some of his artists were crossover candidates who would appeal to the rock audience as well as the jazz crowd, and he wanted to test the idea around New England, with its strong youth market. Steve convinced ABC Records, which owned Impulse, to subsidize a regional tour, and he hired me to do my one-stop thing to produce the concerts and provide the support.

"Support" for Impulse meant everything from renting the venues in eight different cities to designing and printing posters, to placing ads in newspapers and on multiple radio stations in every market, to the care and feeding of an entourage of about 25. It entailed a lot of work in a short time, but that's what we were in business to do. So I left Tony Mauriello to hold down the fort at the nightclubs, and I climbed aboard the Impulse tour bus.

ABC wanted to give away tickets, but I pushed back. I argued for charging $1 instead. Free is just a shrug of the shoulders, just "meh," but a buck—now that's a bargain. That was the price for a ticket to the matinee at Cinema 733! It was a matter of perception, not to mention a heck of a deal.

We kicked off the tour at the Fenway Theater in Boston on April 7, and then every other day over the next two weeks played a different New England college town, seven in all, from good-sized cities like Providence, Rhode Island, to small towns like Sacco, Maine. We wound it up in New Haven, Connecticut, on April 17. For the Boston concert, I went to my friends at WBCN and convinced them to carry it live. It went until 2:00, and WBCN broadcast the whole thing. It was a great way to deliver the Impulse message.

We toured with three acts: pianist and harpist Alice Coltrane with her own group plus a string quartet, the sextet of saxophonist Pharoah Sanders, and violinist Michael White with his quartet. We established our headquarters at the Lenox Hotel in Boston. The artists stayed there, and we traveled to the various places on the day of show by bus.

Steve got what he wanted out of this tour: more recognition for the artists, but also more recognition for Impulse. The tour, and that WBCN broadcast, put Impulse on the map. Before this tour, if you wanted an Impulse record, you had to special order it. The stores didn't carry the label. But afterward, you could find Impulse records in the racks. Nobody at the store counter said "What was the name of that label again?" anymore. For Backer, that was a major accomplishment.

I replayed this single-company concert idea three more times. I did it with Pablo Records in 1976 at the Boston Globe Jazz Festival. Working again with Steve Backer, I produced "An Evening with Windham Hill" in 1982, and that was a runaway success. Then in 2004, at the Tanglewood Jazz Festival, I produced a day with Marsalis Music artists. But this Impulse tour was the only one that hit multiple cities. It was a throwback to the big-band era when the bands traveled the country by bus.

AN EVENING WITH WINDHAM HILL

Steve Backer and I had a second go-round with a 1982 concert called "An Evening with Windham Hill." It starred George Winston, Liz Story, and the rest of that company's New Age roster. The concert was a big success. Steve wasn't with Windham Hill very long, but he delivered the goods while he was there.

Windham Hill had only been around for a few years when Steve and I staged that concert. A guitarist named Will Ackerman started the Windham Hill label in 1976, and he signed a handful of guitarists and pianists who played a similar type of acoustic pop music that was soft and dreamy. It borrowed from folk, jazz, and world music but it was none of those things. People took to calling it "New Age" music, but Ackerman and everybody else who played it rejected the term. One thing for sure, it was not jazz. The label's most popular artist was the pianist George Winston, who liked to play barefoot. The jazz purists hated his music. "It's not jazz," they said. "I'm not a jazz musician," Winston said. That didn't matter, they hated his music anyway.

Steve called in early 1982 to tell me how Winston was making waves in California, and he wanted to find out if that popularity could transfer to the East Coast. I was helping my friend Al Goldman with some bookings at his Cambridge club, Jonathan Swift's, so we decided to try Winston there. We booked Ackerman and Winston for a one-nighter in April. There was a tremendous demand and we had no trouble selling out two shows. Then Steve found out that the Windham Hill records were selling briskly at the Harvard Coop, which at the time was the biggest record store in Cambridge.

That's when Steve decided he wanted to bring the Windham Hill musicians east for some serious concert exposure. And he wanted to record the proceedings in order to create a sampler album for the label's artists. He told me to take the idea and run with it.

Back in 1972, we staged our Impulse concert at the Fenway Theatre. Berklee College had since purchased and renovated it, and renamed it the Berklee Performance Center. The 1,200-seat venue had great acoustics. That's where I wanted this concert, which we'd call "An Evening with Windham Hill."

We lined up Windham Hill's top artists, including Winston and Ackerman, and also pianist Liz Story and two more guitarists, Michael Hedges and Alex de Grassi. We scheduled two shows for the night of October 9, and we sold out the first show and came close with the second. It was a great concert even if it was a little busy with all the performers going on and off the stage, and the reviews were positive. Steve wasn't the only one recording the concert—we had a crew from NBC's *Today Show* filming for the next morning's broadcast.

Windham Hill caught fire in Boston. Deejays would play their records and their phones would light up. We found out that five of the top ten best-selling records at the Coop during the week of the concert were by Windham Hill artists. Backer couldn't get the sampler album out fast enough. *An Evening with Windham Hill* was released in early 1983.

Steve Backer moved on from Windham Hill, but the company established that idea of "an evening with" as a brand, and I don't mind taking some of the credit for it. Windham Hill toured the country with those concerts. It created a situation where the label became well known for a style of music, and the label sold the artist, not the other way around. It was a triumph of branding. If you said "Windham Hill," everybody knew just what kind of music it was. The concerts ended because some of the artists wanted more individual recognition and left the label. I've worked with some of them on and off since. I have no doubt that if they reorganized their label tour, it would be immediately successful.

THE GREAT FRED TAYLOR BARBECUE

Allow me to break away from the concert calendar for a few minutes to talk about chickens, because for a time I was closely associated with them. Yes, chickens. Also bananas; there were several occasions where I donned a banana costume, but mostly it was chickens.

It started with my answering machine. I'll explain. I always liked Louis Jordan and his Tympany Five, the band that recorded "There Ain't Nobody Here But Us Chickens" in the late 1940s. I put that line in my answering machine message. You'd call, you'd hear Jordan singing "There ain't nobody here but us chickens, there ain't nobody here at all." Then I'd come on to say, "That certainly is a 'fowl' situation, but if you leave your message with the chickens, they'll get it to me, and I'll get back to you." And then you could talk after the beep. People started calling just to hear the message. I'd check my messages and there wouldn't be anything but the sound of callers hanging up.

So this started a chicken thing, and I was the butt of many chicken jokes. In June 1982, I had my picture in the *Boston Phoenix*, my head on the body of a big rotisserie chicken. This was to mark the occasion of the Great Fred Taylor Barbecue, where I was roasted by my so-called friends at a gathering at the Bradford Hotel. Norm Nathan was the emcee, and I was roasted but good by Tony Cennamo, Lennie Sogoloff, Ed Halian (the "H" in HT

Productions), Sal Ingeme from Columbia Records, Charles Laquidara from WBCN, and others. The surprise guest was none other than Professor Irwin Corey, who reduced us all to tears by addressing his remarks to Lennie. He claimed he was told that Lennie was the one being roasted that night. I'll never forget it. My roasting was a night of good fun and great friends.

Fast-forward a few years to 1986. Sue Auclair was doing promotional work for Buck Spurr at the Starlight Roof, and she convinced me to climb into a chicken suit and escort her to some event there. Sue found a costume somewhere with the legs, and the chicken feet, and the body—actually it was a modified Big Bird costume—with a big head and two little eye holes in the neck. I could barely see out.

Sue and I walked across Commonwealth Avenue (and of course that prompts one to ask, "Why did the chicken cross the road?" "To get to the Starlight Roof"), and when we reached the other side, we met somebody coming down the sidewalk. Now I'm totally inside this chicken suit, completely covered, and this guy coming down the street says, "Hey, hi Fred!" I couldn't believe it. *To this day* I have no idea . . . *how* did he know it was me? I put the question to Sue.

She rolled her eyes. "Come on, Fred," she said. "Who else in Boston would be standing on Commonwealth Avenue on Saturday night wearing a chicken costume?"

GREAT WOODS 1987: THAT'S DANCING!

The big name in local concert promotions in 1986 was Don Law. Early that year he called to say he was opening a new venue, an outdoor amphitheater called the Great Woods Center for the Performing Arts, in Mansfield, Massachusetts south of Boston. Don wanted to offer a variety of entertainment to appeal to different audiences, and he had already arranged to have the Pittsburgh Symphony Orchestra under the direction of Michael Tilson Thomas in residence for part of the summer. He also wanted a jazz series, and he had lined up the US Trust bank to sponsor it. He brought me in to produce the jazz series—my title was Jazz Programming Consultant. I could concentrate on the creative aspects of developing the program and let Don's organization worry about everything else. We broadened the musical offerings by adding blues, and we had ourselves a three-day Great Woods Jazz and Blues Festival.

In my three years at Great Woods, we had some terrific concerts. In 1986, we had the debut performance of Illinois Jacquet's big band, and he was thrilled to have the opportunity to make his longtime dream of fronting a big band a reality. In 1987, I coaxed Carmen McRae, who was in a foul mood on a day when nothing had gone right, into singing: "Carmen, that was then, and now is now. Let's do a show!" And she sang great, the high point of the night. Actually, I never heard her sing any better than she did at Great Woods. Carmen was a real *jazz* singer.

In 1988, we had an unforgettable Saturday night, starting with the guitar duet of Ralph Towner and John Abercrombie. Then came Herbie Hancock with his Headhunters, followed by Chick Corea's Elektric Band, and our finale was the sextet of Wayne Shorter and Carlos Santana. That was an outrageous night of music, one not to be repeated. How could anyone ever forget that?

In terms of unforgettable memories, though, we had one Great Woods show that topped even Shorter and Santana. Of all the shows I've produced over the years, one of my all-time favorites was the jazz tap spectacular at Great Woods in 1987. It's no secret that I love tap dancing. I cannot tell you when I first became aware of tap, but I know I was immediately drawn to it. Maybe it was watching the Nicholas Brothers dancing down the stairs in *Stormy Weather*, or taking in the stage show back at the RKO Theatre when I was in high school. Whenever it was, I was hooked on the energy and the grace and the sheer fun of it.

I was still working for Serta when I met a tap dancer named Billy in Ogunquit, Maine, dancing to the jukebox at a joint called Bessie's, and I wanted to do it too—I had visions of tapping down a spiral staircase like Bill "Bojangles" Robinson. I started to study tap dance with Stanley Brown, who had been a great dancer himself in the 1930s. He had a studio on Massachusetts Avenue, and he started me doing the basic steps—shuffle-kick, shuffle-kick—but I had problems with my back and had to stop. I never lost my love of tap, though, and was always looking for opportunities to present it.

I had an ambitious goal in 1987—I wanted to present the history of jazz tap. I invited the very best dancers to Great Woods, starting with my old friend Jimmy Slyde, who had me sand dancing with him at Basin Street South 25 years earlier. My next call went to Bunny Briggs, whom I'd first booked in the early 1960s. I had Harold Nicholas of the Nicholas Brothers—the only reason Harold was by himself was that his brother Fayard was having a hip replaced. Chuck Green of the famous team of Chuck and Chuckles was next, and also Lon Chaney, who developed a step called the paddle-and-roll that became a standard part of the tapper's routine. I won't even try to describe it, but you can find it on YouTube. Not to forget the ladies, I invited Dianne Walker, an accomplished Boston tapper and renowned teacher. And finally I had a youngster, Savion Glover, "the tap dance kid." I had all these dancers, the *crème de la crème*, coming to Great Woods! I couldn't believe it.

If you have dancers, you need music, and I put together a tapper's dream band. Pianist Barry Harris had worked with tap dancers in Harlem, and he could play the things they needed. That's why I wanted him in particular. We had Alan Dawson on drums, Major Holley on bass, and Andy McGhee on tenor. Then I added the great drummer Max Roach as a special guest. Max knew all about drum and tap, where the drummer plays something and the tapper tries to replicate the tempo and sound of it. It's exciting and has the improvised feel of a jam session.

Finally, I asked Tony Cennamo of WBUR radio to host the show. And that was the lineup for *An Afternoon with the Masters: Jazz Tap Dance and Drums.*

When the day finally came, the dancers had one of those joyous backstage reunions where everyone's laughing and talking, with hugs all around. A big mutual admiration society. What a day! Chuck Green was holding court, telling stories. I had hired a video crew to tape the show, and I kicked myself for not inviting them backstage beforehand.

Tony started with a little bit of the history of jazz tap, then turned it over to the dancers. The way it worked, the dancers all came onstage together.

They call it getting on line. So they got on line with the band playing and danced in unison. Then one by one they peeled off until only one dancer remained. That dancer did his feature bit, then tapped his way offstage, while the next one tapped his way on. Then that dancer soloed, and then the next, and then the next until they all had their turn in the spotlight. Then the band played a few numbers while the dancers took a break. Finally Max Roach came on, challenging the dancers with his drums. It was an amazing show, one "wow!" moment after another.

This was a show I'd always dreamed of doing, and I was so happy that we got the dancers and musicians together to do it, and so pleased with the way it went. The audience loved it. All I could do was walk around smiling. Days later, I was still smiling.

I hired a crew to tape the show. I knew it was going to be something special, and I ordered a three-camera shoot. It was sensational. At the time, I took it to PBS, but they weren't interested. However, it is an absolutely historic performance by the masters of the art form, and I should try again to drum up interest in it. This performance is too good to leave sitting on a shelf.

AN EVENING WITH DIANA ROSS

I've saved the best for last. Sometimes—but not nearly often enough—everything comes together and you know you can never, ever give up showbiz. The relationships you've built, the media contacts you've made, the story you have to tell, and the public's willingness to hear that story all blend into a nearly perfect picture. It happened to me in February 1977, when Diana Ross brought her big one-woman show, *An Evening with Diana Ross*, from Broadway to the Music Hall. To this day it is one of my most successful concert promotions, and I have great memories when I think back on it. We pulled out all the stops and created a five-star success.

Diana Ross was flying high in January 1977. *An Evening with Diana Ross* broke box-office records at Broadway's Palace Theatre, in a performance that won a Tony award. Her current album, *Diana Ross*, on the Motown label, was in the stores and selling well. That record included "Do You Know Where You're Going To," the theme from Ross's film *Mahogany*, which had been nominated for the Best Original Song Oscar in 1976, and Ross was about to begin shooting her third film, *The Wiz*. Now, in early 1977, Ross was taking *Evening* to some major US cities, including Boston.

Danny O'Donovan was a high-profile promoter from London who was producing this Diana Ross tour. He called me one afternoon in early February, and he said, "Listen Fred, I need your help. We had dates lined up to play Detroit, but they're renovating the hall and it isn't ready, so we're going to move up our Boston dates from the end of the tour, and I need you to promote it." Ross was scheduled to open in Boston on March 1.

I asked him about the new date. "It's in about ten days, February 10."

I just about fell out of my chair. "*Ten days*, Danny! You gotta be kidding me!"

He said, "Yeah, it's tight, I know, but we've got to make do."

I said, "No way. You come in, and if it doesn't do well, then I'm the bad guy because I didn't do a good enough job in promoting it."

He said no, it wasn't going to be like that, and that he understood the situation.

We went back and forth some more. I finally said I'd do it, but I insisted on one condition: "You sign a paper that says that no matter what happens, after the show, you will come backstage, shake my hand, say, "Thank you, Fred, great job," and pay my fee.

He agreed.

I knew I needed help, and the first person I thought of was Wendy Schwartz, whom I met when she worked for the Bob Weiss agency in Boston. We used to talk about promotion and PR, and I liked her ideas. Her big client was Perdue, the chicken processing company, and at some point she told me that Perdue had hired her away from Bob Weiss, and she'd be leaving Boston, moving to Philadelphia. But she said if I ever had something really big, I should call her and she'd talk Frank Perdue into giving her a little time off. So I called in that marker. I said, "Wendy, this is it. Diana Ross. We have 10 days. When can you be here?"

I picked her up at the airport the next day and as soon as she checked into her hotel, we sat down and brainstormed and came up with some good ideas for our campaign—ideas that would turn Diana's first day in town into a series of media events. Wendy set up Command Central in my office and started working the phone.

I went to work on the media kit. We needed an attention-grabbing photo that we could use throughout the campaign, and I selected a shot of Diana in a three-quarter profile, just her face against a black background, a beautiful image, and we sent it out with a press release on the 4th—only one week until opening night, and we were only now sending out a press release! We also used that photo on all the print advertising. The show was starting on a Thursday and running through Monday, so we were able to place big ads in the Sunday papers twice, once before and once during the show. Finally, we printed and distributed posters with that image, and they started popping up all over town.

We wanted to saturate our market, and we did pretty well. Newspapers from Lowell to Quincy to Providence to Worcester added the concerts to their events calendars, and better yet, almost all of them ran an advance photo—our Ross photo with a splashy title and caption. The radio stations gave the concert publicity, and a few of the Boston stations ran contests and gave concert tickets to the winners.

We needed a TV spot. I didn't have Raycraft Studios anymore, but I made arrangements to use the studio at the Boston Catholic Television Center in Newton, where they had a machine that would transfer 35 mm slides to videotape. Danny O'Donovan sent us gorgeous slides of Diana, just beautiful, wearing different stage costumes, so I transferred those to tape. Then I added an opening slide, "An Evening with Diana Ross" coming to the Music Hall, and a closing slide with the ticket info. (By the way, the most expensive ticket was $15, and the least expensive was half of that—and that was for Saturday night!) Then I made an audio track of Diana's music with my voiceover. I gave each slide about 3 seconds of viewing time, so it was bing-bing-bing as the music played. I got a great 30-second TV spot, and the stations started running it.

Everything I've mentioned so far was more or less a part of the standard promotional package in that pre-Internet world of 1977. But now we get to the fine points of promotion. Diana arrived on Thursday morning, and at noon we had her meeting Mayor Kevin White at City Hall. The mayor's reception was one of our main media events. White, for some reason, had been out of the public eye for a time, and we sold him on it as a way to get back into view. He jumped at the opportunity. When a popular celebrity meets a big-city mayor, that's news, and we had heavy radio and television coverage at Government Center. White held Diana's hand and waltzed her around and presented her with the key to the city. We had impressive coverage for noontime, and we needed it. It was opening night, and we still had plenty of unsold tickets.

We followed the mayor's reception with our biggest coup—an open dress rehearsal followed by a press conference at the Music Hall. This was very big stuff. Every important newspaper in our region was there—the *Globe*, the *Herald*, the *Worcester Telegram*, the *Quincy Patriot Ledger*, the *Lowell Sun*, the *Providence Journal*—as well as the smaller papers and the alternative weeklies. There were a half-dozen radio stations, a half-dozen television stations, people from African American media outlets, people from college stations and papers, you name it. To top it off, we got national coverage from the Associated Press, United Press International, and the *Christian Science Monitor*. There were camera crews everywhere and a floor covered with cables.

It was an open rehearsal and Diana worked through a few of the numbers with the orchestra, which was led by Gil Askey, her longtime musical director. I remember her singing "The Lady Is a Tramp" and "Ain't No Mountain High Enough," which of course knocked everybody out. She had her three daughters on the trip, and the little one, Chudney, was still an infant. So there was Diana, rehearsing a song with Chudney on her lap and daughters Rhonda and Tracee on either side. The press ate it up.

Then we had the press conference, and through it all, Diana sat at the edge of the stage, relaxed, kicking her legs, wearing a "Boston Loves Diana Ross" sweatshirt (we helped with that too). She talked about the show, about being a working mom, about Motown and leaving the Supremes, about her next projects. She was modest and open, and when the Q&A was finally done, she sang a few more numbers.

I've put together hundreds, maybe thousands, of press events over the years, but I'd never had a day quite like this. It could not have gone better. For a promotions man like me, *this* was showtime. When the curtain went up at 8:00 p.m. that night, my job was already done. My job was to convince the public to pick up the phone and call the box office for tickets. And they had. Now I could sit back and enjoy the show.

Joe Layton directed *An Evening with Diana Ross*, and he proved that his stellar Broadway reputation was well deserved. Gil Askey did a great job with the music. But what just knocked me out was the stage set. The back of the stage was tiered—three tiers, and each tier was divided into cubes, sort of like what they did on the TV game show *Hollywood Squares*. And there was a musician in each cube. A big show band, 28 pieces, and only the rhythm section was on the floor. The backup singers, a trio called the Jones Girls, were up on ladders. It was quite a set, even before Diana came on stage. During the press conference, Diana assured us she wouldn't be coming onstage in jeans, that she'd have a full wardrobe. And she had that, at one point even turning her gown into part of the projection system. She was singing, and she was joined onstage by two mimes who started unfurling her gown, and she was twirling around, and while they were holding the gown it became a screen showing film of the Supremes in performance. The whole thing was just unbelievable.

The opening night on Thursday was a sellout. Joyce Kulhawik, WBZ-TV's entertainment reporter, had a following, and a good word from her could sell tickets. That night on the 11:00 p.m. news she gave a rave review. Ernie Santosuosso's review in the *Globe* on Friday was glowing. By Saturday morning, every show through Monday was sold out. They added a Tuesday show and sold that out too. Her eight concerts sold nearly 30,000 tickets and grossed over $350,000. That was the biggest box office take in the country, and Diana herself said Boston made the tour for her, with an audience reaction second to none. *Evening* also broke the box office record at the Music Hall, producing the highest gross within any seven-day period for any kind of entertainment.

It was more than just numbers, though. It was people cheering and clapping and shouting for more. I'll tell you, there were some happy audiences at the Music Hall. Every show finished with standing ovations and sustained applause, and people wouldn't leave their seats after the encores until Ross answered one last curtain call.

People talked about this show for days afterwards. Santosuosso called it "Diana Ross's conquest of Boston," and conquer the town she did.

For a promoter, it was heaven. Everything we did—working the media, reaching out to the mayor, setting up the open rehearsal and the press conference—was right. Everything clicked. And that TV spot I made in a rush for basically pocket change? People liked it, and it won an award from the New England Broadcasting Association as one of the best commercials of 1977. As I said, this show is one of my fondest career memories.

There's one last thing. Danny O'Donovan was as good as his word. On opening night, Danny did indeed meet me backstage to shake my hand, tell me I'd done a good job, and pay my fee.

14

BACK IN A NIGHTCLUB

In 1990 I stepped into a sleepy hotel lounge called Scullers and ended up staying there as the entertainment director for 25 years. If you want to know how to build a nightclub step by step and end up with a national reputation, the Scullers Jazz Club story is for you. I worked with the hotel to create a 190-seat nightclub with top entertainers, superb sound, and "night on the town" ambiance.

I faced new business challenges at Scullers. I didn't own or even manage this club, the hotel did, and I didn't always agree with their ideas and expectations. They didn't always agree with mine, either. And over these years the entertainment business itself grew more complex and costly, and the digital revolution turned the whole world of promotion and publicity upside down. I watched this wild quarter-century unfold from my perch at Scullers on the banks of the Charles River, and here's the story.

SCULLERS JAZZ CLUB: THE PREQUEL

We've got to do a little backstory to set the stage for my arrival at the club. In 1989, the Guest Quarters Suite Hotel in the Allston section of Boston opened a small lounge called Scullers, with jazz and cabaret singers providing the entertainment. There were some good ones, like Rebecca Parris, Paul Broadnax, and Wanetta Jackson. Ron Murray, a jazz bassist himself, was managing the club, and Diane Berry was doing the booking. My go-to publicist, Sue Auclair, was handling promotion. Most of their acts were from the Boston area, with a sprinkling of bigger names—they had Houston Person and Mark Murphy, and Dakota Staton sang for the club's grand opening.

It was a good start, but things were going nowhere fast. Sue suggested to Mark Fallon, the hotel's general manager, that he call me to see if I could

offer any advice. I wasn't too involved with clubs at the time. I was helping my friend Al Goldman with some bookings at his Harvard Square club,
Jonathan Swift's, and I was booking concerts and private events. Mainly I was
still digging myself out of the financial hole I'd fallen into when the market
nosedived in 1987. I told Mark I'd be happy to talk.

Just driving up to the Guest Quarters, I saw problem number one.
Scullers had a location I'll describe as "challenging." They were in Allston, on
the western end of Boston, with industrial land to the south and the Charles
River to the north. The hotel was a fortress-like structure at a very busy in-
tersection with no other buildings nearby, poorly served by public transportation, no foot traffic at all. This was not Boylston Street or Harvard Square
with foot traffic day and night. This felt like the exact opposite.

Scullers was in a corner room on the second floor, with the bar along
one wall opposite the windows. It didn't take up the whole length of the wall,
though—half of the wall was open, looking down on the lobby. The club had
about 70 seats—big, plush armchairs that looked like they belonged in the
lobby.

Mark and I hit it off right away—it turned out he used to attend shows
at the Jazz Workshop—and we talked about the club's situation. Mark asked
if I could start consulting with the club's staff, and I did that for about six
months. Then in early 1991, he asked me to take charge of the club's entertainment. That hadn't been my intention, but I saw the potential and couldn't
pass up the opportunity. Mark hired me as an independent contractor, and it
stayed that way through 2016.

Mark had the right idea for marketing the club. He was more interested
in using the club to publicize the hotel and bring people to it than in trying
to make the club into a big moneymaker on its own. He had no intention
of *losing* money on Scullers, but he saw the value in using the club to build
up the hotel's traffic. That's what I always tried to do. And let it be said that
without Mark Fallon, Scullers would not have survived. It was his support
and persistence that saw the club through its first years.

I actually got Mark to dip his toe in the concert business. Nina Simone
was booking dates in 1993, and I asked Mark what he thought about having

Scullers and my concert company, HT Productions, jointly produce Nina at Symphony Hall. That caught him by surprise. He said that would be great, but he'd have to convince the hotel's management. They said, "If you do this, you're responsible. If this doesn't work, you're gone." Mark did it anyway, and the concert sold out. It was a happy ending—the hotel made money, I made money, and Mark's job was secure. It was a pleasure working with Mark.

BUILDING THE BRAND

I came in as entertainment director in February 1991, and Mark and I went straight to work on building up the club. The first thing we did was close off that back wall. I wanted a room, not a loft with a view of the hotel's front desk, so we had that curtained off. Then I spent a little more of Mark's money to improve the stage lighting.

With the basics out of the way, we looked at the revenue situation. Scullers was the hotel's only bar, and it was run as an afterthought by the food and beverage people. There was no charge for admission during the week, and only a low admission on the weekends. I changed that. I said if we were going to present music, it would be ticketed, and there would be a cover charge to get in. And none of it on a tab; I had already fought that battle at Paul's Mall. Even though the number of seats limited what we could do, we started bringing in bigger names on the weekends, like Mose Allison, the singer Sheila Jordan, the father-and-son guitarists Bucky and John Pizzarelli, and the rollicking pianist Dorothy Donegan, a one-woman tornado who became an audience favorite at Scullers. And Mark hired a club manager to work the door and manage the staff.

Our piano wasn't so hot, and I told Mark that we needed a better one. We got it in April 1991, a 6-foot Yamaha C3, a great little piano. We brought in the best jazz pianists our budget would allow to showcase it—we had Geoff Keezer; and Benny Green with Christian McBride on bass, which was Christian's first time in the club; and James Williams, formerly with Art Blakey's Jazz Messengers. James had taught at Berklee and lived in Boston, and he had a good following locally. Then I met a wonderful piano technician, Fred Mudge, who could take care of our new baby. He had just started his own business tuning and repairing pianos. He became a Yamaha specialist and was still with Scullers in 2016.

Things were moving along, but the 70-seat capacity was limiting what we could do with bookings. We couldn't generate the revenue from 70 seats that we needed to bring in some of the artists we wanted. I took a chance and booked the Hammond B-3 organist Joey DeFrancesco anyway. On the day of the show, Joe Anderson, the club manager, and I dragged out all of the overstuffed chairs and brought in banquet chairs from the function room, and that gave us another 30 seats. With about 100 seats, we could make the money we needed. We didn't do this just once, either. Joe and I moved furniture several times to bring in the acts we wanted.

The hotel's senior management was shocked that we would do such a thing. They loved those comfy chairs—they were just the thing for port and cigars after dinner. But they were all wrong for a live music room. I put it to them: "Look, do you want more paying customers or these fancy chairs?" Mark and I finally convinced them to replace the chairs, but then we had to deal with the hotel's design department. Everything had to go through the designer, who came up with a price of $240 per chair. They were deluxe chairs with slanted legs, and I could just imagine a waitress with a tray of drinks tripping over one. But then we got lucky, because the designer left the company before he ordered our chairs. Mark jumped in and we ordered the right chair, the standard club café chair, 18-inch seat, straight legs, nobody trips over it. We bought 125 chairs for about 40 bucks each, and we saved the hotel something like $25,000.

With the new seating, we brought the club capacity up to around 110. I started moving the acts up. We brought in drummer Roy Haynes and saxophonist Lee Konitz and my old friend from the Jazz Workshop, Les McCann. These were bigger names in the jazz field, but not the biggest names. We still weren't ready for an Oscar Peterson.

Then Mark and I started thinking about food. A jazz club in a hotel should have food. Nothing complicated—sandwiches, bar food. Who did we have to go through for this? The hotel's food and beverage manager, who didn't like the idea. It took Mark six months to convince him to put together a simple and small club menu, and he finally came up with something we liked. The actual menu, though, was the size of the restaurant menu: big. I reduced it to a 5 x 7 card, printed it on colored stock, and put it on the tables. On the first night, we sold $300 worth of food. The corporate types were impressed. They saw dollar signs.

Now we had some food, but we had a hotel kitchen at our disposal, and I wanted more. I pitched the idea of creating a dinner and show package, with customers stepping from the hotel's restaurant right into the show. Now like a lot of restaurants, this one had an early bird dinner special, priced at $19.95. I told Mark to round up the chef and the food and beverage manager, and meet me at the club entrance. When they got off the elevator, I pointed to the sign advertising the restaurant's early bird dinner special. The price was $19.95. I said, "That's your dinner show package price. Just extend it for the ticket holders." I saw the light bulbs going on over their heads. So that's how I started the dinner show package at Scullers.

Before we got to "dinner and a show," though, we had "Cookin' with Jazz." This was a little something Sue Auclair and I put together with Ron Della Chiesa, then the host of the *Music America* program on WGBH radio, and his wife Joyce, who was owner and chef at the Turtle Café in Cambridge in the 1980s. Ron served as host, and Joyce took charge of the Guest Quarters kitchen and prepared a special off-the-menu dinner inspired by the artist playing the club that night—so for instance, we had Brazilian specialties for Astrud Gilberto, and *una festa Italiana* with Joe Pass. ("Mama, *Mi*-a!" said Joe.) It was a great promotion and we ran it for about four years.

The club was coming along quite nicely, so in 1994, I went back to Mark with another idea. "Mark, we've got to get more capacity. We could do much more with the entertainment if we had more seats." He asked how many I'd need. I said 200. And I had a plan to get them. I'll omit the construction details, but the plan extended our room by building a deck into the space over the lobby. We'd end up with about 185 seats. The hotel went for it, and Scullers closed just before Christmas 1994, but not without one last memorable night.

BENNETT FINDS A BAND

Tony Bennett, as a rule, does not play nightclubs. For the most part, if you want to catch America's most distinguished singer, you have to hear him in concert. That's why it was a special treat when he walked into Scullers one night in December 1994. I remember it so well because it was our last show before we shut the club down to start construction.

The featured artist that night was the singer Donna Byrne, and the band behind her included trumpeter Herb Pomeroy, pianist Dave McKenna, guitarist Gray Sargent, and bassist Marshall Wood.

Ron Della Chiesa of WGBH was at the club that night, and he mentioned that Tony Bennett happened to be in Boston that weekend. Ron and Tony were close friends. Ron called Tony and invited him to drop by Scullers. Tony accepted the invitation.

Bennett arrived and sat in a corner for a bit, enjoying the band. Then Ron got onstage and announced that a special guest was in the house and was going to sit in for a few songs. "Ladies and gentlemen," intoned Ron, "Mr. Tony Bennett!" To which everyone, band included, said, "Yeah, right." And to the room's astonishment, on came Mr. Bennett.

Nightclub proprietors *live* for moments like that.

The club was all decked out for Christmas, and Tony sang a few songs of the season and spread considerable holiday cheer. The band really impressed him, and there was a hurried exchange of phone numbers before he departed. It turned out that the band had a gig coming at the Village Green in New York and Tony stopped by to hear them. Shortly after that, Bennett's regular guitarist departed, and Tony asked Gray if he was interested. That was more than 20 years ago, and they're still together. Maybe 10 years ago, Bennett's bassist needed time off for health reasons, and Gray suggested that Tony get Marshall to fill in. Marshall did so well the original bassist never got his job back. So Tony found his new band at Scullers, and it reminded me of the similar connections made at the Jazz Workshop years before.

A postscript to this story: Bennett walked into my club unannounced a second time in 1996, on a night honoring Ron Della Chiesa for his long service as a New England broadcaster. Again it was the holiday season, and again McKenna was at the piano, and again Tony got onstage. This was great fun for Tony, who admitted he was a big fan of Dave's and used to catch him when Dave was holding court at the Copley Plaza. They did one tune and it was a swinger, "Santa Claus Is Coming to Town," with Dave hammering out the rhythm with his famous left hand. That night I met Tony's daughter Antonia, who was then a student at Berklee. A good singer herself, we booked her at Scullers in 2003 when she was starting her own career. Like father, like daughter.

NEW YEAR, NEW ROOM, OLD HASSLES

We reopened in our renovated room on April 5, 1995, with pianist George Shearing. The Saturday night was something special, because we added the voice of Freddy Cole to the program. What a beautiful date that was. And I have a recording of a little bit of it. Just before showtime, I was about to ask George if I could record the set—here it was, 40 years after Brubeck and Storyville and I'm still just the guy with a tape recorder—but before I could open my mouth, a reporter got in George's face, upset him actually, and then it was too late. George went onstage. I didn't know what to do, but in the middle of the set I told our sound man to let it roll. I have three beautiful tunes from that set, with my favorite being "You Must Believe in Spring" by the French composer Michel LeGrand. Just delightful.

One week later came the Scullers debut of pianist and singer Diana Krall. She'd been in Boston, at Berklee, in the early 1980s and had been working primarily as a pianist since then. In the early 1990s I heard a tape of Diana, and she sang on only one tune. I told the agent who sent it that I thought Diana should sing more, she had a great sound. In 1995 she was working with producer Tommy LiPuma and singing most of the time, and she had terrific material. She didn't sell out the house like Shearing did, but she did when she came back in 1996 with guitarist Russell Malone. She played a lot of the music from her Nat King Cole tribute album and got great reviews. Diana was a strong draw for us at Scullers in the late 1990s.

Construction was just starting when Mark Fallon moved on to manage a hotel in Rhode Island, and Gary Sims replaced him as general manager. My life got harder with Mark gone. In effect, I was starting over, educating a new GM on what the club brought to the hotel and what I brought to the club. We had a rocky relationship, but we managed to make things work in 1995. But at the end of the year we had trouble.

Gary reviewed the numbers from New Year's Eve and told me we'd lost $5,000 on the night. He wanted to start reducing expenses right away. I thought, no way. That night we featured a swinging band led by Jimmy McGriff, one of the true masters of the Hammond B-3 organ, and saxophonist Hank Crawford, who anchored the sax section in the Ray Charles Orchestra for many years. I was in the house, and there was *no way* we lost money that night. So I did some research and discovered that the accounting department had only reported revenue from the first show. They missed the second show completely!

I put all the information together and went to Gary, but he didn't want to discuss it. So the next time we talked, about taking down the club's Christmas tree or some damn thing, I confronted him. I said, "Look, if you want me out of here, just tell me. Not that I'd like it, but I understand if you want to make a change. But don't use subterfuge, and try to undercut me by talking about how we're losing money. You didn't have the facts—you only accounted for 50 percent of our business on New Year's Eve." I showed him the numbers from the two shows. We *made* $20,000 that night! I told him to confirm it with the accounting department. He didn't have an answer for that. I'm not a guy who likes confrontations, but I had to make that point, about not resorting to subterfuge to discredit me, to get him to listen to the facts about the financial situation.

With that bit of headbutting out of the way, I could again concentrate on taking advantage of our new room. One artist I really wanted to present at Scullers in 1996 was Nancy Wilson. To book an artist like her, you have to start many months in advance, and I started negotiating with Nancy even before the new room was open. But that's another thing about working for a hotel—the GM had veto power over my bookings, and Gary wasn't approving anything. I couldn't start booking and I was getting concerned. Then I found out that he had other plans for the renovated room.

Gary told the operations manager at Doubletree's home office in Phoenix (Doubletree had purchased the Guest Quarters hotels) that he wanted to expand the function and catering work, and to do that, he wanted to close Scullers. Well, that guy at Doubletree knew all about the Allston hotel because he had worked in this area, and he knew all about Scullers, and he was a fan. He simply told Sims "no." And not too long after that, Gary resigned, and in came another GM. During my time at Scullers, I lived through five general managers and at least that many food and beverage managers, and I went back to square one every time, establishing myself all over again.

So while the corporate people were discussing the future of the club, I went ahead and started booking for 1996. That's when I brought in Nancy Wilson, starting October 22, 1996, for six nights. That was a gamble: six nights, two shows a night, 2,400 tickets to sell—and it was my first six-nighter since the Jazz Workshop 20 years before! She was a big success, and we all did well. That was a major step up in the booking. I brought Nancy back in 1998 and 2000. We started with Tower of Power around the same time, and they were, and are, a phenomenon. They can fill the house for four nights, two sets, and we couldn't have afforded them without the bigger room.

Hotels in general are not structured to accommodate entertainment operations. The accounting practices are totally different. I always had to battle that. The hotel looks at one thing: tickets sold. But over the years the club contributed a substantial amount of revenue that didn't show up on its bottom line. We sold as many as 5,000 dinner packages per year, but accounting credited it to the restaurant. Clubgoers who stayed at the hotel overnight booked 400–500 rooms per year, and we rented rooms for the musicians, but there was no "kickback" to the club for those bookings. There was parking revenue night after night, and we got no credit for it.

There was another bar in the hotel, the Fusion Bar, and Scullers customers were in it before or after every show. They wouldn't have been in the building without Scullers. But this didn't show up on the Scullers balance sheet. Every time somebody from hotel management would tell me Scullers was losing money, I'd just shake my head and tell them to look at the real revenue the club was bringing in.

EL PIANISTA DE PANAMA: DANILO PÉREZ

Even though my battles with the hotel could be exhausting, the music made up for it. One of the brightest stars of the 1990s was the pianist Danilo Pérez. He was my first discovery in the Scullers era, and I helped him with his career whenever I had a chance. I first heard him playing in the lounge at the Boston Harbor Hotel while he was a student at Berklee. He was enthusiastic and personable, and we hit it off. He already had a few feathers in his cap—he had worked with Jon Hendricks and Paquito D'Rivera when they came through Boston, and he also toured with Dizzy Gillespie's United Nations Jazz Orchestra. He talked at length about what an incredible experience working with Dizzy was for him.

I brought his trio into Scullers in 1991, and I think that first time we had trumpeter Claudio Roditi with him as a special guest. I'd give Danilo work whenever I could in those first years, letting the public get to know him. I had him accompany the singer Sheila Jordan. He was sideman on one of trumpeter Tom Harrell's albums, so I put together a group with Tom and Danilo. I had him with the trombonist Steve Turre and the drummer Roy Haynes. He was so versatile. Then I helped him get a working band together—his Afro-Cuban Jazz Explosion—with saxophonist David Sanchez. And what's funny is that he didn't want to do it, but I kept after him because I knew he could be more than just a sideman in Dizzy's band.

One thing I could certainly do for Danilo was introduce him to people. I brought him to Ted Kurland, who became his first agency representative, and to Steve Backer, who had started a new label for RCA called Novus. Steve signed Danilo to his first record deal, and he recorded his first album on Novus in 1993, and his second the following year.

It wasn't all work for me with Danilo. I've helped him with personal matters too. When Danilo's wife, Patricia Zarate, gave birth to their first child, she sent me on a mission of great importance: to find her a breast pump. In all my years of producing shows, this was a first. I found one for her, too, at a pharmacy out in the Roslindale neighborhood. Well, what are friends for?

Things were taking off for him, but Scullers remained Danilo's Boston home. He worked with his various groups two or three times a year through the 1990s. He had a loyal fan base here, and he's a great performer. He likes to get an audience joining in with the Latin rhythms, clapping with the *clave* beat. He loves to get that interaction going. We kept presenting Danilo Pérez in the new century, but not as often—he was in demand, literally, all over the world.

Danilo's roots are in Panama, and his family still lives there. And if ever there was someone who believes in "giving back," it's Danilo. He founded the Panama Jazz Festival about 15 years ago, and he still serves as the artistic director. He invited me down to Panama one year, and I was really pleased to see how highly the people regarded him. He started the Danilo Pérez Foundation to organize music programs for the country's kids. He funnels profits from the festival into the foundation's programs. He's a real hero in Panama, a celebrity.

Danilo still tours with his own group and with saxophonist Wayne Shorter's group, and he's been nominated for several Grammy awards. On top of everything else, he directs the Global Jazz Institute for Berklee College. It's almost like he has too many ideas. I don't know how he's able to keep up the pace.

THE SMOOTH JAZZ WAVE

We've never come up with a definition of jazz that everyone accepts, so I'm not surprised we don't have one for "smooth jazz," either, even though it's been around since the 1970s. So let's call it a contemporary jazz/pop sound, but without the improvisation and emotion found at the heart of "true" jazz. The jazz purists hate it—"That's elevator music." But it has a large and loyal audience, and I booked many smooth jazz groups at Scullers, even when the purists criticized me for doing so. But here's the awful truth: smooth jazz paid the bills for straight-ahead jazz, which was always a harder sell. That's just the way it's been for years now. The smooth jazz acts we started presenting at Scullers in the early years, like Dave Koz, Fourplay, and Richard Elliot, were still popular when I left the club in 2016.

We started with smooth jazz in 1992, and we got a big boost from the radio stations that played it. WCDJ, also known as CD 96.9, started sponsoring artist appearances that same summer; saxophonist Nelson Rangell was one of the first, and I was still playing him in 2015. That radio station rebooted itself in 1997 as WSJZ and started broadcasting shows from the club, and that grew the audience even more. I still have some of the original tapes of the club broadcasts, people like Walter Beasley and Kirk Whalum.

Two of our biggest 1990s names, Chuck Mangione and Grover Washington Jr., are sometimes mentioned as smooth jazz artists, but I don't like to assign labels. I had Chuck at the Jazz Workshop a couple years before his monster hit "Feels So Good," which later got a lot of airplay on the smooth jazz stations. His father came along to sell T-shirts—Chuck was into "merch" early on!

He came to Scullers in May 1997, and that's when I really got to know him. At the Jazz Workshop he was kind of standoffish, but when he played Scullers he really enjoyed himself, and we became good friends. And he was there five more times, through 2008, sometimes for three or four nights. I wanted him back, but there was that terrible plane crash in 2009 that killed some of his band, including his sax player, Gerry Niewood, who had been with him from the beginning. Chuck was devastated and has hardly played in public since.

Grover is another one from the Jazz Workshop—in fact, he received his gold record for the *Mr. Magic* album at the Workshop in 1975. He was at Scullers in 1995, not long after the grand reopening, and there was a huge demand for tickets. We actually moved the stage in order to squeeze in a few more seats. Grover was a wonderful, wonderful guy.

Over time, some of the smooth jazz artists have developed a straight-ahead edge. Many of them were always great jazz players who found they could make a little more money producing the smooth sound—artists like Gato Barbieri, Larry Carlton, Russ Freeman. But when they came into the club, they could *play*, and they went outside the limits of what people think of as "smooth." Spyro Gyra is one group that does that. These groups became Scullers regulars, filling the club year after year. When the jazz purists complained, I'd tell them, "Okay, if you've got all the answers, *you* go run a club."

ARTISTS OLD AND NEW

One of my adventurous bookings at Scullers was Eartha Kitt in 1996. She's not a chummy sort, she had a bit of a hard edge. She had it rough growing up. Of course she was famous for her meeting with Lady Bird Johnson at the White House, where she expressed views that got her blacklisted and forced her to find work outside of the country. She spent years in France.

Anyway she was at Scullers, and comes the Saturday, she noticed that *Rent* had just opened at the Shubert Theater, and Nina Simone's daughter, who went by the name Simone, was in the cast. Eartha wanted to see the show, so I offered to take her to the matinee, and we went, the two of us. Afterwards we went backstage, and I introduced Simone to her and they had quite a conversation. After that Eartha and I had a pleasant relationship, and there was always a little tongue-in-cheek banter between us. People were surprised because of her prickly reputation. "You two are getting along!" they'd say. And we did. Speaking of Nina Simone, another one with a reputation for being "difficult," we got along fine too. It's a matter of respect.

Eartha's show was wonderful. I have a video of one of her numbers, which was hilarious. The club's manager then was a good-looking guy named Miguel Rodriguez, and Eartha did a scene where she brought him onstage to play a fellow from room service. She says, "How old are you?" "Twenty-one," he answers. "*Nobody* is 21!" she says. And she's pouring champagne and feeding it to him, and she's got a little song with it . . . Oh, it's a funny bit. And she had such a presence, she could freeze an audience, just stop it cold. That engagement is one of my outstanding memories from that time.

In January 1998, I brought an old, old friend to Scullers: Bobby Short. It was his first club engagement in Boston in over 20 years. What a reunion we had! He was the undisputed king of New York's Café Carlyle, and he was more elegant and sophisticated than ever. The next year he came in with his big band, and performing with a band like that fulfilled one of his longtime dreams. And in 2001 we worked with the Boston Public Library to have one night of his engagement be a library fundraiser. Bobby was very generous with his time when it came to worthy causes, and we were happy to help out.

And I remember him telling me that those gigs back at Paul's Mall in the '60s meant everything to him. He said they kept him alive. Bobby Short—a gentleman and a class act.

And speaking of old friends, another one who gets special mention is Dave Brubeck, one of my oldest friends in jazz. Dave didn't play nightclubs. Dave didn't even like nightclubs. Early on when he had achieved some financial success, he gave up the clubs for the concert stage. He always said he did it because he hated the smoke, not to mention the people who would talk and make noise over the music. But in 1998 he played a long weekend for me at Scullers. And George Wein—I didn't stick with the piano but George did, and he was good enough to turn professional. Yes, along with everything else he's done, George formed his own group, the Newport All-Stars, and toured with it. John Sdoucos and I first booked that group in 1963, and here I was at Scullers in 2012, booking the All-Stars again. George more than held his own with musicians like clarinetist Anat Cohen, who is 50 years his junior. Amazing.

I go back a long way with pianist Ahmad Jamal. I first heard him in the late 1950s at Storyville, in his "Poinciana" days, and I was instantly a fan. Ahmad's playing, his concept—he is totally unique in jazz, and I'm not the only one who thinks that. Miles Davis, for one, always said he learned from Ahmad. I first brought Ahmad to the Jazz Workshop in 1967, and he was with me there until 1977. We used to do concerts during those years, too. I remember one great double bill with Sarah Vaughan at Symphony Hall. We started working together again when I came to Scullers.

In 1999 Ahmad called me and said he was working with a young pianist named Hiromi Uehara, mentoring her, and I had to hear her. She had come from Japan to study at Berklee, and one of her teachers there was Richard Evans, the bassist and arranger, and he was a friend of Ahmad's from their Chicago days. Richard loved Hiromi's playing, and he called Ahmad, and after Ahmad heard her, he called me. He also called his friends at Telarc Records, and that led to a recording contract. I booked Hiromi at Scullers every chance I could get. And she was a Yamaha artist, and helped us pick out a new piano for the club. It's the piano that's sitting on the stage today.

I booked Ahmad to play at the Tanglewood Jazz Festival a couple of times, including at the very first one in 2001. And speaking of festivals, one year I booked him at one in Jamaica. I went down there with Ahmad and Laura, his wife, and the sponsors set us up in a place near the beach in Mona Bay. Very nice. Then we drove over to Kingston for the concert, and we passed through these shanty neighborhoods, poverty beyond belief. I've never forgotten that, the world of difference between Mona Bay and those shanty villages. We stayed over for a few days, and Laura and I got our hair beaded! I wish I had a photo of that to show you.

Don't get the idea that Scullers was just for established stars though. We presented new artists right from the beginning. I've mentioned Danilo Pérez and Hiromi already. We presented Jane Monheit, Christian McBride, Kurt Elling, Peter Cincotti, and Norah Jones. I found Kat Edmonson, and she is now becoming quite a star. We were one of the first with Jamie Cullum; we started him on his first American tour. We showcased Michael Bublé. When Chris Botti, who was Sting's lead trumpet player, went on his own, we brought him to Scullers to do a record release party for Columbia Records. We brought him back six months later, and the next year he did New Year's Eve. By that time his career was in high gear. Chris has always been grateful for that early support.

Esperanza Spalding, the singer and bassist, is another young artist we introduced at Scullers. I first heard her playing at a Berklee event, and then with Maeve Gilchrist, who plays jazz harp. They were playing duets, little concerts, in a music shop near Symphony Hall. I got Esperanza some bookings at corporate events. I kept trying to find things for her to do, because I just knew she was outstanding. I brought her to Scullers in 2005 with a quartet, and then the next year with a trio, and again in 2007. She played at Tanglewood, in our Jazz Café. In 2011, we had that incredible trio of Geri Allen, Esperanza, and Terri Lyne Carrington. That was something else. And in the meantime Esperanza was on the road with Joe Lovano, and things really took off for her.

THE PHENOM: GRACE KELLY

In 2004, I met Bob Kelly, who would drop by Scullers and ask me to audition his teenage daughter, who played alto saxophone. I would put him off. But he was persistent, and one night when Ann Hampton Callaway was singing, Bob and his daughter showed up, and she had her horn. What I did not know was that Ann knew this high school kid and liked her, and had written liner notes for a CD that Bob had produced when his daughter was 12. Twelve!

Ann's doing her show, and she says, "Now I'd like to bring up a very talented young lady, Grace Kelly." I had no idea this was going to happen. Grace was all of 13, and she played "Over the Rainbow," and I'm thinking, "What's *this* all about?" I was floored, instantly a fan, and I met her afterwards and told her I'd like her to do something at the club.

We hosted the release party for Grace's second CD, *Times Too*, at Scullers, and after that Grace and Bob and Irene and I became great friends. I started helping Bob find his way through the business side of the music world. This is not the usual father-of-the-artist story. Bob Kelly made everything possible for Grace in the beginning. You name it, he did it—road manager, booking agent, publicist, website developer, and van driver. Once when the money was tight Bob drove Grace to Chicago to make a gig. Her parents were behind her all the way. They made things happen.

I introduced Grace to the artists playing Scullers, and sometimes they'd ask her to sit in. She sat in with Sax Pack, a great band with three saxophonists, and at the end of the set, Kim Waters, one of those horn players, took the microphone. "Don't lie to me," he deadpanned, "you're really 40 years old!"

Frank Morgan was a giant of the alto saxophone, a disciple of Charlie Parker, and I had him at Scullers when he was staging his comeback after years of addiction and prison. Grace sat in, and Frank flipped over her. He took her along to play the Detroit Jazz Festival, and the Jazz Standard in New York. Frank loved her and worked with her, and after he died, Grace played at San Quentin Prison, where Frank served his time, in a tribute concert organized in his honor.

I'll jump ahead a few years here. A documentary film came out in 2014, *Sound of Redemption: The Frank Morgan Story*, and Grace was in it. That movie was produced by Michael Connelly, who writes the crime novels about a Los Angeles detective named Harry Bosch. Connelly and Morgan were good friends. When Amazon created a web television series about Bosch, Grace was in an episode of that, too, in 2016, playing a tune she wrote, "Blues for Bosch." At the same time, she was in the house band on *The Late Show with Stephen Colbert*. But I'm getting ahead of myself.

When I was programming the Tanglewood Jazz Festival, we set up a small side stage called the Jazz Café and introduced emerging artists there. In 2007, I featured Grace. The people loved her. And I'd introduce her to the main stage artists, just as I'd done at Scullers. One was Marian McPartland, who invited Grace to appear on her national radio program, *Piano Jazz*.

Next I worked with André Menard to get her to the Montreal Jazz Festival, first at the outdoor stage and then with Phil Woods—she recorded that great album with Phil, *Man with the Hat*. Then I introduced Grace to George Wein and he invited her to Newport, opening the Newport Jazz Festival with Jamie Cullum, and Jamie loved her. So just as it was with Danilo, I made introductions for Grace, but it was Grace, upbeat and positive, who always sealed the deal.

So I'm a fan, and since that first night with Ann Hampton Callaway, I've been Grace's biggest booster. Helping her succeed has been very important to me, and continuing to help her is one of my ongoing projects. She's a sweetheart. She loves people and people love her, and I think the sky's the limit for her. She composes, she sings, she plays, she teaches, and she's been all over the world. It's been a joy to work with her, and I talk with her and Bob and Irene often. They're family.

ALL GOOD THINGS

I always felt that I succeeded at Scullers because the people usually went away happy. I did everything I could to make the customers feel welcome and give them a good show. I liked to stand by the door afterward, mingling with the people leaving. I was gratified whenever someone said, "Keep this music going, this is wonderful." It made me feel like I was the keeper of the flame.

I also felt we succeeded because we were a little more than just a nightclub. Like Paul's Mall before it, Scullers presented the best in musical entertainment regardless of style or genre. I didn't know of any other club in the country that had a similar variety of music. Scullers crossed all the boundaries, with straight-ahead jazz, smooth jazz, Latin jazz, R&B, cabaret, world music, blues, funk . . . You can only offer that variety of music if you have an audience that supports it, and Scullers did. I worked especially hard to bring in the Latin jazz groups, and the R&B and soul groups, because no one else was. Scullers was the only place in Boston you could hear black artists who were not catering to the youth market, and I worked to develop Scullers as being a comfortable place for the black community to enjoy music. Not many places in Boston could say that. I always thought that if Scullers didn't exist, the people who loved these kinds of music would have nowhere to go.

Thoughts of success aside, my last few years at Scullers were hard for several reasons. The nightclub business seemed tougher than ever. People, or at least the people who came to Scullers, weren't going out as much. Second sets especially were becoming an endangered species. That was part of it, but a bigger part was the increasing tension in my relationship with hotel management. The last of the hotel-hired club managers I worked with was Annmarie Blyth, who arrived in late 2011. She got a new boss two years later when Jayne Barrett became the hotel's general manager.

The shoe dropped the first week of January 2017. Jayne asked to meet, and she told me the hotel would not renew my contract as entertainment director. I was to complete the business I already had in the pipeline and be out at the end of February. I asked why. She said that Scullers, and me, had been doing the same thing for a long time, and it was time for a change. Jayne fired Annmarie, who was an employee of the hotel, at the same time.

You always hear that the coaches of professional sports teams are hired to be fired, and that sooner or later they're going to be out. It's a "What have you done for me lately" business. Well, the entertainment business isn't so different. Sometimes, for strictly personal or political reasons, you're gone. And so it was for me with Jayne. I didn't have a poor relationship with her, I had no relationship. We had almost no contact with each other over the years, and I honestly don't recall her ever attending a show at the club. She just decided that she wanted her own team at Scullers, and Annmarie and I were out.

My long ride was ending after 26 years. "Upset" and "disappointed" don't even come close to how I felt. I was hurt. I hadn't expected to get the axe, but I have to say, I wasn't shocked that it happened. But the local press was, and so were people on the big social media sites. There was an outpouring of protest, and hundreds of letters and comments expressing disbelief. The community support was great. It's nice to have friends.

What, and give up showbiz?

15

A LITTLE MORE SONG AND DANCE

Throughout my career I've always found time to get involved in projects that I can only fit into a category I call "none of the above." Surprising new things are always turning up. Sometimes the end results are good, sometimes they aren't, but it's always time well spent. Here are a few of those projects.

WHO'S LINDA CHORNEY?

I was backstage at Great Woods in 1987 when Linda Chorney approached me. It was the Saturday of the jazz festival, and backstage access was restricted, but Linda found her way in—she's very good at finding her way into places she's not supposed to be—and she says, "I want you to manage me." Total stranger. Never saw her before. I asked her what she did. She said she was a singer and songwriter. I said, "Okay, I've got to hear some of your stuff. If you can record some of your material, I'll listen." So the next week she's at my office, with her recordings and her guitar, and she played some of her songs, and I thought they were good.

And she says, "You're gonna be my manager, and I'm gonna be a star!" Her mind was made up. She talked me into it.

She put together a good little band and I got her some dates—at the Channel and Copperfield's, places like that—and she kept writing new material. We decided to see if any of the record people on the West Coast were interested. My old friend Al Coury, who was then with David Geffen, got us in with Geffen's A&R guy. He listened to Linda and said, "That's not what's happening right now."

And that bothered me. I said, "I'm sorry to hear you say that. I'd rather have heard you say 'I don't like the material,' but to tell me 'That's not what's happening now,' that's a wrong answer. That just means you want something that sounds like what's out there now, not something that's fresh and original. If you don't like it, that's an honest answer. But don't tell me that it's not what's happening now."

It didn't do any good, but at least I got to deliver my sermon. We went to see a couple of other companies too, but we never got to first base.

But we did go to Disneyland one afternoon, which was a first for me. The best Disneyland moment came when we came across a shooting gallery, where you win a prize if you knock down all the targets. Linda wanted me to try it. So they gave me the pistol, and instead of aiming the thing, I got in my gunslinger stance with the pistol hanging down by my side, and said, "Alright, draw!" And bang! I knocked everything over, and won a giant teddy bear for Linda. Talk about shooting from the hip! And for some reason she dubbed me Monk after that. Not the stuffed bear, me. To this day she still calls me Monk.

One of Linda's bright spots came during Nelson Mandela's visit to Boston in 1990, and there was a big tribute and concert at the Hatch Shell, where Mandela himself spoke. My old friend Mae Arnette sang that day. Paul Simon was there, with Ladysmith Black Mambazo. Linda walked right up to Simon backstage and started talking about guitar playing. She's very gregarious, and there's no hesitation with Linda. Anyway, she sang at that concert, a wonderful tune that she wrote, "Love from All Over the World." She sang the word *love* in 13 languages throughout the song. Really it was a great song, a very appropriate and wonderful thing to hear on a day dedicated to Mandela and freedom.

Linda left Boston after that, and she's done many things since—released CDs, made films, and written a book, *Who the F&*% Is Linda Chorney*. That's about her quest for the 2012 Grammy for her album *Emotional Jukebox*. She's an indie musician, no big record company or public relations firm behind her, and she found a way to earn a Grammy nomination, although she did not win. She made the music establishment furious, this outsider, who's always been pretty good at finding her way into places she's not supposed to be.

She called me not long ago, and when I answered, she said, "It's me, the star who still hasn't made it yet." She's a good friend, and I don't understand why after all this time, over 30 years, she isn't a star. Who knows why things happen in this business. I say that success in show business is 30 percent talent and 70 percent chance, or luck. Some people make it, and Linda, she just keeps on paying her dues.

EVA CASSIDY: AN ANGEL ALMOST LOST

One of the things you need if you book bands for a living is a big mailbox. Record companies send you music, agents and managers send you music, artists send you music. First it was cassettes and then it was CDs, and now it seems my email box is filled to bursting with MP3 files. There's no end to it. I literally have CDs stacked in waist-high columns in both home and office. I sample as many as I can, but they come in faster than I have the ability or appetite to listen to them. Many will never be played. I used to feel guilty about it, but there just isn't enough time in the day to listen to even a tune or two from each.

One Sunday morning in 1998, I grabbed a CD off the pile that had taken over a corner of my bedroom. The cover photo showed a smiling blonde-haired woman, a kind of country look. I was curious, so I popped it into the player. I was walking out of the room, and this voice came at me and I stopped in my tracks, in a "What is this?" kind of reaction. I looked to see who was singing.

The CD was titled *Songbird*, and the smiling blonde was Eva Cassidy. The CD was still playing and I was already making plans to book her at Scullers—I'm telling you, her voice was really something. I started reading the notes, and bang, my heart just dropped. Eva was already gone. She had died about a year before this recording was released, of skin cancer, at age 33. Oh my God. But I kept listening, because *I loved that voice!* Sting's "Fields of Gold" was gorgeous, emotional. Then one of Pete Seeger's folk tunes, "Oh, Had I a Golden Thread." Then a powerful version of the standard "Over the Rainbow." There was even a spiritual, "Wade in the Water." It didn't matter what type of music it was, she sang them all equally well. I thought hers was a fresh, new voice, and her story a poignant one, because that voice would never sing again.

The next day I was winding up a phone call, and I started talking about this Eva Cassidy CD. I mentioned it to everybody, on every call, all day long. I kept it up all week, because it was one of the most emotional experiences I'd had in a long time. I just kept talking about it.

Then I got the idea that just telling people about it wasn't enough, and I had to enlist some help to get this music noticed. I thought about approaching Robin Young, who was doing a morning show on WBOS-FM. I thought Robin would be the perfect person to hear this, because she had a news background and might appreciate a story with a good feature flavor. I sent her a note with the CD. I called her a few days later and asked if she'd had a chance to listen to the music. "Have I ever," she said. "I went on air with it. I gave a little intro and played "Fields of Gold," and I don't think we were more than 15 seconds into it when the phone board just lit up. And it hasn't stopped!"

Then I got a call from Bill Straw with Blix Street Records, the company that released *Songbird*. He asked me what was going on in Boston, and I asked him, what do you mean? He said, "We can't keep Eva Cassidy's CD in stock, we're sending everything we've got up your way, and we can't get copies in fast enough." I told him that Robin Young had been playing it and getting good response, and I was personally pushing Songbird because I was very moved by it. His response? "Incredible!"

My passion for Eva's music was not letting up, and I decided I had to do something else to promote it, so I brought the story to the *Boston Globe* and convinced the editor to assign a writer to it, to find out who Eva Cassidy was and how the music came to be. So the *Globe's* Joan Anderman traveled to Maryland to interview her parents and her fellow musicians, and wrote a long story for the paper in late January 1999 called "Eva Cassidy's Gift."

In her article, Joan mentioned me and what I was doing to promote Eva's music. I got a call from a friend of mine in Texas about a week later, and he told me he read this article—the wire services had picked it up—"and your name was in it, so I thought I'd call. Who's Eva Cassidy?" I started getting more and more of these calls.

Now we jump to late 2000, early 2001. The only radio deejay in the US who was playing Eva's music was Robin Young here in Boston. For some reason, the station programmers and music directors couldn't hear it. But somebody sent *Songbird* over to the UK, because it was number one on BBC Radio 2 in London. How did that happen? Nobody played Eva on the radio here, but despite that she became a huge hit on BBC Radio 2. Then the television side of the BBC picked up the story, produced a documentary on Eva, and showed it on *Top of the Pops 2*. That made its way back over here.

Because of the exposure through the BBC's radio play and documentary, *Billboard* got excited about *Songbird* and put it on their front cover. *People* magazine did a big feature story. Then Ted Koppel and *Nightline* picked it up. *Nightline* usually had two or three feature stories per show, but they did the whole half hour on Eva Cassidy. And just after that, *Songbird* become the top seller on Amazon.

This thing just mushroomed! I heard stories about people who made *Songbird* part of their life. There's one about a woman who was going into the hospital, and asked if they could play *Songbird* during her surgery. I'd go to my health club and listen to Eva Cassidy while riding the stationary bike. Eva's music was just everywhere.

I learned a little story about Eva a few years later. She auditioned for Blue Note Records, but they didn't know what to do with her. They paired her on tour with Pieces of a Dream, a funky R&B group, which was totally wrong, and they never signed her. Bruce Lundvall, the president of Blue Note, called Eva during her final days and apologized for not signing her. He was determined not to repeat that mistake.

A few years later, I brought Norah Jones into Scullers the first time on the strength of a demo her agent sent me, before her first album came out. Norah and I had dinner together before the first show. I asked her, since she was a Blue Note artist, if she knew about Eva Cassidy. She said, "Oh, yeah. Bruce Lundvall told me he wasn't going to make the same mistake with me that he made with Eva Cassidy." Lundvall told her he was going to sign her the same afternoon he heard her sing. She didn't have an agent or a lawyer at the time, and I think she was still waitressing, but Lundvall started the process that afternoon. He didn't let another one get away.

I look at my experience with Eva Cassidy's music and I think of two things. The first is the part that fate, or luck, plays in this business. I grabbed this CD out of all the CDs I had that Sunday morning. If I had grabbed a different one, *Songbird* could have sunk down in the pile, and I might never have listened to it. There would be no Robin Young, no Joan Anderman, no Boston buzz to start what became a global phenomenon.

The second thing I think about is how grateful I am that I got to hear this music and care about it and be able to do something to tell people about it. I took what Eva's circle of friends had done, and what Bill Straw had done, and pushed it a little further down the road. And someone else was able to take what I did in Boston and push it even further—even across an ocean. I'm proud of what I did for Eva's memory. I never made a dime off it and never intended to, but I do know that what I did was appreciated.

In 2001 I got a package in the mail that didn't contain CDs. It was a framed gold record from Bill Straw at Blix, thanking me for my role in making *Songbird* a hit on both sides of the Atlantic. It hangs in a prominent spot on my office wall.

Eva Cassidy's story is one of those bittersweet things, a great talent lost too soon, but a great talent also finally heard. And I'll tell you, here we are 20 years later, and I hear that music, and it still gets to me.

TONY SANDLER, CHEVALIER, AND ME

Sometimes I get into a project and get completely carried away with it. I think, "There's something really good here," and I want to put it together. I can get myself into trouble that way. Exhibit A: working with Tony Sandler on the production of *Chevalier—Maurice and Me* in 2004.

My friend Buck Spurr, who loved musical theater as much as anybody, introduced me to Tony Sandler. He had been working on his own since his partner of many years, Ralph Young, retired from performing. The duo of Sandler and Young had been very popular, with Tony, the debonair European (he's Belgian), playing the foil to Ralph's gregarious New Yorker. When they stopped clowning around they'd sing, and the formula brought them great success. Anyway, Buck said Sandler had a show based on the life of Maurice

Chevalier, the legendary French song-and-dance man, and he was looking for backers. Buck insisted I meet him. So Sandler came to Scullers, and we talked, and the 2004 version of his musical biography of Maurice Chevalier began to take shape. The show reviewed Chevalier's entire career, from the Paris music halls through his film and stage career on both sides of the Atlantic. Tony would perform the one-man show and we would film it. Then we'd produce an edited version of the show for the broadcast and home video markets. The DVD could serve as a calling card that would lead to more stage bookings. The project looked solid and I got excited about it.

I went all-in as producer and set about staging the show. First I chose the Cutler Majestic Theater on Tremont Street, which I thought was just the right kind of venue. It had just been restored to its early-20th-century glory, and with about 1,700 seats, it would be ideal for a one-man show. I started the publicity machine and hired musicians, including a great accordionist from Belgium, Ludo Mariën. We brought in a first-rate camera and sound crew to capture everything. Opening night was April 26, 2005.

We had our week at the Majestic, and those who attended said it was a wonderful show—but we didn't do much business. We weren't helped by the *Boston Globe's* tepid review. And the people who saw the show didn't get on the phone to tell all their friends they had to see it. We didn't generate any momentum from the Boston show. I lost money on it.

But we had film, and we had hopes for that. Tony had worked previously with IPTV, a public television station in Iowa known for high-quality studio work. IPTV's executive producer, Jerry Grady, saw *Chevalier* in Boston and agreed to edit the film and produce a show for public television. Just when the editors told us they were about three-fourths done, Sandler threw a wrench into the works.

Tony decided to go to Belgium for a homecoming concert with a big band and film that for video. I tried to talk him out of it, saying we should finish *Chevalier* first. But off he went, and that delayed *Chevalier's* completion by six months. He returned with concert film and wanted to go straight into production with it. I looked at the film and it didn't grab me. It was a good concert, but there was nothing exceptional about it, and I still thought

Chevalier was the better bet. Tony insisted on editing the concert first. So *Chevalier* waited, and we finally finished production in early 2006. PBS picked it up, with over 30 stations broadcasting it. But like the Boston show, it didn't create any buzz.

I booked a few shows in Florida, and we presented *Chevalier* in New York at the annual APAP (Association of Performing Arts Presenters) convention. That's *the* place to catch the eye of people in my line of work. We didn't get any bites.

Then the bills from the Belgian concert started coming in, and Tony wanted me to invest more money but I said no. I was in as far as I wanted to go. There were disputes about money and who owed what, and *Chevalier—Maurice and Me* got lost in all of that. In the end, it sort of fizzled out. People just weren't interested, and I think that's too bad. We released the DVD in late 2006, with the PBS show and a fascinating interview with Tony. He's a charming guy. It's great entertainment—and if you'd like the DVD, contact me, because I've still got boxes of copies.

Why wasn't *Chevalier—Maurice and Me* a success? Part of it might have been the subject matter, Maurice Chevalier himself. He didn't connect with the American audience of 2005, who knew very little about this entertainer who stepped out of history. Even his famous role in the movie *Gigi*, where he sang "Thank Heaven for Little Girls," was 50 years in the past. Something else came up too. Maurice Chevalier was accused of being too close to the Nazis in occupied France during World War II. Tony maintained that was not true, and that although he did perform for German troops, he only did it to save his Jewish girlfriend. But the Nazi association dogged Chevalier, and maybe that turned people off.

It came down to this: I was the producer, I invested in the show and the video production, and I took a loss on it. It happens. And that's my story about a creative venture where I got carried away.

What, and give up showbiz?

16

SPLENDOR IN THE BERKSHIRES

Tanglewood, an idyllic estate in Lenox, Massachusetts, has been the summer home of the Boston Symphony Orchestra (BSO) and a beloved destination for music lovers since the late 1930s. With its beautiful Berkshire Mountains setting and relaxed atmosphere, there is no finer place in New England to enjoy an outdoor concert.

On a lesser scale, Tanglewood has also been home to a popular music series for decades, and everyone from Liza Minnelli to Willie Nelson to perennial favorite James Taylor has performed there. There's been jazz too, but never anything too ambitious. Maybe a jazz weekend or a few single concerts mixed into the popular series.

In 2000, the BSO organization thought the time was right to reconsider summer jazz at Tanglewood. That year, I was attending Boston's annual Fourth of July extravaganza on the Charles River Esplanade. Sometime after the *1812 Overture* and before the fireworks, I fell into a conversation with Tony Beadle, the director of the Boston Pops. Beadle asked if I might be interested in "doing something with jazz" at Tanglewood, and I said yes. That's all it took to get started.

SETTING THE FESTIVAL STAGE

I was very excited by this opportunity. One of my favorite parts of what I do is planning and packaging shows. I enjoy putting different people together to make a great event, and festivals have always been a place for innovative musical pairings. I couldn't wait to get started.

We made our plans that summer, scheduling our first events for summer 2001. I was named artistic director, reporting to Tony, who would be my liaison with the BSO organization. As I'd done with all my major projects since 1981, I brought in Sue Auclair to handle publicity.

Our first decision involved concert dates. Instead of having concerts spread across the summer as part of the popular music series, we would concentrate the jazz programming over the Labor Day weekend, the end of Tanglewood's classical season.

I wanted to create an identity for the jazz program, so we called it the Tanglewood Jazz Festival. That established the name and the concept, and separated our program from everything else in the pop realm scheduled earlier in the summer.

There are two stages at Tanglewood, both named for past conductors of the BSO, and we planned to use them both. The 1,200-seat Seiji Ozawa Hall is on the western edge of the grounds, and the 5,100-seat Koussevitzky Music Shed is right in the center of everything. Both open onto the lawn, which stretches between them and can accommodate another 13,000 patrons. Lawn seating is one of the things that makes Tanglewood special. People can spread their blankets and picnic on the lawn while enjoying the music, weather permitting. We did have some rainy nights that kept attendance down. But when Mother Nature cooperates, Tanglewood is an incomparable setting.

THE FIRST FESTIVAL

Tanglewood 2001 set the basic structure that we used every year thereafter. We started with a press party and opening concert on Friday evening. Then we staged two separate shows on Saturday, in the afternoon and evening, and finally two more shows on Sunday afternoon and evening. The Saturday and Sunday evening shows were in the Music Shed, and the others in Ozawa Hall. We stayed away from the holiday Monday itself. There was already enough traffic on the roads that day without us contributing to it.

We started the festival weekend with a press party early Friday evening, at the Highwood Manor House, a restored Victorian with a function room and a patio outside. We put the food inside and the party outside, and while everyone was doing their meet-and-greets and arranging interviews, we'd have soloists or small acoustic groups playing. That was a nice way to introduce new artists to the press. Alto saxophonist Grace Kelly, who was all of 14, was at the press party one year. Guitarist Jonathan "Juanito" Pascual entertained another year, as did Edmar Castañeda, the jazz harpist from Columbia.

We wanted to make a mark with our first festival, so I chose artists who were proven performers, people I knew and had worked with before. I was looking for established mainstream artists to set the right tone and appeal to the "typical" Tanglewood attendees, who tend to be an older crowd. We weren't programming music with college students in mind. That first Friday concert had the New York Voices opening for Chuck Mangione. John Pizzarelli's trio and Jane Monheit were our Saturday afternoon event, followed by a three-hour evening show with Spyro Gyra, Ahmad Jamal, and Sherrie Maricle's DIVA big band with their guest vocalist, Nancy Wilson. We had Sonny Rollins on Sunday afternoon, and the finale included George Benson, Poncho Sanchez, and Nicholas Payton's Louis Armstrong Centennial Celebration Band. There was nothing extreme on this program, just solid mainstream jazz with headliners we thought would attract the broadest possible audience.

In 2002, I made two additions to the festival that were so well received they became permanent parts of the program. First, I introduced Latin jazz, because Latin was a category many festivals overlooked. I knew from what was happening at Scullers that it was a growing and mostly untapped audience. Friday night became Latin Jazz Night, and we featured the groups of Arturo Sandoval and Nestor Torres.

Our second addition took place on Saturday afternoon at Ozawa Hall. I thought it would be a great idea to broadcast Marian McPartland's longrunning public radio program, *Piano Jazz*, from Tanglewood. I approached Marian with the idea, and she was all for it, and we did it for the first time in 2002. Her guest was Roland Hanna. NPR did not broadcast the program live—they recorded it and, after editing, broadcast it nationally in early 2003. We hosted Marian and *Piano Jazz* every year I was at Tanglewood, and NPR always broadcast the program in the winter months, when memories of pleasant summer afternoons were most welcome. We preferred this arrangement, because her show provided the festival with a midwinter shot of publicity.

Marian and I go way back. I recorded her at Storyville, about the same time I recorded Brubeck, in the early 1950s. So we were celebrating a 50-year friendship at Tanglewood. She played at the Jazz Workshop and at Scullers. And on one of her Scullers visits, Sue Auclair and I took her out to lunch, to Harvest on Harvard Square. Now I've known Marian a long time, and I've listened to her talk, and she has this lovely British accent, refined. And she was telling us a story about playing the Hickory House, her longtime haunt in New York City, and she remarked that "Someone kept asking for some stupid tune, and finally I had to tell him to *fuck off*, you know." And Sue and I just backed up in our chairs. Wait! This lovely lady with this delicate accent—but I found out Marian was a trouper and could really let go with the language. She could go toe to toe with the boys, but I had never heard it, and there it was in the middle of this lovely conversation. Oh, it was a funny moment.

In later years at Tanglewood, Marian's *Piano Jazz* guests were often young artists just emerging on the national scene, including pianist Taylor Eigsti and singers Norah Jones and Madeleine Peyroux. One year she featured the husband-and-wife team of Elvis Costello and Diana Krall.

THE TANGLEWOOD JAZZ CAFE

Prior to the 2003 season, I pitched another idea to Tony Beadle. On the hill behind Ozawa Hall was a tent selling refreshments named the Hawthorne Tent. (Everything at Tanglewood has a picturesque name.) I suggested to Tony that it would be an ideal place to stage music featuring upcoming artists before the main shows. We could call it the Tanglewood Jazz Café. Tony liked it, so we got that under way.

The Jazz Café was not created without headaches though. When I came up with the idea, the BSO people said there was no money, and they showed no inclination to go out and find it. The BSO's marketing group was tasked with raising funds for BSO activities, presumably including Tanglewood, but

they weren't being much help. So I reached out to people I knew and presented the concept of the Tanglewood Jazz Café and what it would cost. And we
found receptive ears. Volkswagen of America and *Travel + Leisure* magazine
were willing to support us, at a cost of about $4,500. Volkswagen would dis-
play two cars on the property in front of the Jazz Café, and *Travel + Leisure*
would run a full-page ad with the cars sitting on the Tanglewood lawn. Done.
We had our Jazz Café.

Then Tony called to say we couldn't do it. "What do you mean, we can't
do it?" I said. He said the marketing department wouldn't allow it. "They
won't *allow* it?" I shrieked. "We needed funding, they didn't come up with
it, so I beat the bushes and found what we needed." He said all such funding
requests had to go through the marketing department. It was a policy. I said,
"Well, Tony, we have to go through with it. There's a full-page ad in *Travel +
Leisure* magazine. If you cancel this now, and they have to change the magazine at this late date, they'll sue you." So his marketing people grumbled, but
they "allowed" it. Then we had a debate about whether Volkswagen could
park their automobiles on the lawn, and we finally resolved that, too.

The festival opened, and we had our Jazz Café. I stationed myself there
to see how the concertgoers took to it, and they enjoyed it, as I suspected they
would. They could have a little nosh, listen to some music that was probably
new to them, and then stroll down the hill to their concert. Not one person
told me they were bothered by Volkswagen's sponsorship, or by a couple of
cars parked on the grass. The Jazz Café was a success, and it contributed
mightily to the ambiance we were creating. Over the years we presented some
terrific young jazz artists there, including pianist Taylor Eigsti with guitarist Julian Lage, saxophonist Grace Kelly, vibist Warren Wolf with vocalist
Rachael Price, and bassist Esperanza Spalding.

When the time came to make plans for 2004, I remembered my bruises
from the battles with the marketing department the year before, and I said
we wouldn't do the Tanglewood Jazz Café. "No, no!" said Tony. "They want
to do it!"

What, and give up showbiz?

FESTIVAL ON THE AIR

In 2004, I found a way to extend the festival's reach across the Northeast. I formed a partnership with two powerhouse public radio stations, WBGO serving New York, and WGBH serving Boston, to broadcast our Friday night show live. I think about a half dozen other stations picked up the concert through them. We were now on the air in these two major markets, but it got better: National Public Radio recorded the concert for rebroadcast on Labor Day itself, and they made it available to affiliate stations nationwide. Talk about a promotion opportunity! That Latin Jazz Night broadcast featured Eliane Elias followed by Eddie Palmieri's ensemble, La Perfecta II.

I have a few other strong memories of that 2004 festival. I was one of the first music producers to back a little-known New Orleans pianist and singer named Harry Connick Jr. He wasn't getting much attention until I had him open for Al Jarreau at the Great Woods Jazz Festival in 1988. His set that day opened a lot of eyes and ears. So I was pleased to have him bring his 16-piece big band to the Koussevitzky Music Shed on Saturday night. His father, a former district attorney in New Orleans who also happened to be a singer, joined the band for one number. Then on Sunday, Harry played a solo piano set, no singing, reminding everybody what a great jazz pianist he was.

A pianist figures into my second strong memory of that year too. Dave Brubeck closed the festival on Sunday with a performance by his quartet, accompanied by an 18-piece string "symphonette" conducted by his longtime associate, Russell Gloyd. They recruited many of the string players from the ranks of the Boston Symphony Orchestra. It was Brubeck's first performance of that piece before an American audience.

In 2005, I assembled a jazz supergroup for the Latin Jazz Night: harmonica legend Toots Thielemans, Kenny Werner on piano, Oscar Castro-Neves on guitar, and Airto Moreira on drums and percussion. Toots told me one night at Scullers that he regretted never playing at Tanglewood, and he was elated when I booked him. I felt pretty good about making it happen, and what a gorgeous concert that was.

That Sunday afternoon, I featured Sonny Rollins, who was then probably the greatest tenor saxophonist in jazz. Sonny doesn't do many encores.
He puts everything he's got into his sets. On this day, he did his show and left
the audience clapping and cheering and on its feet. He came off the stage at
Ozawa Hall, and I pointed out at the crowd, which was still yelling for more,
and he said, "Okay, this one's for Paul's Mall." And he went back on stage and
played a beautiful rendering of Duke Ellington's "In a Sentimental Mood."
That was just the best, my favorite Tanglewood encore.

I was feeling very good about the state of the festival. We were five years
in, and we were growing and gaining stature. We presented the top artists in
jazz, from across all its genres, and we mixed things up for the widest audience appeal. We had the nationwide reach of radio through our Latin Jazz
Night and Piano Jazz broadcasts. We had the Tanglewood ambiance. The
buzz was positive and we had gained a reputation as a boutique festival, and
one of the better new festivals in the country.

STORM CLOUDS OVER THE BERKSHIRES

I saw the first storm clouds threatening the festival after the 2005 season. The
BSO said we could no longer use the Shed, because it was too expensive to
operate. There may have been sound reasons for this decision, but saying "too
expensive" didn't make sense from a business point of view. In 2004, I produced a big Saturday night show with Tony Bennett singing with the Count
Basie Orchestra. When I was planning it, I asked the BSO for summary of
their costs, so I could be sure we had everything covered when I negotiated
our contract with the artists. I specifically asked what it cost to run the Shed
for the night, and they said about $40,000. When I built the offer, I used
$80,000 for the split point. That's an industry term that means the point
where you've covered all your fees and costs, and everything after that is split
between the artist and the producer. We did well with Basie/Bennett, and we
passed the split point and netted the BSO something like $35,000 on the
night. When they came back and said it was too expensive to run the Shed
during the jazz festival, I didn't buy it. There's always the risk that you don't

sell enough tickets and lose money, but that was not the case with our festival. Something else was going on.

Perhaps there was some truth to a rumor that was in the air at the time regarding the BSO organization. When the classical season ends just before Labor Day, the people who work at Tanglewood want to close down for the season, and the organization was having trouble keeping a full working staff in place over the Labor Day weekend. As I say, it was a rumor, but you could run the place with a smaller staff if the Music Shed was dark all weekend.

It was after the 2007 season when those storm clouds I saw a few years before let loose with a downpour. In January 2008, I got a call from Keith Elder, the producer and stage manager I had worked with for the past three years at Tanglewood. A great guy, and we'd worked well together. Keith wanted to meet. I said sure—I thought we were going to talk about the next season. I got there, and he said, and I'll never forget it, "I was told to tell you that your services are no longer needed."

My first thought was, "What?" My second thought was that the festival was being discontinued, and that's what I asked Keith. He said, "No, they just told me to tell you that your contract isn't being renewed for the next year." The decision came from down from the top, from Mark Volpe, the BSO's managing director. I never saw it coming—we were actually doing better numbers than Newport. I felt like I was being fired for being successful.

To this day the decision makes no sense to me. We had established a world-class event and the audience was growing year by year. Nobody did anything wrong. We didn't lose money. I can only guess that they figured they could save money by directing the festival themselves.

Tony Beadle had replaced Sue Auclair with another publicist, Dawn Singh, so she and the BSO's in-house staff organized the next festivals. And although it continued until 2011 and presented great acts every year, the festival gradually diminished. Marian McPartland left after 2008. They dropped the Latin Jazz Night, and I never learned the story behind that. I'm not sure how much longer the WBGO broadcasts continued. The BSO finally pulled the plug on the festival after 2011.

I'm still hearing from people who tell me they miss the Tanglewood festival. Hell, I miss it. The Tanglewood Jazz Festival was one of my greatest achievements as well as one of my greatest disappointments. It ended badly, but I am proud of the fact that I created something positive that many thousands of people enjoyed.

Tanglewood will always be a wonderful place and its summers are still filled with music, but you want to know something? I've never been back.

17

ENCORES AND ACCOLADES

The Tanglewood episode left me down in the dumps for a while, but I couldn't stay there long—I had a business to run. There were concerts and private events to produce, and Scullers was still going strong. I had eight more years at Scullers after the BSO showed me the door.

A funny thing happened to me after Tanglewood though. That was about the time people started calling me a local legend, and I'll let you in on a little secret: if you live long enough, you too can become a legend. There are no tests to take and no swearing-in ceremonies. You just keep doing what you're doing, and keep making things happen, and sooner or later somebody's going to notice and call you a legend. The last time the great jazz trumpeter and perpetual optimist Clark Terry came to Scullers, he was asked how he felt about being called a legend. He said something like, it means you've lived a long time. Clark had it right.

So I became a legend, and then something really wonderful happened: people said, "Thank you, Fred." There was the 2008 Dimock Hall of Fame award, for 15 years of supporting the Dimock Community Health Center's fundraising. In 2010 I was presented with the Jazz Hero Award by the Jazz Journalists Association, honoring my lifetime commitment to jazz. In 2013, I received the Lifetime Music Mentoring Award, "given with love and thanks for a lifetime of contributions to the Boston Music Community," by the Over My Shoulder Foundation, a Boston-based mentoring organization. JazzBoston honored me in 2014 with their Roy Haynes Award, presented "for exceptional contributions to jazz and the jazz community." The Arts & Business Council of Boston presented me with its Lifetime Achievement in the Arts Award in 2017. Finally, Mayor Marty Walsh declared February 28, 2017 to be Fred Taylor Day in the City of Boston. And of course I can't forget where we began the story, at Scullers in March 2015, receiving the very first George Wein Impresario Award, granted by the Berklee College of Music, and presented by Berklee president Roger Brown and George Wein himself.

To be honored by the mayor of Boston, and by Berklee, and by George, for my life's work . . . I thought it could never get any better than that. Until it did.

AN HONOR TO TOP ALL HONORS

In 2017, not long after I left Scullers, I got the word that after several months of behind-the-scenes activity, the Berklee College of Music was going to announce the creation of an endowed scholarship in my name, coupled with an annual fundraising concert.

This absolutely floored me. You get older, you start to wonder if you made your mark, if you have a legacy that will be remembered after you're gone. Here is the answer, in the form of a scholarship in my name to be awarded every year to a Berklee student of promise. It will make a powerful impact on that student's life, and whatever triumphs he or she achieves in music, I'll have contributed to it. Now *that's* a legacy. And I can't begin to tell you how humbling this is for me, a not-very-distinguished student of economics in my own college days. The first scholarship was awarded in 2018.

Nothing this good comes without a lot of work, and I want to thank the people who did it. The idea for a scholarship was hatched by my friends Bob Kelly and Irene Chang, Grace Kelly's parents; and trumpeter Bo Winiker, who, with his brother Bill, has led a band in Boston as long as I can remember. Bob and Irene took the plan to Grace, who loved the idea of a scholarship at Berklee, where she studied. She proposed it to Roger Brown, and he liked the idea too. While Brown and company worked on scholarship details, Grace, Bob, and Irene planned the fundraising concert, working with the Berklee Performance Center and lining up logistics, sponsors, and promotion.

Grace recruited the musicians for the fundraising concert, which was set for September 12, 2017. It was an amazing lineup, and—another humbling fact—they all volunteered their time and talent. Grace herself played, and Bo Winiker too. How about Danilo Pérez, John Patitucci, and Terri Lyne

Carrington for a rhythm section? How about Kurt Elling, Catherine Russell, and Kat Edmonson to sing a few tunes? And I can't forget pianist Monty Alexander, bluesman James Montgomery blowing his harp, and trumpeter Jason Palmer, who also arranged all the music.

My friend Pat Metheny was in the house. He sat with me down in the front row, and when the time came to step onstage to say a few words, Pat helped me up the steps. I wouldn't have made it without him. My legs were like rubber. I honestly don't remember much of what I said. I know what was in my heart, though: I will be eternally grateful to everyone who made the Fred Taylor Scholarship Fund a reality. None of us can go on forever, but maybe with things like this, the music will.

WHAT? AND GIVE UP SHOWBIZ? (REPRISE)

That brings me to the end of my story—but what a finish! I'm still here, though, and still booking shows around town. People ask me, "Fred, when are you going to retire?" I always answer the same way—I enjoy what I'm doing too much to retire. A reporter once asked Duke Ellington, then in his 70s, if he thought about retiring. "Retire to what?" Duke replied. He was leading his orchestra, composing new music, and fully engaged in the work that brought him joy. I share that sentiment. I'm engaged in my life's work too, immersed in the world of music, discovering new talent, producing events, and chatting with the people who attend my shows and concerts. What else would I do, spend my days staring at a computer screen? And I still love listening to the music, and I still laugh out loud when I hear Dizzy sing, "Salt *pea*nuts! Salt *pea*nuts!" What can I tell you, my friends—I'm going out with my boots on.

I spent 60 years bringing entertainment to countless thousands of people. Despite all the bumps, bruises, and near bankruptcies along the way, it brought me a profound sense of satisfaction, and I can certainly live with that.

Give up showbiz? Not this guy.

INDEX